E-moderating: The Key to Teaching and Learning Online

Second Edition

GILLY SALMON

RoutledgeFalmer
Taylor & Francis Group

LONDON AND NEW YORK

For Glenn

First published in 2000
Reprinted 2000
Reprinted 2001 (twice)
Second edition published 2003

Taylor & Francis Books Ltd
11 New Fetter Lane
London EC4P 4EE

British Library Cataloguing in Publication Data

A CIP record for this book is available from the British Library.

ISBN 0 415 33543 4 (hardback)
ISBN 0 415 33544 2 (paperback)

Typeset by JS Typesetting Ltd, Wellingborough, Northants
Printed and bound in Great Britain by TJ International, Padstow, Cornwall

Contents

Exploring online:

Preface

E-moderators are the new generation of teachers and trainers who work with learners online. I hope this book will 'strike a spark' and help make the online world a creative, happy, productive and relevant place for successful learning.

Human use of computing is vast and growing. Networked technologies such as the Internet and the World Wide Web have been called 'transformational' because of their wide-ranging impact. Electronic networking creates communications across terrestrial boundaries, across cultures and on a global scale. Concepts of space and time are changing, and of how and with whom people can collaborate, discover communities, explore resources and ideas and learn.

Computer Mediated Communication and its collaborative sister, Computer Mediated Conferencing (CMC), actually arrived before the Internet and the World Wide Web became widely available. CMC has encouraged teachers to challenge perceived and received wisdom and practice about learning online and to reflect on their experiences. In this book I call attention to the mediator, or e-moderator, in online learning processes. Successful online learning depends on teachers and trainers acquiring new competencies, on their becoming aware of its potential and on their inspiring the learners, rather than on mastering the technology.

Investigating the use of CMC has many facets and aspects. Web utopians are predicting virtual universities with very low cost learning and truly effective 'any time, any place' student interaction. They say that the need for expensive campus buildings or large corporate training facilities will disappear along with the requirement for learners to physically congregate. The 'Web-phobes' are very worried that the benefits of learning together may be lost and that it will be a bad day for knowledge, for feelings, for the joys of gatherings and groups.

Meanwhile, some of us are getting on with it! Small factions of teachers, researchers and trainers have led the way. Like all pioneers, they have a tough time. For them, and for the thousands of online teachers that will follow, I hope this book will be of interest and of use. It's time to start the wagon train again but this time with a rough and ready trail to follow!

There are many definitions of an online course. At one end of the spectrum of 'online-ness', these include classroom-based teaching supplemented by lecture notes posted on a Web site or by electronic communication such as e-mail. At the other end of the spectrum, materials may be made available and interactions occur exclusively through networked technologies. This book is concerned with more or less the full spectrum (and not-yet-created combinations), but the key issue is that the teacher, instructor, tutor or facilitator – the e-moderator – is operating in the electronic environment along with his or her students, the participants.

I have drawn on my own experience of Computer Mediated Conferencing, as well as that of many other people. I have selected case studies and experiences where the storyteller is the academic, teacher or e-moderator involved, where implementation occurred within the regular training or teaching situation, and where there was some evaluation or at least serious reflection on practice.

For some years, I have been able to study and practise the art of e-moderating, particularly within the Open University (OU). I began learning online in 1988, when I was a student on the first OU course to use CMC on a large scale. The software and systems we had at that time were primitive, although they felt revolutionary to me! I was excited by the experience and by CMC's potential. In 1988, we used a system called 'CoSy' (short for Conferencing System) that worked on commands from the keyboard. Offline readers, point and click mouse commands, graphics and ever increasing sophistication of functions followed as software systems developed. Each new function seemed like a great step forward at the time. When I joined the OU Business School (OUBS) as a lecturer in 1989, I was able to experiment with CMC for teaching management courses at a distance. In the last few years I have been responsible for training hundreds of e-moderators for the School.

You will appreciate the irony of writing a book about something I strongly believe needs to be experienced in the electronic environment itself. So while I have been putting the book together, I have thought of you, the readers, as potential collaborators in an online experience. I think of you as:

- academics, teachers, course managers, teaching assistants, tutors, instructors, moderators and trainers of any discipline at post-secondary level in any country or training department, who are planning to move from conventional teaching to teaching online or who are working in open and distance learning;
- developers of 'corporate universities', training departments of large companies, brokers of and agents for online training.

I believe there may be some 'lurkers' or 'browsers', too. They are likely to be:

- software designers who are working on education and training projects;
- developers considering the use of CMC in educational programmes;
- teachers working in primary and secondary schools;
- staff in community programmes or local government departments dealing with health and social welfare who are planning to use CMC for building communities or for democratic purposes;
- managers and academics responsible for assessment of trainees' and teachers' performance.

In Part 1, Chapter 1 explains what I see as e-moderating and explores it. The next chapter offers a research-based model for understanding training and development for CMC. Chapter 3 explores the roles and competencies of e-moderators, with examples. Chapter 4 explores the key issues in training e-moderators and Chapter 5 looks at the learners' experiences. No book of this kind, with the use of CMC in its infancy, can resist a peek at the future, which you'll find in Chapter 6.

Part 2 of the book changes tack and offers a set of practical resources based largely on my own practice as an e-moderator and e-trainer. I hope you will find them useful for meeting this exciting challenge.

This book will provide you with support in thinking through your online teaching, for your topic, your subject, your organization, your programme, your teaching practice and your learners. This is the way to take part and *shape* the future of teaching and learning online – through the actions of the e-moderators.

Gilly Salmon
Epping Forest
February 2000

Preface to the second edition

This second edition of *E-moderating* offers something of a renewed and refreshed rather than changed vision of the role and training of the online teacher or trainer, the person I call the e-moderator. There is a little more about his or her role in synchronous technologies. There is a new chapter about the future for e-moderating, which I hope will help you better prepare for what's around the corner.

Since the first edition of *E-moderating*, times have been changing across levels of education throughout the world. Drivers in education are many and complex. Borders and boundaries between physical locations, disciplines and levels are reducing and sometimes disappearing. The use of information and communication technologies (ICT) to support easy access to learning or flexibility of all kinds is often a central tenet of educational missions. Some countries, like Australia, forged ahead using leaders and champions to show direction. In others, such as the UK, government initiatives have promoted new institutional forms or technological systems approaches. Naturally, the allure of the technology has received the lion's share of attention. Although the ideas of increasing access, participation, skills and competencies for new forms of societies of the 21st century are at the heart of many intentions, the investment in the role of human intervention and support to harness the technology into the service of teaching and learning has been meagre by comparison. I hope this new edition will play a little part in redressing the balance.

One notable development in the last few years is the increasing exploration around the nature of teaching and learning itself, which has been fed, stimulated and challenged by the increasing use of computing in most educational arenas. Many educationalists are excited that networked technologies provide a new kind of window on the world of information, but feel uncomfortable that they also may serve to reduce the social and collaborative aspects of learning. The debate about how to fully engage students online continues, and about what kinds of technologies, provided by whom, create the right kind of environments for what! My book *E-tivities* attempts to address some of these.

Three key themes have emerged since I wrote the first edition of *E-moderating* around the turn of the millennium. First, there is less reason to convince the world that we need support for online teachers, trainers and facilitators (from a happy and successful band of e-moderators) to make e-learning work well. Thinking has moved on a little from believing technology may do away with teachers, and towards how they can be trained and supported to work online. Second, researchers have stopped counting online messages, making spurious comparisons between online and face to face, and started instead to explore when and what we need to do to make online really worthwhile. I have included some of their published literature for this edition. Third, and as yet largely unresolved, are ways of scaling up the e-moderating task force beyond the early adopters, without consuming huge amounts of diminishing resources. I hope you will find this edition inspires you to e-moderate more, more effectively, more efficiently and with joy! Good luck!

Gilly Salmon
G.K.Salmon@open.ac.uk
Epping Forest
November 2003

Acknowledgements

The first edition of this book was touched by the experience of many different people, mainly through their keyboards. David Hawkridge's patient exploration, critique and insightful comments throughout the book's development have been incredibly valuable to me. My recently retired colleague from the Open University Business School, Ken Giles, is always supportive and creative online and offline and has tracked the research and the book's progress from beginning to end with full encouragement.

My thanks go to case study contributors, who shared their online experience with me: Haydn Blackey, Tony Fiddes, David Hawkridge, Marie-Noëlle Lamy, Sandra Luxton, Gerry Prendergast, and Claudine SchWeber. And thanks too to all of their online participants – a cast of thousands!

Many others offered me inspiration, suggestions, comments, sources, help and experiences and encouragement: Gary Alexander, Anne Armstrong, Edis Bevan, Carol Daunt, Margaret Debenham, Roger Dence, Tom Kernan, Jan Kingsley, Robin Mason, Bob Masterton, Norman Maxfield, Patricia McCarthy, Dave Meara, Caroline Middleton, Grant Miller, David Murphy, Peter Neal, Emir O'Healy, Daxa Patel, Anita Pincas, Jenny Preece, Andrew Remely, Sally Reynolds, John Scully, Cynthia Sherwood, Dale Spender, Robin Stenham, Denis Tocher, Jo Wackrill and Jazz Webb.

I am also grateful to the developers of FirstClass software, Centrinity for permission to show screen shots using FirstClass software.

Some 400 or so Associate Lecturers from the Business School ploughed through the online training and then e-moderated for real. Many of the checklists in Part 2 are based on their experiences and feedback. I hope their online 'voices' shine through. Many of them I've got to know very well online over the years, but have never met.

Thanks to my partner, Rod Angood, my sister Jackie Bocchiola for critical reading and meals and my grown-up-networked children, Glenn, Emily and Paula for loving support and encouragement.

I thank my faculty, the Open University Business School, for the brilliant opportunities to work online and for some leave to think and write away from the everyday excitement.

Acknowledgements for the second edition

This second edition has benefited from feedback and discussions with many colleagues, their experimenting, critiquing and developing of ideas and their exploring, systemizing and modelling. Scholarship and reflection rolled into practice. The many questions, illuminations and challenges offered to me during face-to-face or video-delivered conference speeches have poked and prodded the ideas of e-moderating from every angle.

Special thanks to All Things in Moderation Ltd E-convenors – the people at the sharp end of e-moderating – Christine Bateman, Frankie Forsyth, Ken Giles, Paco Gonzalez, Pat Mela, Val Robertson, David Shepherd, and to Learning Networks' Bill Seretta. Ken Giles also assisted with the weeks-long search for relevant research papers of all kinds. There were many more of these than when the first edition of the book was written.

Further appreciative acknowledgements for their time, thoughts and examples include Shirley Alexander, Alejandro Armellini, Ros Baston, Tim Bilham, Len Bird, Susan Clayton, Curt Bonk, Chris Cheers, Robin Cheeseman, Stephen Coleman, Carol Daunt, James Davenport, Mike Dempsey, Yolanda and Ernest Elsener, John Hedberg, Bob Hunter, Tirzah Kengoo, Mark Keough, Sally Joy, Naomi Lawless, David Lloyd, Steve Little, Bernard Lisewski, Barry Marcus, Judith Margolis, Janet Macdonald, Mina Panchal, Irving Rappaport, Nick Russell, Noreen Siddiqui, Tim Wales, Martin Weller and Ann Wilson.

Steve Little, Lesley Shield, Mirjam Hauck and Regine Hampel, all from the OU, were most helpful in exploring and updating issues around synchronous e-moderating. Thanks to Sandra Luxton for her reflections and updating of her case studies and for Gillian Roberts for her new ones for this book. Thanks to Emily Salmon for her work on analysis of exit questionnaires, recommendation for improvements to courses and her development of e-moderator online recruitment and selection. Thanks to Jason Newington for his work on the book's Web site.

My Visiting Professorship at Caledonian Business School, Glasgow, during the development of this book brought me into contact with many new colleagues in 'transformation' from campus to online and blended learning. Many thanks for their work, time and insights. My visits to Monash, Melbourne and Northern Territories, Darwin Universities in February 2003 were most helpful in establishing a taste of 'where we're at' with online teaching.

Chapter 6 is new for the second edition. Many thanks to the following, who commented on early drafts and contributed ideas about future technologies, pedagogies, assessment and the scenarios: Rod Angood of University of Bath, Dr Joanna Bull of Eduology, Brian Elkner of Deakin University, Professor Trisha Greenhalgh of University College London, David Mercer and Professor David Hawkridge from the Open University, Charles Jennings of Reuters, Mike Sharples of Birmingham University and Nancy White of Full Circle Associates. Glenn and Paula Salmon enlightened me about Star Trek (Classic).

Many of the new example messages are from participants in e-moderating and e-tivities courses from the Ngee Ann Polytechnic Singapore in March and April 2003, Hansard courses 2002–3 and Learning Networks programmes 2003.

Many thanks to Steve Jones of Taylor and Francis for his unstinting support and encouragement. And the Open University Business School for more study and writing leave, and for colleagues at the OUBS who 'covered' my teaching and administrative responsibilities during that time.

Part 1:

CONCEPTS AND CASES

Throughout this book, I use real online messages from courses that I design or run as illustrations. I indicate a screen message by shading, like this paragraph. Messages have had to be pruned to reduce the amount of space they take up in the book, but I have not attempted to correct their grammar or informal language. By the way, looking at selected messages in print after the interactive event makes them seem more organized than they really were. Live e-moderating is likely to be messier!

Chapter 1

What is e-moderating?

This book is set in the context of the rapid development of Information and Communication Technology (ICT). Its key focus and emphasis are on the changes to learning made possible by ICT, but I look at these changes through the eyes of online teachers, for whom I have used the term 'electronic moderators' – 'e-moderators'. This chapter introduces e-moderating to you and explores the contexts and environments in which it thrives.

The term 'online' came from the days of the telegraph, when messages could be tapped directly onto the line rather than prepared 'offline' on perforated tape, for sending when the machine was connected later to the telephone line. Today, 'online networking' covers a range of technologies. In education and training, technologies that concentrate on computer mediated communication are commonest. They fall into three broad categories as defined by Santoro (1995):

1. Informatics, particularly involving electronic access via telecommunications to catalogues, library resources, interactive remote databases and archives, including those on the World Wide Web.
2. Computer-assisted instruction, also known as computer-assisted learning and computer-based training, which may or may not require telecommunications.
3. Computer mediated conferencing is based on computers and telecommunications.

Now we have a new view of 'generations' of online learning environments (Dirckinck-Holmfeld, 2002). These are:

1. First generation: computer conferencing, asynchronous and text based.

2.   Second generation: Web based, still asynchronous but now including more linked (hyper) texts and multimedia resources.
3.   Third generation: includes more synchronous communication.
4.   Fourth generation: looking to the future including virtual reality and mobility.

E-moderators undertake most of their work at present with first and second generation technologies, and most of this book is about those. However, I include a little on synchronous e-moderating in Chapter 3 (third generation) and Chapter 6 is about the future (fourth generation).

A moderator is a person who presides over a meeting. An e-moderator presides over an electronic online meeting or conference, though not in quite the same ways as a moderator does. Computer mediated conferencing (CMC) actually requires e-moderators to have a rather wider range of expertise, as I shall explain and demonstrate.

There are many different definitions and applications of e- or online learning. One main difference is between those who see online as based on instruction and transmission, and those who see the learner's experience as central to knowledge construction. In this book I focus mainly on the second definition. This is the world where the role and skills of the e-moderator are critically important.

I hope you will come to see the word 'e-moderating' as an active verb – like learning and teaching. The essential role of the e-moderator is promoting human interaction and communication through the modelling, conveying and building of knowledge and skills.

An e-moderator undertakes this feat through using the mediation of online environments designed for interaction and collaboration. To learn to undertake an e-moderating role, whether coming to it fresh or as a change to previous teaching, coaching or facilitating practice, takes a mixture of new insights and some technical skill, but mostly understanding the management of online learning and group working.

Jane's diary

Here are a few pages from Jane's diary. She's an e-moderator, and it will give you the flavour of what this job can be like. Jane is a university teacher, like me, and she's an enthusiast too.

Day 1, Thursday, 10 pm

Just back from swimming. I check my course list: 16 students this time, from four continents. I hope they've all received the first mailing in the post, including their log-on instructions and my first requests. I try not to plead too hard for them to get started really early on the conferencing!

How many will have logged in by Day 1? I click on the Cross-cultural Management conference icon. Then into the 'Arrivals' thread. And there it is on my screen! The 'new message' flag. The conferencing begins! It's great getting to know new students. Abraham is confident:

> Hi there.
>
> ABRAHAM HAS LIFT OFF! OR IS IT LANDING?
> I'VE ARRIVED IN THIS INTERESTING NEW PLACE AND I'M
> READY TO BEGIN.
> Who can tell me what's what around here?

This one's perhaps timid:

> I hope I'm posting this message in the right place. Can someone tell me?
> Marianne from Manchester

Out of my 16, 8 have got there so far and have announced their arrival, as I asked them to. Another two have e-mailed me. Paula in Moscow says she's having connection problems. Ben can't find the Cross-cultural Management conference icon on his screen. I e-mailed both back with ways of contacting technical support and diaried myself to follow up in a few days.

So, I e-mail the arrivals to thank and encourage them for their first conference messages. I mention to Abraham that capital letters are equivalent to shouting online. I check the message history for the arrivals conference – two more have been reading the messages but haven't contributed yet. I'm sure they will soon. I make that 12 on the runway.

I check the conference for their second task: to use the 'resume' facility to tell the group a little about themselves. Time online: 45 minutes.

Day 3, Saturday, 10.45 am

Super! Two more in arrivals, one from Beijing, one from London. Fourteen on the runway now. Some chat occurring in arrivals between those already there. I need to archive to avoid too many unread messages (especially as 6 were from Abraham) for the final arrival I post a message asking people to move across to the café conference and put a couple of chatty messages in there myself. Time online: 15 minutes.

Day 5, Monday, 10 pm

Out for a pizza then log on. Fifteen chatty messages in café conference and one more new arrival – Sylvia from Vienna.

Set first conference for carrying out course activities. As a 'warm-up' activity, I post this message:

> Task 1 Over the next few days, visit a local store that sells soft drinks. Try and find the cheapest of the kind on offer of:
>
> Coca Cola
> Local cola brand.

Check out how each type of cola is priced, the place where you found it and the type of promotion it was being given. Please give price per can or bottle.

Then convert your currency into sterling through a currency converter Web site.

Post your results in this conference by next Sunday 7 pm GMT.

Abraham and Marianne have agreed to collate and post comparative results.

As an example, I went to my local supermarket in Loughton in North East London in the United Kingdom.

Here are my results:

Price for Coca-Cola: £0.38, ie 38p (but sold only in packs of 6 for £2.25)
Price for local cola: Safeways 'Select' Cola £0.28 (but sold only in packs of 6 cans for £1.69)
Promotion for Coca-Cola: displayed at eye level on soft drinks shelf (Pepsi Cola was below eye level)
Promotion for local cola: displayed at eye level along with options, e.g. caffeine-free. The packaging and colour very similar to Coca-Cola.

Time online: 10 minutes.

Day 10, Saturday, 6.45 am

Going out for the day so I log on early.

The facilitators for the cola activity, Abraham and Marianne, report by e-mail that they have 13 results in. They are chasing the other two.

Check message histories throughout the conference. I'm still one participant completely missing online. Check participants' list, this is a Philip Brown from Dublin. Time online: 10 minutes.

Phone technical helpline. They've had no requests for help from P. Brown. Fax him to ask what problems?

Day 13, Tuesday, 7.15 am

Log on before leaving for work.

Marianne has posted a spreadsheet giving 15 results (14 from students plus mine) for the 'cola' exercise. I set up a sub-conference with starter questions:

> What do the results tell you about the way soft drinks are marketed in your home location, compared to the others? What do they tell you about:
>
> 1.   The economy of your location?
> 2.   The habits of cola drinking throughout the world? Are there any indications of cultural differences?
> 3.   Your views on the nature of global brands?

Time online: 5 minutes.

Day 18, Sunday, 7.30 pm

Log on quickly while the family are clearing up the garden after a barbecue.

E-mail from the course administrator that P. Brown from Dublin has dropped out of the course due to connection problems. Very annoying, wonder if it's recoverable? I will compose a snail-mail letter to him.

The cola exchange sub-conference has really taken off. There are 36 messages in it. I do a quick analysis:

4 people had posted 1 message each;
3 people had posted 5 messages;
4 people had posted 2 messages;

3 people had posted 3 messages;
1 reading everything but not contributing.

I summarize the relevant contributions into one 'key points' message and archive the originals so participants can access them if they like. Two people – Anton and Jeremy – had started a conversation in the cola conference about alcohol and their local driving laws. I archive these messages with the rest but e-mail A. and J. to suggest they continue this conversation by e-mail. Time online: 35 minutes.

Day 20, Tuesday, 12.30 pm

Log on from the office in my lunch break to set up the first assignment.

I divide the 'class' into two groups for this exercise – one group of 8 and one of 7. I mix up activists and reflectors in the groups, based on my experience of them so far. Post URL with notes on forming virtual teams and online collaboration. Appoint facilitators for each team, and e-mailed them basic e-moderating points to help them

Make as clear as I can the requirements for assessment and deadlines for submission. Time online: 35 minutes.

Day 30, Friday, 4 pm

Log on from office and look in on Assignment 1 discussions.

Team A have built themselves a clear objectives and a triple conference structure for their team. They've spent the first few days in dividing up tasks and responsibilities. In Conference 1 'Data', the student facilitator has asked each participant to post a set of data about themselves. In Conference 2 'Concepts', Peter's summarized the data in Conference 1, and put his views on how this relates to Hofstede and there is the start of a discussion. Conference 3 'Meanings?', is currently empty except for its introduction message, saying this is the place for developing the written assignment!

Team B has started with just one conference, where they introduced themselves, explained their backgrounds, education, families, interests and the places they had lived in the world. People seem to be enjoying explaining about themselves and only two messages have gone over the suggested 'one screenful' in length. There are several interesting threads, where participants are finding their similarities and differences. No leader has emerged yet but two participants appear to be taking responsibility for progressing the discussions, while another is complaining about the two who are reading but not posting messages – saying this is not 'fair'. I'll wait for a few more days to see if they start putting some structure into this before intervening.

I post a message in our 'information' conference to say I'll be away for three days and offline. Time online: 20 minutes.

E-moderating, a new way of teaching

E-moderating along the lines of Jane's conference, is becoming a new way of teaching, particularly in higher education. The rest of this chapter examines the context of e-moderating.

Tony Becher and Paul Trowler in their preface to the second edition of *Academic Tribes and Territories* (2001) highlight the impact of a decade of profound changes in education across the world, and the proliferation of the complexity and strengths of forces acting upon us. As a result, the territories that academics and teachers thought were their own have altered and adapted. The features of the landscape of our universities and colleges have changed, and over the land hangs the star of new technologies.

The early adopters of teaching with computers were considered mavericks. They found it necessary to substantially change their teaching practice, to welcome computers with open arms, took online course for themselves, incessantly asked questions of experts, acquired the earliest computers at their school or for home use. Some worked out how to use computers to enhance their usual ways of teaching, others saw computers as a way of transforming their agenda for student-centred learning (Cuban, 2001). Since then there has been an increase in the adoption of networked computers for teaching and learning, but most of the staff involved are still considered 'innovators' or 'early adopters' (McNaught, 2003).

We are now at something of a crossroads; some would say a watershed. Many colleges, universities and training organizations are 'moving online', with the associated issues of student satisfaction and quality, and much professional uncertainty about the value of e-learning. Many of us are now competing as well as cooperating with each other for the first time. The role of the online teacher or trainer is often referred to as part of the 'human factors' of e-learning, and is known to be a major influence on success (Coldeway, 2002). I find this a confusing perspective since I cannot see how teaching or technology can exist without humans!

What we do know is that concepts of time, motivation and the quality of support and training are the key factors in e-learning success. We need to improve our online teaching in terms of both quality and quantity, whether in a blended, online only or technology enhanced mode. We cannot succeed in scaling up without enabling the role and training of the e-moderator. E-moderators need new attitudes, knowledge and skills, and ways of operating successfully and happily in the online environment (Barker, 2002).

The availability of networked computers in homes and at work is rapidly increasing, while costs to online users are falling, making online conferences accessible to large numbers of participants. Online learning raises extremely challenging issues for education, however, including complex partnerships, funding, intellectual property. Most of all, online learning calls for the training and development of new kinds of online teachers – the e-moderators of this book – to carry out roles not yet widely understood.

As the Internet and the World Wide Web have expanded, opportunities to use it for teaching and learning have expanded too – some people call this 'networked learning'. Educationists all over the world are experimenting with various forms of distance, open and flexible learning. Networked computing offers the chance to build a learning community: this can be in a university or college, in an industrial or commercial setting, or based on common interests or objectives rather than geographical location. I have met many academics and trainers who are very keen indeed to adopt these new ways to enliven teaching and learning in their subjects. Their institutions and organizations are investing heavily in technological systems, thus creating conditions in which networked learning can be widely available.

Training e-moderators at Monash

Monash University in Melbourne, Australia, was one of the first universities in the world to explore and exploit networked computing for learning, and to train academic staff and e-moderators. After nearly a decade of online involvement, it continues to be committed to the philosophy that effective e-moderation underpins the delivery of quality education in the online environment. Sandra Luxton, Senior Lecturer and Director of the online Master of Marketing, reports on the role that e-moderation has played in the development and delivery of online marketing education at Monash.

> The Marketing Department at Monash University has been involved in distance education since the late 1980s and multimedia education since the mid-1990s, with the initial development of an online version of the undergraduate foundation subject, 'Marketing Theory and Practice'. From this experience in electronic course delivery, a second development phase was undertaken; that of an entire graduate program – the 12-subject eMaster of Marketing. The eMasters is based on a hybrid educational model comprising a print-based study guide, CD with multimedia enhancements and networked learning through WebCT.
>
> Expansion from one online undergraduate subject to an entire postgraduate degree program was a major feat, and not without problems! The scaling up included servicing a much larger cohort of students than earlier and ensuring a consistent, high quality experience for them as they completed each subject throughout the degree program. Furthermore, the target market shifted from

young, computer savvy, full-time undergraduate students to groups of middle and senior managers, studying part-time, returning to study after many years, travelling often, time poor and with varying computer literacy. So an effective approach to maximizing time spent in the online environment became paramount.

We needed to increase the numbers of staff involved quickly, so our first leap was to take WebCT to the on-campus faculty. The reaction from staff was varied. Some staff were excited and have since become great advocates, but initially were somewhat the 'cowboys' with their own ideas about how they would manage this new environment. At the other extreme, some staff became involved reluctantly. In both instances, the need for careful management became evident. This realization encouraged us to explore online teaching models, and subsequently adopt Gilly's five-stage model for e-moderation to support staff in systematically building the confidence and competencies of the students.

Monash e-moderator training takes place with faculty staff who are accustomed to face-to-face classrooms in a traditional university setting. We introduce them to teaching and learning in the online medium. This involves a major change to their workplace culture and their comfort zone. We find a combination of on and offline training is most effective for them.

Approximately 60 per cent of the training is offline for local staff. We conduct this training in a computer lab so that they can participate in online activities. The WebCT discussion forum provides staff with an opportunity to learn in a familiar environment. We find we can then assist their transition to working in the online environment whilst minimizing their anxiety. Our experience suggests that e-moderation training increases confidence and comfort with online teaching and dispels preconceived ideas about the 'unmanageable workload', as well as fears and myths of the unknown online world.

We also remotely train lecturers working outside Australia as e-moderators. Their training takes place 100 per cent online. These staff members are selected on the strength of their pre-existing familiarity with the online environment. The absence of face-to-face or offline training proves unproblematic for them.

On completion of training, each staff member is given an e-moderation CD and a mentor appointed from the pool of more experienced e-moderators.

Teaching and learning online

The most optimistic commentators see a whole new world for learning:

Every learner can, at his or her own choice of time and place, access a world of multimedia material. . . Immediately the learner is unlocked from the shackles of fixed and rigid schedules, from physical limitations. . . and is released into an information world which reacts to his or her own pace of learning.

(Benjamin, 1994: 49)

This renaissance view of teaching and learning is not universally shared, however, nor is it based on the record of what has been implemented to date (Kaye and Hawkridge, 2003). Millions of words have been written about the technology and its potential, but not much about what the teachers and learners actually do online.

Thousands of online discussion groups have started up among people with shared interests (Preece, 2000). Some prosper, others wither. Many change and grow with very little structure and no one person providing direction. Networked computers can provide vehicles for learning materials and interaction but students still need the 'champions' who make the learning come alive – the e-moderators.

Education and training are always undertaken for a purpose. Unlike casual browsing or playing computer games on the Web, a key distinction of online education and training is that they are very purposeful. Like their classmates on campus, students online need goals, usually ones provided by their teachers. Like their colleagues on campus, the e-moderators have to think through the design of structured learning experiences for their students. To exploit online for teaching, they must understand its potential, which is different from that of any other teaching medium.

At the Open University, with its well-established distance learning methodologies, most courses include some face-to-face sessions and many include online. Some courses have a small proportion of online working based on e-mails only. Others have a Web site with online exercises and study guides. A few courses, ranging from small to extremely large in student numbers (from 35 to 10,000), include no face-to-face meetings and provide a good deal of teaching through online. In all OU courses, the students are never 'left on their own' with no support, direction or leadership. This is where the e-moderator comes in!

Open University Business School in Wales case study

Haydn Blackey is an Associate Lecturer with the Open University Business School in Wales. He describes using online networking for analysing case studies. Haydn highlights the importance of transferring to online what we know about the dynamics of small face-to-face learning groups.

B820 is an MBA course on business strategy that puts much emphasis on developing students' case study skills, which are normally reinforced in face-to-face meetings. For two successive groups, I developed practice sessions online for strategy case study analysis.

For the first group, I used a short printed case (Case I) but focused on students sharing their understanding and developing their analysis through online conferencing. I laid out a clear timetable at the beginning, with start and finish dates for each activity:

Week	Activity
1	Analysis of the context of the case and exploration of the key issues
2	Where are they now? (Developing SWOT, STEP and resources and capabilities analyses)
3	Where would they like to be? (Stakeholders, option development, option analysis, and option selection)
4	How are they going to get there? (Strategic selection)

As e-moderator, I was most active in weeks 1 and 2, when students were exploring which models might be used to undertake the analysis. My main roles were as group facilitator, developer and content provider. My first message suggested an approach to make best use of the conference. I set the conditions of the conference and the element of trust students should expect from each other in sharing ideas.

The work in weeks 1 and 2 was structured. I acted as adviser to the students in their exploration of the use of models. In weeks three and 4, when judgement was more important than model identification, I withdrew from active conference participation. By this time, the students' commitment to each other and the work they were doing became taken for granted and the conference became more reflective. They did not then need me to act as the 'expert'.

Four participants proved better at resource investigation than critical thinking. They used the course books and suggested models and concepts useful for the case analysis. Their approach was useful in the first two weeks of the conference. It appears that these students felt comfortable enough with the material in formal ways, but were less willing to take the risk of sharing their own ideas and interpretation.

Some students did not feel they could contribute, although these same students contributed in a face-to-face group. Perhaps they were unwilling to 'take a risk' with their ideas in a written form online than with a spoken non-stored medium? Of course, the ability to go back, delete or alter messages can help make participants feel that their mistakes are not going to be a long-term source of embarrassment. The e-moderator needs to be aware of the potential for embarrassment and allow for such deletions in the initial conference arrangements.

Watching the case study conference develop was fascinating, I could see how ideas were developed, reinforced, revisited and reformed. The online environment offered as good, perhaps a better, learning environment than a face-to-face tutorial. This was because students read messages, went away and thought about the issues and ideas, and came back the next day with a reflective and thought out comment. Such a process isn't possible in a face-to-face meeting.

After this initial success I used a similar approach with another group of B820 students, with Case 2. This time there were seven potential students: six participated fully. They had either failed or marginally passed their first assessment. Therefore, I used Case 2 as remedial support for learning about strategy. Case 1 went to the students as hard copy, but for Case 2 I generated and collated material about the automotive industry and delivered it online through the conference in timed chunks. Again I used weekly periods for debate:

Week	Activity
1	Discussion of the case – two companies before a merger
2	The merger – who were the winners and losers?
3	Who got it wrong?
4	Where next for the company?

This group of students had worked together online in preparing their first assignment, so the socialization elements of conferencing had taken place. They were already aware of their individual strengths and weaknesses and were able to share out tasks between them in a way that does not always happen in online conditions. I have seen online groups fail because no one is willing to lead, no one to reflect, and no one to do. I consider it necessary, if the group does not realize this for themselves, for the e-moderator to remind them of the need to set up groups, roles and processes through the online facilities.

These students quickly split this work between them and shared the strategic analysis process. Two of them logged in four times a day, but all six logged in at least once every day for all of the four weeks. Thus the group came to have a more synchronous feel. They were not online at the same time, but the flow of discussion felt continuous. My experience is that conference participants are better able to follow and contribute to one dominant thread rather than many. E-moderators need to sum up and archive frequently, otherwise the ideas and arguments become tangled. Students may then look at the archive if they wish but focus on the topic under discussion. The advantage of online is that the texts of previous debates are still accessible and can be drawn on to enhance and develop the current discussion. Students may notice these linkages for themselves but the e-moderator can help make the connections.

I have to be abreast of the conference issues, and also have some knowledge of the material in the discussion. Only then can I be a summarizer, reflector and source of external support if group process fails, able to push along discussion if it becomes stilted, and to link discussion. My experience shows that these roles are important at the early stages of group forming rather than later. The group members become more capable of undertaking the roles for themselves once they are practised in the conference process. After the first two weeks I step back and allow them freedom to develop their ideas. If a member of the group is competent with the software, the e-moderator can also let the summarizing and archiving become the group's responsibility.

During week three of Case Study 2, the conference developed over 200 messages. I regularly archived the messages into online folders for ease of use. However, my interventions were light and I indicated if a particular approach was moving away from the case itself. As the participants saw more of value to them as individuals emerging out of the exercise, they became more committed to the process. I find this point in a conference most challenging to e-moderate. It is like a parent shaking a child free from the apron strings – a strange and uncomfortable feeling. Overactive e-moderating at this point will not enhance group working and may cause it to break down. This is the skill of e-moderating by silence!

When I asked the students why they thought these conferences were so successful, their answers were:

> It was always worth logging-in.
>
> It wasn't like popping into a conference to check if there is anything interesting, it was like catching up with your favourite TV show or magazine.
>
> Not going into the conference was like coming off an addictive drug. I was at work wondering what new insights tonight would bring. I'd rush to the PC when I came in.

Although this level of interaction did not continue after the four-week case study was over, the group continued to work well together throughout the course and provided good support to each other for revision and examination preparation. They all achieved marks in the middle range for the final two assignments and had good passes in the examination.

On reflection, offering parts of the case over a fixed period was more effective than simply breaking the case into four areas of analysis (the Case 1 approach). By the end of four weeks of Case 1, students were fed up with it. For Case 2, the story kept moving on and a key strategic lesson was learnt, that the same tools and approaches were shown to work differently, even in the same organization, because of changes occurring in the internal and external environment of the organization. I therefore prefer this drip-feed approach, which is only possible through asynchronous online working, to an 'upfront' case analysis.

Systems

If you have already used online teaching and learning software, you may want to skip this section, in which I want to say just enough to introduce the software to those who have never seen it.

Computer mediated conferencing (CMC) provides a way of sending messages to a group of users, using computers for storage and mediation. A computer, somewhere, holds all the messages until a participant is ready to log on and access them, so online conferences do not require participants to be available at a particular time. For this reason CMC is often called 'asynchronous' (not operating at the same time), although synchronous (at the same time) 'chat sessions' use similar technology.

Online networking serves people almost anywhere, because participants need only have access to a computer, a network connection and password, a modem and a telephone line to take part. You may have been in a cybercafé recently. They have appeared in many cities, world-wide. You can join a network through any of them.

Three types of technology are involved in computer mediated conferencing:

1. **A server (special computer) and software system:** the server can be anywhere, though often it is maintained and housed by the institution or organization that sets up the platform. It is a special computer, with its own software, that can store and organize well the messages, of which there may be tens, even hundreds, of thousands in a year. Fast, powerful hardware and reliable, sophisticated software enable many thousands of users to access the platform through a single server.

2. **A terminal or personal computer for each user:** there are two main ways of accessing the server. For the first, client access, an application program must be installed on each user's computer. Client software is produced by the same software company that designs and distributes the server software. It has powerful functions and features and is normally fast and reliable.

    Until recently, online networking was typically delivered through client software. However, it is now common for access to be delivered through standard Web browsers and interfaces. Access to online networking through Web browsers needs no special installation and is catching on quickly since free browsers are now factory-installed on computers. This method of access at present provides fewer features and slower communication, and is not as 'slick' as client software.

3. **A telecommunications system to connect the computers to the server:** connections for the computers can be through local area networks that link the computers in a department, campus, region or country, or the computers can be connected through modem and telephone lines or increasingly through always-on broadband connections. Increasingly, networks are being linked, so that a message may cross several networks before it arrives in the relevant conference in the server. Students and trainees are able to access conferences through a home computer and telephone line, a work or campus computer or a computer at a study centre or student residence. Connection is becoming available through wireless networks.

Networking software

Some universities have developed their own software and systems, but most educational and training providers choose a commercially available system because they want the benefits of support and development, year in, year out, at a reasonable cost. Lotus Notes, Blackboard, FirstClass and Web CT are examples of popular systems. There are many others. Each has its own underlying software 'engine', a different 'look and feel' for the participants, and different facilities and functions for e-moderators. Of course, all systems have certain features, but there are real differences.

For example, Lotus Notes provides a shared database system that is very powerful, therefore commonly used in industry. It offers good facilities where large groups are involved, with high security. However, the screen looks rather like a filing cabinet and there are few opportunities for e-moderators to choose graphics of any kind.

FirstClass, by contrast, provides a wide choice of icons for organizing conferences and discussion areas and is very popular in the United Kingdom. It can be accessed either through the Web or by 'client' software that is loaded on each user's machine. WebCT, developed in Canada, offers bulletin board systems for conferencing but also an easy-to-use authoring tool for developing online learning materials. There are some free Web-based systems that are easy to set up and try.

The examples throughout this book are drawn from e-moderating experiences using many different systems. Some of these platforms have since merged, disappeared or become highly marketed commercial systems. It's probably true that if the e-moderators are keen and competent, having the best software system is rather less important as long as it doesn't crash!

Online networking for education and training

Working together, perhaps informally, in groups, for learning purposes is a tradition in many parts of the world. For example, a group of Scandinavian educators write about the concept of 'folkbildning' (Axelsson, Bodin *et al*, 2001). They say the term is not really transferable to English (although their book about it has been translated). Nordic folkbildning traditions of over 100 years are based on meetings intended as learning and opportunity-generating groups, stimulating curiosity and critical thinking. The democratic nature of the meetings promotes tolerance towards differing opinions and respect for developed arguments. Courses are also structured in this way, and participants are involved in the shaping of their learning processes with others. When we move such concepts online, and restrictions of travel and location are no longer significant, then we open much new potential.

Compared with face-to-face group teaching, for example, online is readily available, and does not require participants to travel to a certain place. Many users find that the time lags involved between logging on and taking part, encourage them to consider and think about the messages they are receiving before replying, rather more than they would in a class situation. Participants can ask questions without waiting in turn. Because of these characteristics, rather different relationships – usually based on shared interests or support – can develop compared to those between learners or teachers who meet face-to-face. Although many people find the lack of visual clues strange, messages are 'neutral' since you cannot see whether the sender is young or old nor need to consider their appearance or race. This characteristic tends to favour minorities of every kind and encourages everyone to 'be themselves'. Of course as online includes more pictures, as it certainly will, this situation will change again. Meanwhile with text-based conferencing it is possible to 'rewind' a conversation, to pick out threads and make very direct links. Therefore online discussions have a more permanent feel and are subject to reworking in a way more transient verbal conversation cannot be. This means that the medium is good for giving praise and constructive critiques.

Working online can be viewed as a new context for learning, not just as a tool. It enables individuals and groups of people to carry on 'conversations' and 'discussion' over the computer networks. At present, online relies on the typed word, although audio and visual links are being added. Networking works like a series of notice boards, each with a title and purpose. For example, an individual may set up a conference and post a message on it to begin a conference. This message could be, 'This area is for our discussion on your next assignment'. Each participant then logs on through his or her personal computer, reads the message and can post one of his or her own. When the originator of the first message logs onto the conference a few days later, 20 others may have made their contribution to the discussion and perhaps responded to each other's questions. Participants continue to log on, read the contributions of others and the discussion proceeds. Online networking's ability to engage its users is remarkable.

The asynchronous nature of bulletin boards relates to many of their special characteristics. The benefits include the convenience of choice over when to participate. Participants can have 24-hour access to the system and can log on when they wish, for as long or short a time as they want or need to. Many participants can be logged on at the same time although each message appears in a list. Online is less intrusive than face-to-face conversations or telephone tutorials because participants can choose when to read messages and when to contribute.

Online networking involves a hybrid of familiar forms of communication. It has some of the elements of writing and its associated thinking, and some of the permanence of publishing, but it also resembles fleeting verbal discussion. The discursive style of the typical participant lies somewhere between the formality of the written word and the informality of the spoken. An experienced e-moderator wrote to one of his online students, 'Consider this medium as like talking with your fingers – a sort of half-way house between spoken conversation and written discourse' (Hawkridge, Morgan and Jelfs, 1997).

Being able to reflect on messages and on the topic under discussion, in between log on times, has always seemed important to researchers into computer mediated conferencing, and to some at least of the e-moderators I have known. It does seem that quite a few participants reflect on issues raised online and then mould their own ideas through composing replies. For example, a very experienced Open University teacher describes his first participation in an online conference:

> I was struck by how I'm still in touch with the conference even when away from my computer and busy with other activities. Somewhere in my unconscious I continue to debate and new lines of argument keep occurring to mind unbidden. And it is always so tempting to take just one more peep at the screen to see if another participant has come up with something new or built upon the last message one posted oneself.

> (Rowntree, 1995: 209)

Online networking can offer the opportunity for a whole series of ideas to be pulled together, too. Many computer conferences promote openness and, except in conferences that are deliberately and rigidly pre-structured, participants expect freedom to express their views and to share their experiences and thoughts.

The online environment mediates the communication but also shapes it. Large groups of people or selected sub-groups with common interests or purposes communicate (Preece, 2000). Participants do not need permission to contribute and individuals can receive 'attention' from those willing and able to offer it. Face-to-face identities become less important and the usual discriminators such as race, age and gender are less apparent. Successful participation online does not depend on previous computer literacy and it often appeals to inexperienced computer users.

Authority and control of the conferences may shift, at least temporarily, from teachers to students, trainer to trainee, the more frequently as the students become more competent and confident online. Existing hierarchies and relationships can change and even fade. The social and contextual cues that regulate and influence group behaviour are largely missing or can be invented during the life of the conference. It is easier to leave the conference unseen – and unembarrassed – than is possible in face-to-face contexts and synchronous chat sessions. It is also easy to 'lurk' or 'browse' – read conference messages but without contributing.

The lack of traditional hierarchies and its ability to support synthesis of knowledge lead to somewhat different styles of communication and knowledge sharing, compared to synchronous meetings. Programmes of study aiming at a spirit of wide access and openness, or at crossing industry, professional and international boundaries, are therefore well served, though such programmes are demanding in terms of technical access and learning support. The online environment is such that mistakes are rather public and recorded for all to see. Tardiness, rudeness or inconsistency in response to others tend to be forgiven less easily than in a more transient face-to-face setting. Minor complaints can escalate when several individuals in a conference agree with each other and create a visible 'marching about with banners' online.

For all these reasons, working online has attracted the attention of leaders of graduate level courses, those involved in professional development of people such as managers and teachers, and those attempting to build online learning communities. In addition, many campus-based universities are seeing the benefits of enhancing classroom-based work with technology, some of them very successfully. For example, Hopson's study in Texas found that technology-enriched classrooms resulted in more student centredness, more group working and more applied learning. Most importantly, Hopson and coworkers note that the role of teacher was transformed. They say, 'As the students began to use the technological resources to manage their learning, the role of the teacher was transformed from lecturer to guide. The availability of vast amounts of easily accessible information freed the teacher from the role of purveyor of facts. . . to encourage the students to use the computer as a tool for problem solving and decision making (Hopson, Simms *et al*, 2001–2: 117).

Costs

Anyone interested in introducing computer mediated conferencing into a course or teaching programme is likely to be asked the basic questions, 'What will it cost?' and 'Will it save money?' These are tough questions to answer, because every system is different, the technology is changing rapidly and opinions differ about how to estimate costs. Accountants, academics, administrators and politicians all have their own way of judging what is value for money. Accountants want to look at the 'bottom line'. Academics are conscious of the opportunity costs (such as time taken away from research or working with more familiar teaching systems). Administrators look for gains to the institution. Politicians want to foster national development.

As yet, there is no widely agreed method for working out online costs, despite concern about the costs of using online applications as additions to courses (Brown, 1998; Hawkridge, 1998). Nor is there a standard way to measure the educational or other benefits of using online (Bakia, 2000). In any case, what students and teachers actually do changes when online is introduced, so meaningful comparisons are difficult. The costs and measured benefits of e-moderating alone have not been studied, since e-moderating is always associated with online systems, which in turn are based on courses or programmes. However, some studies are starting to show that by using online, higher student: faculty ratios can be achieved, with a satisfactory or perhaps increased learning experience. Innovation and collaboration cost money, too, for resources and time, and for the training and support of individuals (Bacsich and Ash, 1999). As Rumble (1999) says, costs of online learning depend so much on the context.

Structured, paced and carefully constructed e-tivities reduce the amount of e-moderator time, and impact directly on satisfactory learning outcomes, adding value to the investment in learning technologies (Salmon, 2002a). Cost savings also occur from the ability to reuse and re-version course resources (Thorpe, Kubiak et al, 2003).

Skilled and trained e-moderators can often handle large numbers of students online, if well-constructed programmes are used. Using lower cost people, such as graduate students, to support participants often helps. There seems to be an overall optimum point on costs around 30 or 40 participants to one e-moderator (Rumble, 2001). Most well-designed e-tivities run successfully with a ratio of up to 20 participants to one e-moderator, so it is best to have one (well-trained) e-moderator running two groups for optimum cost–benefits.

Average costs per student depend to some extent on scale but less so than expected due to the investment required in computer systems and the increased interaction between e-moderators and students (Mason, 1998). A virtual campus that saves on most of the capital and recurrent costs of buildings is not free, because at least some of the capital and direct costs of ICT infrastructures must be paid, but it may be cheaper (Tiffin and Rajasingham, 1997) or it may be possible to establish a 'crossover' point where the benefits of economies of scale come into play (Jewett, 1999).

Some costs may be transferred or displaced. Hidden costs include the purchase of computing equipment and students' time. But savings may be gained through students using online instead of travelling to class (Bacsich and Ash, 1999). Rumble (1997) explores the accounting categories for online learning and gives an example of online costs on one large OU course in the early days.

Costing each activity related to online staff development is difficult, but not impossible. Much depends on the assumptions behind the figures. For example, I compared the estimated costs of training Open University Business School e-moderators face-to-face with the actual costs of training them online. My estimates were based on costs in 1996 of a face-to-face weekend for 180 e-moderators, drawn from all over the United Kingdom and Western Europe, including travel and subsistence, attendance fees and set up costs, but excluding staffing costs and overheads. These came to £35,000 in 1996. The actual costs of the online training for 147 e-moderators totalled £8,984, again without including staffing costs and overheads. The two sets of figures do hide quite a few assumptions, but the cost advantage of using online was apparently consider-able, in that particular context. For the Business School, there is a very substan-tial competitive advantage in having a large cohort of trained e-moderators, plus a proper induction programme for students, for all courses that use online, now and in the next few years. This advantage, if it could be costed, is probably worth far more than the total cost to date of networked technologies.

Rumble (1999) provides a comprehensive review of costs of networked learning including transfers of costs and qualitative cost benefits. Bacsich and Ash's approach suggests that networked learning costs should be based on all stakeholders – and that we will soon need to find a way of both planning for and recording the use of staff time (Ash and Bacsich, 2002).

Why bother?

In the OU Business School, I chair a large open entry course leading to our Professional Certificate in Management. The programme developed as a response to customers' requests for flexibility in learning provision for the 21st century. We deploy the well-rehearsed OU-supported open learning method, including high-quality materials together with on and offline tutor support for individuals and groups. We use custom-built Web sites and FirstClass online conferencing for interaction.

The programme is highly modular and customizable, with a wide range of choices for participants, including four start and finish dates each year, special versions for some employment sectors, study breaks and online options. It attracts around 4,000 registrations a year in Western and Eastern Europe. The programme is popular and successful with students and sponsors but very demanding and costly to run. We recently completed a survey of current students to explore their experiences of such flexible provision.

The management students defined 'flexibility' in 73 different ways! Their top requirements could be met by online provision. They want fully searchable, portable, course materials and extensive help with pacing of their study. They expect any time, anywhere assessment and feedback on their exams of the same quality as the feedback provided on assignments (personalized and individually crafted by their tutors).

The management students' greatest wish is for increased access, not to technology, but to human support. Their expectations are demanding: an 'always on, broadband tutor'! The issue of access to tutors and to others is a key aspect of making the course not only more flexible but also friendlier, more motivating, achievable and satisfying. How can we do this successfully?

Ultimately providing for the kind of flexible provision expected by students needs loving adoption by the experienced e-moderators, and rather more than promise and the hand of fate from technology provision. I hope this chapter has introduced e-moderating and its context to you, and the rest of the book will show you some pathways towards flexibility and success. Chapter 2 goes on to introduce my research in the area.

To explore further the ideas in this chapter, look at the following Resources for practitioners:

11 Costs p 176
16 Communicating p 189
23 Parable p 207
24 Myths p 210
25 Future p 211
26 What call? p 214

Chapter 2

A model for online in education and training

About the OU

My research into online networking for education and training was carried out in the Open University of the United Kingdom (OU), therefore you should know its context.

The OU is an excellent 'test bed' for new ways of teaching because it:

- is 'open as to people, places, methods and ideas' – and to new media;
- is one of the largest distance teaching universities with over 200,000 students world-wide;
- provides a wide range of supported self-study courses;
- awards its own internationally recognized degrees and other qualifications;
- is known for the quality of its teaching and research – and the success of its students.

Course design, production and distribution are located centrally at the OU's headquarters in Milton Keynes, England, together with personnel, finance and administrative systems. As the OU Website shows (http://www.open.ac.uk), on the Milton Keynes campus are the academic schools, faculties and institutes, as well as the administrative and operational departments. I work in the OU's Business School at Milton Keynes.

Services to OU students, such as registration, advice and arrangements for residential schools and examinations, are devolved to 13 regional centres in cities of the United Kingdom. These are manned by administrative staff and faculty representatives with responsibilities for students and tutors. They look after some 300 study centres, in which the face-to-face tutorials take place, and they organize the residential schools, essential for students taking certain courses. They also recruit, appoint, induct, develop and supervise tutors, who are employed part-time by the OU as Associate Lecturers.

Tutors (mentors, instructors or teaching assistants as they are called in North America) have always had important roles in the OU system. Many people believe that the OU's success can be attributed to the support it gives to its students, through the tutors. Until the advent of ICT, each one tutored up to 25 students, mainly through the postal system but also through face-to-face group tutorials in the local study centres. They marked and commented on students' assignments, and students could phone them for support, direction and counselling.

For OU courses without conferencing, this work has continued, but conferencing has vastly changed some of these roles and functions for tutors, as I shall explain in this chapter (Hawkridge, 2003). If you would like to know more about the development of CMC in the OU's courses, read Salmon, 1999a.

Building a model of online teaching and learning

Although e-mail was available to some OU students and tutors much earlier, computer mediated conferencing (CMC) was first introduced in 1988, in a new course made by a team from the Social Science and Technology Faculties (*DT 200 Introduction to Information Technology*). As you can see from the title, CMC was peculiarly well suited to such a course. The course team, the tutors and the students were very keen to try it, if a little apprehensive about how successful it would be. The software available was CoSy; today, it looks very primitive, and it did cause some problems.

The DT200 course served about a thousand students a year for four years. The experiment was sufficiently successful for other course teams to want to include CMC as part of their media mix. By 2000, there were 160 courses, being studied by about 100,000 students, and by 2003, 150,000, in which CMC was used. For the first time, one very large-scale foundation level course (*T171 You, Your Computer and The Net*) was taught entirely online (Weller and Robinson, 2001). Many more courses with CMC were being made.

In 1991, the Open University Business School (OUBS) started experimenting with CMC in its Master of Business Administration (MBA) courses. During the early 1990s general interest conferences were provided covering topics of the students' choosing. They were available to those MBA students and tutors who wanted to use them and could – typically 20–30 per cent of students or 100–200 individuals per course. These first online discussions were seldom e-moderated except to start and stop conferences and to ensure that nothing obscene or inappropriate occurred (this was extremely rare).

I used these early voluntary conferences in the MBA to build simple working models of CMC use in the Business School. I developed a framework for action research, which allowed for pathways, ideas and feedback to be explored (Salmon, 1998a). My action research was aimed at solving problems rather than establishing theory. However, the models I created and developed provided a set of constructs that could be tested as well as a basis for later online induction and training programmes.

Methodology

My model as described below in some detail is therefore grounded in my research. Here is a very brief summary of my content analysis and focus group work, for those interested in exploring action research in online environments.

First, I analyzed the content of messages. I concentrated on understanding the naturally occurring online behaviour. I was the observer. In online, every piece of information entered into the system, including all the messages, is stored and can be accessed. These messages are suitable units for content analysis (Holsti, 1968). There are many possible methodologies for studying communication patterns, but apart from content analysis they are too complex for non-specialists and not suitable for analyzing a huge volume of messages (Henri, 1992). Online messages are in textual form but they have little in common with printed texts, the usual medium for content analysis, since they have been produced in collaborative and asynchronous ways. Each person's contribution has its own meaning and can be considered individually, although patterns of interaction and discourse can be ascertained. Messages online have several advantages over printed texts when it comes to content analysis: the exactness of expression and the direct, brief and informative styles limited by software; the messages also form a distinct body, usually united by a joint purpose (Mason, 1993).

For my research, I printed around 3,000 messages over two years from the voluntary MBA CMC. I used 'idea units' for analysis (Potter and Wetherell, 1989). An idea unit is a single idea or piece of information, with its context attached. It forms a 'unit of meaning'. Like Halliday and Hasan (1989) I divided the idea units into univocal (received and understood) and dialogical (the text ceases to be a passive link in conveying information, and becomes a thinking provocation device).

Later, I did a content analysis of the responses to feedback from OUBS tutors undertaking online Tutor Training (described in Chapter 4). I created special conferences called 'reflections' where tutors could give feedback messages. I drew on Kelly's construct theory (Kelly 1955). I used a computer programme, COPE, based on cognitive mapping for data entry and analysis of the tutors' statements (Eden, Ackermann and Cropper, 1992.) (COPE is now called Decision Explorer, see http://www.scolari.co.uk.) COPE provided a powerful way of capturing the natural language used by the individuals in the conferences. I copied each statement from the reflections conferences in its entirety into the COPE software. I entered words and phrases exactly as the respondents gave them in their messages. COPE then acted as a database and enabled manipulation of the data to determine the most important ideas in a quantitative way, without loss of the original text.

After I had entered all the phrases and statements from the reflections conference, I searched for relevant text using the word search facilities and by listing concepts. The COPE database then provided a vehicle by which tentative classifications were made, changed, or extended. It provided basic retrieval and presentation commands and a variety of text-based and graphic displays and printouts of data (Pidd, 2003). This enabled me to build a more complete picture of the statements. At any point in the analysis, I could ascertain the source of any statement. I colour-coded the statements according to whether they appeared to refer to technical aspects of the software, learning aspects, or e-moderating and teaching. This analysis led me to revise the categorizations of some messages, and to a greater sense of the sequence of activities pursued by the online participants. In this way I was able to discern patterns of behaviour without resorting to intervention or questioning.

Second, I used focus groups, a rich source of qualitative data, to improve my understanding of participants' experiences (Morgan, 1988). I ran focus groups of 35 CMC participants who produced lists and mind maps. They employed brainstorming techniques and nominal group techniques (Van Grundy, 1988). I also asked them to draw causal maps of their experience. The focus groups provided a large amount of data in a short time, answering specific questions I had formulated from the content analysis.

From the lists and causal maps, I created process diagrams of what the participants considered were key activities for learners online, the significant technical skills needed, and the kind of support and help required. I built a simple model first, then obtained feedback and comment by showing the diagrams to further groups, to add to focus group results.

From 1996 onwards, with my OUBS colleagues I built and ran an e-moderators' training programme based on the first model. I was able to extend and test out the grounded ideas in the model. At the end of the first training programme in February 1997, accessed by 187 trainee e-moderators, I developed an extended model based on participants' experiences and opinions. I collected my data through online evaluation and reflection conferences during the training. Online training of a further 200 e-moderators in the OUBS during 1997–9 provided even more data, through 'reflection' conferences and exit questionnaires.

From 1999 to 2003, research took place through the analysis of interaction, online messages and exit questionnaires from 600 participants on 40 courses, using 10 different online platforms.

> Action research is highly appropriate to the development of e-learning, where experience suggests that significant modifications are required to the traditional paradigm . . . changes imply not only alterations to course models but also development of new attitudes. (Baptista Nunes and McPherson, 2002: 17)

My ongoing research continues the traditions of the action research started in the mid-1990s (Salmon, 2002a, 2002b, 2002c). The wide methodological and ethical challenges of researching online teaching and learning are starting to be addressed in the wider literature, along with the huge possibilities and opportunities (Kleinman, 2002). Many researchers are pointing to the importance of using a range of participatory methods for data collection and analysis to explore ways in which knowledge is constructed and transmitted through online networking (Somekh, 2001).

Five-stage model

The consolidated model that I built from my action research is below. I hope you will explore it and use it in your own context wherever you can.

First let me summarize the model, before going into detail. The underlying assumption to the model is that learning involves very much more than undertaking activity on a computer. Indeed, online 'Learning . . . Includes an intricate and complex interaction between neural, cognitive, motivational, affective and social processes' (Azevedo, 2002: 31). Also, learning is a transformation where the energy and impetus take place, not smoothly, but in leaps and bounds. Learners move from the known to the unknown (Dirckinck-Holmfeld, 2002). A further assumption is that participants learn about the use of computer networking *along with* learning about the topic, and with and through other people. Much literature until now has distinguished between learning *about* ICT and learning *with or through* ICT (Cloke and Sharif, 2001), whereas in practice, success comes from integration.

Individual access and the ability of participants to use online are essential prerequisites for conference participation (stage one, at the base of the flight of

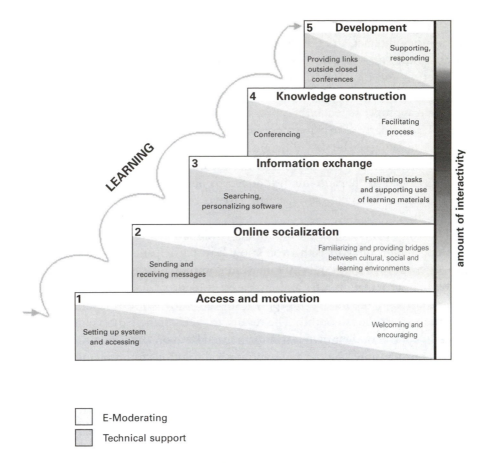

Figure 2.1 *Model of teaching and learning online*

steps). Stage two involves individual participants establishing their online identities and then finding others with whom to interact. At stage three, participants give information relevant to the course to each other. Up to and including stage three, a form of co-operation occurs, ie support for each person's goals. At stage four, course-related group discussions occur and the interaction becomes more collaborative. The communication depends on the establishment of common understandings. At stage five, participants look for more benefits from the system to help them achieve personal goals, explore how to integrate online into other forms of learning and reflect on the learning processes.

Each stage requires participants to master certain technical skills (shown in the bottom left of each step). Each stage calls for different e-moderating skills (shown on the right top of each step). The 'interactivity bar' running along the right of the flight of steps suggests the intensity of interactivity that you can expect between the participants at each stage. At first, at stage one, they interact only with one or two others. After stage two, the numbers of others with whom they interact, and the frequency, gradually increase, although stage five often results in a return to more individual pursuits. The nature of the interaction and the kind of information and messages that participants exchange also change through the steps and stages of the model.

Given appropriate technical support, e-moderation and a purpose for taking part online, nearly all participants will progress through these stages of use. There will, however, be very different responses to how much time they need at each stage before progressing. The model applies to all online software, but if experienced participants are introduced to new-to-them software, they will tend to linger for a while at stages one or two, but then move on quite rapidly up the steps.

The chief benefit of using the model to design a course with online networking and group work is that you know how participants are likely to exploit the system at each stage, and you can avoid common pitfalls. The results should be higher participation rates and increased student satisfaction. E-moderators who understand the model and apply it should enjoy working online, and find that their work runs smoothly. The results are likely to be participants who are more in control of their own learning, focused both on tasks and processes, and able to pursue more obscure and hypothetical solutions to problems (Hopson, Simms *et al*, 2001–02: 117). But let me go into more detail about the stages of the model.

The five-stage model can be used not only to give insight into what happens with online discussions groups, but also to scaffold individual development. The more successful and scaled networked learning courses use scaffolding approaches: see Cummings and Bonk (2002) for another detailed example. Scaffolding is also a way of gradually moving from what we might call directed instruction to a constructivist approach, from short-term needs to the longer term, and from immediate to more holistic learning (McNaught, 2003; Roblyer and Edwards, 2000; Salmon, 2002d).

Stage one: access and motivation

For e-moderators and students alike, being able to gain access quickly and easily to the system is a key issue at stage one. Participants' attitudes towards computers and their ability to get effective help are the two main variables at this stage (Tsui, 2002). Another key issue is being motivated to spend time and effort.

In short, participants need to know what they will get out of the system when they are involved in logging on. The purpose at this stage is to expose participants to the platform (not train them), and to enable them to become successful in using technology and see the benefits.

New e-moderators try out their stage one ideas

I kicked off my own e-learning unit this week. Really interesting timing now that the Poly is shut down for 3 days! So I have been thinking a lot about 'sparks' to get the students going. I set up a group discussion forum for them and invited them to post their feelings about launching into e-Learning – I told them it was perfectly fine to say they were uncomfortable or nervous. There was zero response! They all had their laptops yesterday so I got them to go into the online discussion board and I (jokingly) said no-one goes to lunch until I get a posting from everyone – then there was an explosion of responses! There were some great posts and they had a lot of fun. What was happening, of course, was that no-one wanted to be first to post (even though I had posted my own feelings to give them some idea of what to do). It is interesting how a little hesitation can lead to a big block. BM

I associate this online discussion with a new swimming pool. Everyone's perhaps waiting along the sides for the other person to jump in first. Test out the water. How do we get them in?

1. Be in the water and do the coaxing or
2. Get behind them and do the shoving. KP

If, like me, you are an organizer of online provision for education and training, you want to be sure that the student or trainee (I'll use the term 'the participant' for short):

- gets to know about the availability and benefits of the system;
- sets up his or her own system of hardware and software;
- obtains a password, dials up or accesses the system through a network;
- arrives in the conferencing environment at the point where the conferences are available on the computer screen.

The participant needs information and technical support to get online, and strong motivation and encouragement to put in the necessary time and effort. Like learning about any new piece of software, mastering the system seems fairly daunting to start with. Many participants need some form of individual technical help at this stage, as well as general encouragement. Problems are often specific to a particular configuration of hardware, software and network access, or else related to loss of a password. Access to technical support needs to be available, probably through a telephone helpline, particularly when the participant is struggling to get online on his or her own.

Marc Eisenstadt, Chief Scientist at the Knowledge Media Institute at the OU, feels that the key issue in successfully working online is the ability to touch type – fast. He claims that the prospect of using a keyboard is the single biggest block to staff acquiring ICT skills: 'It breaks my heart to see members of staff having to hunt and peck their way through the keyboard when a few hours of touch typing lessons would improve their productivity for life' (Eisenstadt, 2003: 3). Marc recommends we provide staff with good touch typing training products.

If you happen to be a participant who is paying for access to the Internet, or for dial-up calls, the amount of time spent online becomes an issue from the first log in. Time online is money . . . and if you make a mistake online there is the added embarrassment of doing so in front of other people (not just the computer). No wonder some participants get nervous and need help!

Strong motivation is a prime factor at this stage, when participants have to tackle the technical problems. Stage one is when e-moderators can look out for any sign of life online from new students. This is the time to welcome participants and offer them support, by e-mail and/or telephone.

Motivation to take part, and continue to take part, occurs as a balance between regular and frequent opportunities to contribute, and the capacity of learners to respond to the invitations. The best participant experiences occur when both the challenges, and their skills to respond, are high (Csikzentmihalyi, 2003). The difficulty is that what is challenging to one person may be a barrier to someone else, so it is always necessary, at all stages of the model, to expect to offer some individual support. However, try to avoid dependency on this mechanism being set up. Usually, the need for individual support is higher at stage one than later in the model, before the establishment of personal online identity, and group dynamics kick in (Salmon, 2002d).

It is also motivating at the start to make it very clear to participants the value of online, its links to and integration with the rest of the course, its role in assessed components (tests and assignments) and the amount of time they should allocate to its use. It is a great mistake to assume that any participant will want to divert hours and hours to online conferences without good reason. Clarity of purpose from conference designers and e-moderators is critical from the very beginning.

Stage one is over when participants have posted their first messages.

Stage two: online socialization

John Seely Brown and Paul Duguid's influential book (2000) argues that technologies that do not have a strong social 'scaffold' are inadequate and may even be harmful. An underlying assumption to the model is that learning involves very much more than a simple shift in cognition or the experience of using a computer. Online learning offers the 'affordance' of online socializing and networking. Affordance means that the technology enables or creates the opportunity, that is, it has an inherent social component. However, online conferencing will not in itself create the social interaction (Preece, 2000). Sensitive and appropriate conference design and the e-moderator's intervention cause the socializing to occur.

In stage two, participants get used to being in the new online environment. There are two motives for groups of people to work together. One is self-interest, and the other, common interest (Csikzentmihalyi, 2003). The first can be promoted through extrinsic factors, such as incentives, but the second needs trust and mutual respect. So from the start of stage two, e-moderators should seek a climate of strong enhancement of the well-being of the online group, based on respect and support for each other, rather than corner cutting in the service of instrumental personal goals. In this way, intrinsic motivators will gradually emerge, and learning will be promoted.

Many of the benefits of online networking in education and training flow from building an online community of people who feel they are working together at common tasks. However, such power is not inevitable but depends on the participants' early experiences with access to the system and integration into the virtual community. Online, people have the ability to convey feelings and build relationships (Chenault, 1998).

A century ago, Émile Durkheim, the French sociologist, explored the issues and consequences of socialization and the implications of shared customs, beliefs and heritage for human behaviour and welfare. He is perhaps best known for his concept of 'collective representations', the social power of ideas stemming from their development through the interaction of many minds. He was of course writing long before anyone thought of the Internet but perhaps we could learn from the basic ideas as we start to build online societies? Durkheim showed that a sense of security and progress depends on broad agreement both on the ends to be pursued and on the accepted means for attaining them. Every grouping of people develops its own culture with formal and informal rules, norms of behaviour, ways of operating and sanctions against those who fail to understand or conform. An individual cannot easily replace a familiar culture or values with those of a new community – he or she is more likely to selectively adapt or modify features of a new group that seem attractive or useful. In this way a newcomer to an environment is assimilated but also changes the nature of the environment and the interpersonal interactions within it.

If e-learners become alienated, they may 'distance' themselves also from the topic (Mann, 2001). Therefore, at stage two, e-moderators should create opportunities for socialization not only into the online group, but also to understand how online contributes to learning for *their* topic, *this* course, *this* discipline.

If there is hope that a community of practice will develop, then the e-moderator needs to give very explicit attention to enabling and promoting all aspects of online socialization. To succeed in fully engaging the participants and promoting their active involvement, imaginative and creative images will be needed. Energies can be harnessed towards the shared enterprise and purposefulness of the learning community. In a sense, e-moderators create a special little cultural experience belonging to this group at this time and through discussion and negotiation (Bruner, 1986). This is called a virtual 'third culture' (Goodfellow, Lea *et al.*, 2001). Although these socialization components can gradually develop throughout the five stages of online provision, success comes with a strong foundation at stage two.

Working online is a new and potentially alien world for many partici-pants. An influential discovery from the early research on CMC was the impact of the lack of non-verbal and visual clues in online interaction. Some partici-pants regard this as an inadequacy that can result in a sense of depersonalization and hence negative feelings. Others consider the lack of face-to-face interaction to be a freedom and prefer that participants are undistracted by pictures of or the accents of participants, or by social games. Participants can disagree without arousing excessive emotion by creating a positive emotional atmosphere (Tsui and Ki, 2002), they can debate without clashes apparently based on conflicting personalities and without shyer individuals having to 'fight their way in'. Some participants find it easier to ask for help online than face to face. Trust cannot be over-emphasized (Castelifranchi, 2002).

The virtues of a sense of time and place are those of finding 'roots' – provided by continuity, connectedness with place and others who share it and our own internalized set of instructions for how to behave, how to make judgements, feeling comfortable and 'at home in one's world' and the reassur-ance of the familiar. Working online fragments and expands this sense of time and place and the usual pillars of well-being may be less available. There is evidence at stage two that individuals struggle to find their sense of time and place in the online environment. Hence the importance of enabling induction into online to take place with support and in an explicitly targeted way. When opportunities for induction into the online world are taken, participants report benefits to their later online learning.

> I am now coming to regard the adjustment to working online as if to one to a different culture. My first language and cultures are British English, my second are Japanese and my third North American (most of my social interaction is with people from that part of the world). Therefore I am something of a hybrid, which has advantages and disadvantages and affects my interaction with indigenous members of all cultures.

For example, British people find me excessively courteous to the point of thinking me uptight, sarcastic or humorous (my Japanese influence). They also find me too enthusiastic, friendly, or gung-ho (the North American influence).

When entering any other culture there are initially acclimatization problems. With Japanese, it took me a long time due to not only great cultural differences but also learning the language. In North America the process was thankfully a lot quicker. With both, the acclimatization was fraught with emotional peaks and troughs of elation ('Wow! Japanese trains are so punctual', or 'Great! Americans are so enthusiastic') and depression ('Why are the Japanese people so uptight when I am 2 minutes late?', or 'Why are some Americans so warm at first and then go cold?'). Gradually the amplitude and frequency of these extreme emotions decreased as I acclimatized, defined my identity and started to function to my full potential in the new culture.

I currently feel I have been through the maximum and minimum amplitude of troughs and peaks of acclimatization last week during the first stage of our online course. There were messages I sent, and have since unsent, that I now look at and cringe. There were also moments when I thought I had been kicked off the course because I had posted something extreme and by chance the server had gone down a few hours after: effectively denying me access. I know the amplitude and frequency (feelings of insecurity exacerbated by distance) will continue to decrease from here on in. I apologize to those of you who happened upon some of my more extreme postings. There are some interesting ideas behind them which I intend to explore in due course.

I thank everyone on the course for treating us newbies with support and compassion, and I hope that, one day when I am an old hand, I too will have the wisdom to read through the emotional rantings of newbie postings, like my own, to the heart of what they are trying to say. Thank you for your time.

Nick

In my experience, online participants display all these behaviours, needs and feelings, immediately following their gaining access to the system, when they reach stage two. They recognize the need to identify with each other, to develop a sense of direction online and they need some guide to judgement and behaviour. A wide range of responses occurs. Some are initially reluctant to commit themselves fully to public participation in conferencing, and should be encouraged to read and enjoy others' contributions to the conferences for a short while, before taking the plunge and posting their own messages. This behaviour is sometimes known as 'lurking', although the term can cause offence! 'Browsing' is perhaps a safer word. Some e-moderators become annoyed with lurkers but it appears to be a natural and normal part online socialization and should therefore be encouraged for a while as a first step. It is also important that the e-moderators are tolerant of 'chat' conferences and online socializing. As Ari Leino, of the University of Turku said, following an online course across 22 countries, 'Chatting increases belongingness' (Leino, 1999).

Among the huge variety of issues recently studied in ICT, cultural factors are often cited as especially important (Gaillard, 1998). When participants feel 'at home' with the online culture, and reasonably comfortable with the technology, they move on to contributing. When we interact with other people through oral communication (face to face or by telephone) we use much more than words. We use gestures, breaks, intonation and body 'language', all of which we are skilled in 'reading'. Online, this kind of communication must be made more explicit through the medium itself. For example, you might shrug your shoulders in answer to a question from someone who is standing in front of you (Mathiasen and Rattleff, 2002). Online you would need to type 'don't know' or 'I don't care!'. If you failed to reply at all, the questioner would not know whether you had left the computer or were outraged at the question. However, the benefits of writing are huge for the development of thinking skills, especially if written messages are exposed to the responses of others and to feedback (Tsui, 2002).

E-moderators really do have to use their skills to ensure that participants develop a sense of community in the medium. Group discussions on the Web frequently demonstrate how quickly and easily group thinking and shared understanding can develop, often around the simplest of identity-bonding issues such as PC versus Mac, Canon versus Nikon. All of us who teach through groups know the tricks to get small face-to-face groups working quickly together – handing out a badge or a flag, allocating a space to sit, or working with a flip chart. We wouldn't dream of facilitating a learning or collaborating group without applying such basic principles!

The empathy developed through this stage of online interaction provides an essential prerequisite ingredient for later course- and knowledge-related discussions (Preece, 1999). At this stage e-moderators should take the lead in promoting mutual respect between participants, defusing problems and counselling any apparently alienated or offended individuals. They should also try to help those participants with similar interests and needs to find each other.

At this stage, it is essential to create an atmosphere where the participants feel respected and able to gain respect for their views. E-moderators should deal with strong differences of opinion or objections to procedures. The best way is in private through e-mail rather than allowing participants to 'flame' and cause discomfort in conferences. This is quite different from encouraging productive and constructive exchanges of views, which occurs at stage four.

Some e-moderators assume that varying cultural backgrounds and experiences from participants result in very different approaches to learning, and try to adapt their e-moderating accordingly. See Resources for practitioners for tips on avoiding common pitfalls online. It is extremely difficult to get to know and understand someone else's culture, and attempts to do this can result in unhelpful stereotypical views. Instead we find it's best to promote interest and respect for the backgrounds of all participants. The nature and support of the learning environment are just as important as participants' cultural backgrounds. We find that online students are very adaptable and able to respond to challenges and new opportunities, and we avoid simplistic views of cultural influence on online learning. Building a 'third culture' which values different perspectives and strokes seems the best way (Goodfellow, Lea *et al*, 2001)

Recent research supports exploring feelings along with reflection (Taylor, 2001). Transformations happen through reflection, but also through experience and feelings, thoughts and actions. In other words e-moderators should try and promote emotional literacy as much as information technology literacy (Taylor, 2001).

This stage is over when participants start to share a little of themselves online. E-moderators should ensure that the social side of conferencing continues to be available for those who want it. Usually this is done by provision of a 'bar' or 'café' area and through special interest conferences. Skilled e-moderation will always be needed to ensure scalability of conferences beyond small groups. The balance between delegating the e-moderating responsibility and avoiding creating many, many small, unproductive conferences is a delicate one (Preece, 1999). E-moderating these can be time-consuming, and some large online programmes allocate e-moderators specifically for the social host role, perhaps recruited from experienced participants or alumni.

A trainee e-moderator reflected:

For me, the key learning point from taking part online is the realization that I am not alone in the problems I encounter. This is where this medium of communication scores over all others. Through reading the other messages you quickly find that whatever is concerning you, others have faced the same problem and that gives you confidence to carry on. CR

Stage three: information exchange

If stage two has been successful, your participants will have gone beyond seeing your system as a 'fast food' IT tool and into viewing it as an active and lively human network. A key characteristic of working online is that the system provides all participants with access to information in the same way. At stage three, they start to appreciate the broad range of information available online. Information exchanges flow very freely in messages since the 'cost' of responding to a request for information is quite low. In my experience, participants become excited, even joyful, about the immediate access and fast information exchange. They also show consternation at the volume of information suddenly becoming available (Barker, 2002). E-moderators can help them all to become independent, confident and enthusiastic about working online at this stage.

Critically, by this stage, ensure that every participant has a role to play and is actively participating. I'm not suggesting you should treat browsers or vicarious learners as criminals, but instead you should continue to both design and e-moderate for active participation and workable online relationships.

For participants, their learning requires two kinds of interaction: interaction with the course content and interaction with people, namely the e-moderator(s) and other participants. Whether on campus or in a distance learning programme such as OUBS's, content is usually best sent to participants as well-designed and carefully prepared print, or by using Web sites, CD-ROMs and other pre-recorded media. Participants often find that references to course content, including links to online resources such as Web sites, provide welcome stimuli during, and sparks for, conferences (Salmon, 2002a).

E-moderators and participants alike soon find that the 'messiness' of conferencing is in stark contrast to well-crafted print or multimedia materials. Networked learning makes demands on the participants: they have to find what they really want. As two e-moderators in management education put it:

> It is very easy to see conferencing as a fun medium. This is possibly a valid use but my advice to participants would be to focus very clearly on what they want to get from conferencing and to pursue this objective as in any other management activity. RA
>
> What a lot of files/conferences/folders – call them what you will. If I imagine a shelf of files for the various topics covered by our various conferences then it doesn't look too large and unwieldy but I must confess to a slight degree of cross-eyedness when scanning through all this. Having said the above, it is a super facility and great fun – as long as it stays manageable! CT

At this stage, e-moderators should ensure that conferencing concentrates on discovering or exploring known (to them) answers, or on aspects of problems or issues. Presenting and linking of data, analysis and ideas in interesting ways online will stimulate productive and constructive information sharing. E-moderating at this stage calls for preparation and planning, as in any good teaching. At this stage there will be evidence of participants able to take strategic approaches with particular interest in assessment (Mann, 2001).

Participants develop a variety of strategies to deal with the potential information overload at this stage. Some do not try to read all messages. Some remove themselves from conferences of little or no interest to them, and save or download others. Others try to read everything and spend considerable time happily online, responding where appropriate. Yet others try to read everything but rarely respond. These participants sometimes become irritated and frustrated. They may even disappear offline. E-moderators need to watch out for each of these strategies and offer appropriate support and direction to the participants. Information overload and time management are much less of a problem for those participants who are already well organized, or who rapidly learn to share the workload in teams.

At this stage, participants look to the e-moderators to provide direction through the mass of messages and encouragement to start using the most relevant content material. Demands for help can be considerable because the participants' seeking, searching and selection skills may still be low. There can be many queries about where to find one thing or another online. E-moderators should be introducing some discipline online through providing guidelines and protocols (Resources for practitioners 6 p. 162). For participants, learning how to exchange information in conferences is essential before they move on to full-scale interaction in stage four. If participation starts to flag at this point, e-moderators have an important role to play in empathizing and encouraging.

Hi everyone

Well, I went offline for a few days and all sorts of exciting things happen!

I'm shocked to hear about the SARS problem in Singapore. I guess we in West Australia are next in line to feel the effects. I know you probably feel under stress from all directions with SARS and the terrible things happening in the Middle East. I'm still trying to catch up with all the postings from session 5 so I can empathize with those of you who have been distracted from the course.

If you are trying to catch up, try to concentrate on the SUMMARY or the later postings to the e-tivity to gain an overview of the learning.

> But NOW time for a diversion. Check out the Discussion e-tivity in Session 6. Carrie and Paul have been very provocative, obviously wanting some energetic debate from their colleagues.
>
> Have fun Your convenor, Christine.

> Hi,
>
> Hope you've found reading the messages in the conference interesting. The number of messages can seem a bit overwhelming but selecting messages, especially summaries, and using the 'collect' option is a good way to save time and effort.
>
> It would be great to see some messages from you in the conference (perhaps I've not spotted them?) – just one or two to start with. Pick on something that interests you and send a short comment to start with.
>
> If Christine or I can help in any way, don't hesitate to let us know.
>
> Best wishes, Ken

The temptation at this stage may be to provide some kind of 'automatic' answering of frequently asked questions (usually called FAQs). See Masterton (1998) for an interesting researched example. It is common for overstretched e-moderators to insist that participants check electronic FAQs before asking online. This may work for technical issues or rules and regulations about the course if a good search programme is provided. However, it is unlikely to inspire appropriate communication around course content and best practice or lay the basis for more in-depth interaction at stage four. At this stage, the motivation and enjoyment come from personal and experiential communication (Preece, 1999).

Supportive, formative feedback is motivational and will contribute to modification of participants' thinking. A key skill from e-moderators at this stage is to look beyond the obvious in participants' questions (Castelfranchi, 2002). E-moderators should celebrate, give value to and acknowledge contributions to discussion processes and knowledge sharing by participants, and give credibility, authenticity and verification of information offered. Summative feedback and assessment can be introduced at stage three, especially if aligned with the online processes and achievements.

Stage four: knowledge construction

You may feel tempted to skip to stage four. However, the previous stages provide an important scaffold for success. At this stage, participants begin to interact with each other in more exposed and participative ways. They formulate and write down their ideas or understanding of a topic. They read such messages from other participants and respond to them frequently and often successfully. As conferences unfold and expand, many (but not all) participants engage in some very active learning, especially through widening their own viewpoints and appreciating differing perspectives. Participants' grasp of concepts and theories is enhanced through the debate and by examples advanced by other participants. Once this process begins, it has its own momentum and power. Rowntree puts it this way:

> Participants are liable to learn as much from one another as from course material or from the interjections of a tutor. What they learn, of course, is not so much product (eg, information) as process – in particular the creative cognitive process of offering up ideas, having them criticised or expanded on, and getting the chance to reshape them (or abandon them) in the light of peer discussion. The learning becomes not merely active. . . but also *interactive*. The learners have someone available from whom they can get an individual response to their queries or new idea and from whom they can get a challenging alternative perspective. In return, they can contribute likewise to other colleagues' learning (and themselves learn in the process of doing so).
>
> (Rowntree, 1995: 207)

Discussion has centred more recently in the literature around the ideas of communal constructivism and ICT (Leask and Younie, 2001). Communal constructivism puts emphasis on the building of knowledge in groups, and drawing on real situations and experiences (Wenger, McDermott *et al.*, 2002). The use of networked technologies enables access to the communication and sharing of such knowledge, the opportunity to present and publish individual and collective views, and easy ways of building on the ideas of others. At stage four these are the aims! At best, highly productive collaborative learning may develop. As one OUBS e-moderator says:

> Conferencing is a medium that can add an extra dimension to developing ideas and increasing understanding of the course material. It gives the opportunity to stop and think and refine ideas without immediately

losing one's place in a debate, and holds on to those ideas for future reference. It is important to accept that it has to be structured and focused in order to do that. IN

The issues that can be dealt with best by online participants at this stage are those that have no one right or obvious answers, or ones they need to make sense of, or a series of ideas or challenges. These issues are likely to be strategic, problem- or practice-based.

By this stage it's important that participants appreciate knowledge is not something that is fully 'fixed' and can easily be codified and transferred from one person to another. However, some participants may feel uncomfortable at expressing controversial views (Tsui, 2002). It takes skill in online activity design and interventions by the e-moderator to overcome such reluctance. E-moderators may need to ask more questions, seek more discussion, motivate, challenge, compliment and encourage all participants. Attempts can be made to gradually reduce dependency of the virtual group on the e-moderator. E-moderators should design for group interaction, create a feeling of 'presence' (see Resources for Practitioners), but also make it clear they are not always available, perhaps 'handing on the baton' to participant leaders of small groups.

However, e-moderators have important roles to play at this stage. The best demonstrate online the highest levels of tutoring skills related to building and sustaining groups. Feenberg (1989) coined the term 'weaving' to describe the flow of discussion and how it can be pulled together. Online forums make weaving easier to promote even than in face-to-face groups, since everything that has been 'said' is available in the conference text. The best e-moderators undertake the 'weaving': they pull together the participants' contributions by, for example, collecting statements and relating them to concepts and theories from the course. They enable development of ideas through discussion and collaboration. They summarize from time to time, span wide-ranging views and provide new topics when discussions go off track. They stimulate fresh strands of thought, introduce new themes and suggest alternative approaches. In doing all this work, their techniques for sharing good practice and for facilitating the processes become critical. While it is important to allow interest groups to flourish, it is also critical to allow them to die naturally away. The value of an online discussion can be very high while interest and focus last. There is no need to artificially extend these.

Here is an example of a woven message.

Week 2 started with a shock e-tivity. We were asked to simulate affordances of the online environment but in the physical one, with small groups of colleagues or family. Simulating the online environment offline was quite an eye opener! On her review, Gilly suggested 'real learning here!' and asked 'whether anyone might choose to do a summary of it?' I volunteered . . .

Here is my woven summary.

This activity aroused in some the feeling of 'virtual frustration' as Patty put it. 'The pace of conversation and contact needs to be steady or students will be deluged by, possibly, conflicting instructions.' The typical chat-room scenario? Patty suggested also 'instructions need to anticipate likely problems . . . If ignored the student may well . . . disappear.'

But Frankie was quick to point out that 'for online to work well, it has to be useful or interesting enough to move individuals beyond negative feelings'.

Wanda bravely started the exercise 'moments after Ricky arrived home from 2 days in Berlin'. She experienced similar irritation: 'Frustrating that the object of our messages didn't always read them immediately, odd to not be acknowledged and understood immediately' and of course 'lacking in that extra dimension that accompanies a f2f message – so information was flat if not read in detail and with concentration'.

Communication problems – communication out of sync – were highlighted by Tony: 'The exercise was a real eye-opener for me', as for many, concluding a 'need for simple structure and language, for empathy, for reformulation to check meaning', and 'for awareness of time and constraints on communication'.

Participants chose to solve real-life problems using this exercise. Dylan 'tried this exercise with my wife on discussing where to go on holiday this year' and found progress slow!

I found my own experience of the virtual offline activity to be 'a good demonstration of the online messaging environment. . . to highlight what we are missing when we communicate online.'

Anton observed that 'When somebody doesn't answer a message . . . I feel . . . more affected than I would be if fellow students in a class were not to pick up on an observation or an interjection I've made.'

The discussion now became more interesting and reached new depths. The focus shifted to the dynamics of online communication.

Rupert noticed how 'the core group were communicating far more often than the others, including myself, but I was reading all the messages'.

. . . and communication breakdown: Jonathan said, 'My subject area is TQM'. Anton said, 'Whatever is TQM, Johnnie? I've no idea!'

. . . and the issues facing on-line communication – as Myrna says 'on one side pushes you on revealing more of yourself but on the other hand you can hide more easily' while Anton finds the medium 'all so strange isn't it'.

The focus then shifted again to the importance of the words themselves in this environment.

Bertie became 'much more aware of the starkness of the online environment – all the missing cues of voice, tone, nuance, body language, and getting the messages in the wrong sequence! Yet we find ways to compensate – online or otherwise – perhaps through better use of words?'

To which Frankie added that 'seeing *through* the words to the person behind them . . . someone's personality still comes through strongly online despite (because of ?) the focus on just one medium.'

Prompting Bertie to respond that 'we sometimes reveal more of ourselves this way than in face-to-face verbal communication' but Myrna was '. . .not so sure . . . It seems to me that you can either create very deep relationships or completely false.'

Anton agreed – 'This thought is often at the forefront of my mind as I read people's messages and as I post my own.'

The importance of language came to the fore, as illustrated by Myrna 'It is really important to pay careful attention to the language you are using . . . think of how many times you got angry for a misunderstood e-mail.' Barry continued 'the written words themselves become more important and more subject to scrutiny than in a hasty verbal utterance', and Patty graphically illustrated the point 'I can't remember the last time I spent so long deliberating over a sentence . . . but . . . as time goes by and the correspondents become more familiar, then you slip into easier patterns of speech. Just like making new friends.'

Wanda observed that online communication 'does feel odd at times . . . but . . . the opportunity to plan your contribution carefully seems to make up in part for not being able to read body language.'

So, to summarize we explored:

- the importance of careful use of language and words
- the absence of non-verbal cues and ways of compensating and benefiting
- and the permanence of the written word and its impact on group dynamics and our communication.

For me I found this a really educational e-tivity that helped us discover the advantages, how the careful use of language and extra time available in this environment can lead to greater depth and expressiveness. BM

The locus of power in more formal learning relationships is very much with the tutor, teacher or academic expert. At stage four, however, there is much less of a hierarchy. You could say there is a 'flattening' of the communication structure between e-moderators and participants. E-moderating is not the same as facilitating a face-to-face group. In stage four, it may be necessary to explain this to the participants, especially if they expect the e-moderator to provide 'the answers'. At stage four, we see participants start to become online authors rather than transmitters of information.

Particularly in distance learning, online networked technologies have the potential for knowledge construction (not just information dissemination) at stage four (Murphy, 1999). Jonassen *et al.* assert that:

Dyads and groups can work together to solve problems, argue about interpretations, negotiate meaning, or engage in other educational activities including coaching, modelling, and scaffolding of performance. While conferencing, the learner is electronically engaged in discussion and inter-action with peers and experts in a process of social negotiation. Know-ledge construction occurs when participants explore issues, take positions, discuss their positions in an argumentative format and reflect on and re-evaluate their positions.

(Jonassen *et al.*, 1995: 16)

At this stage, e-moderators need to appreciate the differences between cognitive methods of teaching and learning, where new information is assumed to be directly assimilated by participants, and constructivist approaches, where learners create their own meanings (Fibiger, 2002). Stimuli for this construction process can happen through interaction with other participants' messages, by the introduction of 'sparks' of information, or through the interventions of the e-moderator.

At this stage, there is a tendency to engage in 'feature creep' and introduce more text, more visuals and links (Salmon, 2002a). These should be used cautiously if group collaboration is required.

During my own research I undertook a study of groups of participants who had already reached stage four in their use of online conferencing. I examined three conferences in an OUBS MBA course (*B820 Strategy*). The participants were charged with discussing the strategy of their chosen industry, with a view to deploying this new knowledge in their assignment. Extracts from these conferences can be found in Resources for practitioners 27.

In each of the three conferences different approaches developed. One group discussed the voluntary and not-for-profit industry. This sequence of messages started with a participant posing a series of questions. The e-moderator behaved like a participant and was unafraid to express a personal opinion. Message three, from a participant, suggested a structured way of capturing opinion – based on an audit. Several participants responded to this message and the audit reports became interwoven with a debate on stakeholders as customers. The participants were very aware of the need to be supportive and build on each other's contributions and of the communications protocols of conferencing in terms of length of messages, avoidance of mere lurking, and so on.

The second group discussed strategy in the brewing industry. This group had an interesting mix of participants, widely scattered geographically, who had never met. They appeared confident communicators and were operating in only information sharing and knowledge construction modes – there was no 'socializing' or technical discussion. The e-moderator was the managing director of a successful local brewery. Of the participants, around half were working in brewing and the rest were 'users', accustomed to drinking beer. The conference began with a participant drawing attention to a report on the brewing industry. He suggested that what he saw was the impact of the data and he asked for views. He also used a little self-disclosure about himself and his own job. Message two suggested that although the statistics were interesting, a wider view of the industry should be taken. Message three knitted together the first two messages and resulted in a very productive sequence of messages that attempted to weave understanding of quantitative ideas with notions of wider strategy. Many participants stated a view or gave information and then finished their messages with a question. Several messages from participants and e-moderators summarized and modelled ideas as well as supporting the contributions of others. The designated e-moderator had to do very little. About halfway through the sequence he too threw in a short message based on a question. The sequence closed after a participant commented on how useful the discussion was for the assignment.

The third conference was about strategy in the information technology industry. This conference also included a mix of participants, all managers working in the IT industry and customers. It had 30 active participants plus some lurkers. Although it had an e-moderator, this is an example of a conference where the participants effectively adopted and shared the e-moderating role, with one participant taking the lead. The participants spent considerable time and effort in defining their task and sharing ideas on how to collaborate. One participant adopted the e-moderating role by posting a starter suggestion and then continued to weave together other contributions. He then posted a plan which he later said '. . . has now been read by 31 members of the conference, ie a majority, without any objection'. He continued to facilitate the discussion throughout and his fellow participants much appreciated his role. This probably contributed later to their negative reactions to the official e-moderator's well-intentioned but directive interventions.

The conference continued by others posing questions, suggesting an online brainstorm and adding links to relevant Web sites. At the right moment, specific questions proved helpful in summarizing and focusing. While some participants interacted regularly, others came in only occasionally but nevertheless contributed effectively to the collaboration. Other participants acted as cheerleaders and timekeepers and reminded of the need for focus. They were extremely supportive and encouraging of each other's contributions which led to continuous development of the information sharing and knowledge construction. One participant managed a little humour – which is not easy online due to the lack of non-verbal expression. One 'lurker' apologized for his absence. There was good demonstration of search and share skills and of summarizing by participants.

The appointed e-moderator eventually felt he had to assert the requirements of the assignment in a very structured way, thereby establishing his authority rather than participating in the discussion. He thus gave the impression he was the teacher/assessor rather than adopting an e-moderating role. He asked for contributions from lurkers but this seemed to have no effect. He also asked participants to reduce the amount of 'techie' debate and for them to focus on the strategic issues. This resulted, some four days later, in one participant suggesting that they should join another conference. The e-moderator gained access for them and signed off with a 'good luck'. I conclude that the participants felt that the e-moderator was not helping them in the way they expected and that he was less skilled and understanding of online working than they were. Because of his inappropriate e-moderating approach, they sadly failed to succeed in tapping into any expert knowledge he had to offer.

All three of these e-moderators had been through the training programme using the model. Two had become very effective and successful e-moderators, one somewhat less successful. The latter continued to assert some authority, to the detriment of knowledge construction online, although he was known as a valued and effective face-to-face facilitator. I conclude that face-to-face facilitation skills, while having many of the same attributes as online e-moderation, are insufficient in themselves to ensure successful interactive conferences. Most participants have not 'grown up' with online (indeed, some may still be mourning the passing of print), but this may change as the next generation enters professional and higher education. However, if some participants are also trained and experienced in conferencing skills, they may be able to take on successfully some at least of the e-moderating roles.

Stage five: development

I hope by now you have become convinced that technology itself does not lead to independent learning, but there is much that e-moderators can do to promote and build increasingly productive use of the system. There are powerful reasons to scaffold online learning, not only for gradual knowledge construction but also to promote individual cognitive skills and reflection. Cuevas, Fiore *et al.*'s study (2002) shows us the importance for learning of supporting metacognitive processes. Metacognition promotes integration and application of learning experiences. Therefore stage five is just as important as the other four!

At stage five, participants become responsible for their own learning through computer-mediated opportunities and need little support beyond that already available. Rather different skills come into play at this stage. These are those of critical thinking and the ability to challenge the 'givens'. At this stage, participants start to challenge the basis of the conferences or the system. They demand better access, faster responses or more software. They become extremely resistant to changes to or downtime on the system. It is also at this stage, however, that participants find ways of producing and dealing with humour and the more emotional aspects of writing and interacting. Experienced participants often become most helpful as guides to newcomers to the system. Indeed, a few who resent 'interference' wish to start conferences of their own and ask the designated e-moderators to withdraw. The participants are sometimes confident enough in the medium to confront an e-moderator when his or her interventions seem unhelpful or out of place. Some e-moderators are naturally concerned or upset about this since their roles are then difficult to negotiate.

At stage five, e-moderators and participants are essentially using a constructivist approach to learning. Constructivism calls for participants to explore their own thinking and knowledge building processes (Biggs, 1995). This personal knowledge includes not only ideas about the topic area under study, but also the teachers' and participants' responses to the experiences of teaching and learning themselves (Hendry, 1996). A key principle of constructivism is that the meanings or interpretations that people give to incoming information depend on their previous mental models and maps of the topic area or issue, drawn from experience (Seel, 2001). Challenge and argument at this stage will foster deeper thinking and reflection.

When participants are learning through a new medium such as online, their understanding of the processes of using the software and of the experience of learning in new ways is being constructed too. It is therefore common at stage five for participants to reflect on and discuss how they are networking and to evaluate the technology and its impact on their learning processes. These higher level skills require the ability to reflect, articulate and evaluate one's own thinking. Participants' thoughts are articulated and put on view online in a way that is rarely demonstrated through other media. In that sense, the role of reflection contributes in a unique and powerful way to each individual's learning journey (Hunt, 2001).

When conferences are set up to discuss the role of online conferencing in learning, they are always well populated with messages and ideas. The discussion probably includes uncertainties and problems with the content and design of conferences and an awareness of the social, ethical and technical dimensions of the experience of conferencing. E-moderators need to be prepared for this and should welcome it as evidence of real cognitive progress in their participants. E-moderators, for stage five, should set up exercises and online events that promote critical thinking in conference participants, such as commenting on each other's writing.

If suitable technical and e-moderating help is given to participants at each stage of the model, they are more likely to move up through the stages, to arrive comfortably and happily at stages three–five. These stages are the ones that are more productive and constructive for learning and teaching purposes.

Blumer's (1969) view of action learning is of people involved in directing their actions, individually and collectively, around shared understandings of their world. Each carry cultural, philosophical, physical and psychological luggage and shape their learning experiences to meet ends associated with these. The aspect of meeting online with colleagues, sharing views and receiving support, especially in terms of actions, is commented on time and time again in the conferences.

> I'm an enthusiast for getting in touch with someone (with more experience, or generous-spirited, or patient, or in an appropriate formal position, or stimulating to talk to. . .) and asking for help. All of you are here with me! RB
>
> I do like having the opportunity to computer conference. It breaks the isolation, it enables self-help, it networks, it allows for all kinds of learning styles. I wish I'd had this when I was studying my MBA. CB

There was evidence that the tutors going through the OUBS training were considerably altering their overall view of the world of online and their role within it. They seemed to be enjoying this experience: this is a first message from JD, a new e-moderator.

I've never been in such an interesting new place. I'd just like to wish all conference members a happy New Year and to say how pleased I am to be starting this strange new programme. JD

Thanks for the Christmas cheer giving me much food for thought, and so little thought for food! KH

This experience has forced me to rethink, review and refocus! JB

An eclectic approach will not do the trick if you want to introduce online networking. If you want to encourage participants to move up through the stages, use online induction before a course starts (see Chapter 5). E-moderators also need online training beforehand (see Chapter 4). I am going to say more about e-moderators and their roles, with some examples, in Chapter 3.

The following Resources for practitioners will help you use the model:

2 Socialization p 153
10 Using the five-stage model p 170

Chapter 3

E-moderating qualities and roles

This chapter considers the knowledge and skills that the best e-moderators probably have, and uses examples to explore and illustrate their roles. I say 'probably' because what makes for good teaching has been the subject of many debates over the centuries, and a new debate is now going on in relation to online teaching. My intention in this chapter is to explore the qualities of e-moderation and to place the e-moderating roles firmly and significantly into the online learning environment. This chapter includes recruiting e-moderators and key aspects of their roles. It also offers you three examples of e-moderation in practice.

What do e-moderators do?

You already have some idea from Chapters 1 and 2 of what e-moderators commonly do. In the Open University, and many distance learning systems, the various aspects of teaching are divided up among several people. Usually, for example, the authors of course materials do not look after groups of students studying at a distance, whose progress is guided and evaluated by tutors. Authors are subject matter specialists and they may have training and experience in preparing print, audio and video materials. Tutors know something of the subject matter too but have training and experience in dealing with students. E-moderators could be described as specialist tutors: they deal with participants but in rather different ways because everyone is working online. An e-moderator, like a tutor, does the job part-time and probably has another job too: typically, this might be teaching, but it doesn't have to be.

Is online networking a unique communication medium? It lacks social and contextual cues and is not strictly controlled. It also generates new communication patterns. I have noticed that OU Business School course teams with conferencing communicate much more directly and widely with tutors than those without. The tutoring community builds up online and tutors' exchanges are much more prolific and productive than when tutors meet only occasionally face-to-face. There is more sharing of experiences than is possible in face-to-face meetings. The style of writing online is an unusual combination of informal and formal. All these aspects are largely enjoyed and considered highly beneficial by the participants once they have become accustomed to using online. I think it is indeed a new context for learning and interacting, rather than simply mediating teaching. The conference users, both students and e-moderators, are creating and shaping the learning environment rather than having it imposed upon them.

As discussed in Chapter 2, each level of the five-stage model involves somewhat different activities for the participants. What the e-moderator does online, and how much, varies according to the purposes, intentions, plans and hopes for a conference – and of course with the motivation, knowledge and skills of the e-moderator.

Online has often been adopted where programmes of study involve the sharing of professional or sectarian knowledge, such as management, teaching and technology. Interacting with peers and practitioners is especially important when the learning impacts on practice. Online networking is equally as important where there is little consensus about key concepts or rapidly developing knowledge and practice (Ahlberg, Kaasinen *et al*, 2001). Working online enables the sharing and assimilation of a wide range of experiences of practice. This form of knowledge is often informal, tacit and continuously developing. The participants create knowledge for themselves through dynamic processes as explained by levels three and four of the model. Therefore, in e-moderating there is very little teaching in the conventional sense of instruction or 'telling'. Online learning offers participants opportunities to explore information rather than asking them to accept what the teacher determines should be learnt. They construct knowledge for themselves through interacting online with peers, under the guidance of their e-moderator.

The e-moderator's main role is to engage the participants so that the knowledge they construct is usable in new and different situations. So you can see the goal of the e-moderator for this kind of learning is to enable 'meaning making' rather than content transmission.

E-moderator competencies

In Table 3.1 I have shown the qualities and characteristics of successful e-moderators – the competencies they should acquire through training and experience.

Recruiting e-moderators

The e-moderators you recruit should of course be credible as members of the learning community. They do not, however, need a long string of qualifications, nor many years of experience. Nor do they need to be experts or gurus in the subject – as a rough rule of thumb, I suggest that they need a qualification at least at the same level and in the same topic as the course for which they are e-moderating.

I am going to assume that you will be looking for e-moderators able to understand their roles and willing to be trained online. They will need reasonably good keyboard skills, and some experience of using computers, including online networking. However, given those requirements, you will find that good e-moderators come from many different backgrounds, with very varied learning and teaching experiences. If they do not need to meet face-to-face with their course participants, you can select them on the basis of their suitability rather than their geographic location.

I suggest that you try to recruit e-moderators with the qualities from columns 1–2 of Table 3.1. At the moment, there are very few people available with these abilities (Goodyear, Salmon et al, 2001; Weller and Robinson, 2001). I tend to select applicants who show empathy and flexibility in working online, plus willingness to be trained as e-moderators. Before asking them to work online, I train them in the competencies described in columns 3–4 in Table 3.1. I would expect e-moderators to be developing the skills in columns 5–6 by the time they had been working online with their participants for about one year.

The most successful e-moderators have some particular qualities. These characteristics can be found in traditional lecturers but are often surfaced and developed by those teachers and trainers more familiar with the online environment. For example, e-moderators need to be able to support text-based communication, know how to 'weave' and classify, and be able to handle relationships without physical meetings (Bygholm, 2002).

The ideas of emotional intelligence are controversial, but acknowledge that a great deal more is going on than cognitive capabilities in learning processes. Emotional intelligence includes aspects such as motivation and intuitiveness (which act as goal drivers) together with resilience and conscientiousness

Table 3.1 *E-moderator competencies*

| Quality/ characteristic | RECRUIT | | TRAIN | DEVELOP | | |
	1. CONFIDENT	2. CONSTRUCTIVE	3. DEVELOPMENTAL	4. FACILITATING	5. KNOWLEDGE SHARING	6. CREATIVE
Understanding of online process A	Personal experience as an online learner, flexibility in approaches to teaching and learning. Empathy with the challenges of becoming an online learner	Able to build online trust and purpose for others. Understand the potential of online learning and groups	Ability to develop and enable others, act as catalyst, foster discussion, summarize, restate, challenge, monitor understanding and misunderstanding, take feedback	Know when to control groups, when to let go, how to bring in non-participants, know how to pace discussion and use time online, understand the five-stage scaffolding process and how to use it	Able to explore ideas, develop arguments, promote valuable threads, close off unproductive threads, choose when to archive	Able to use a range of approaches from structured activities (e-tivities) to freewheeling discussions, and to evaluate and judge success of these
Technical skills B	Operational understanding of software in use, reasonable keyboard skills, able to read fairly comfortably on screen, good, regular, mobile access to the Internet	Able to appreciate the basic structures of online conferencing, and the Web and Internet's potential for learning	Know how to use special features of software for e-moderators, eg controlling, weaving, archiving. Know how to 'scale up' without consuming inordinate by using the software productively	Able to use special features of software to explore learner's use, eg message history, summarizing, archiving amounts of personal time,	Able to create links between other features of learning programmes, introduce and e-tivities and to online resources without diverting participants from interaction	Able to use software facilities to create and manipulate conferences and e-tivities and to generate an online learning environment; able to use alternative software and platforms
Online communication skills C	Courteous and respectful in online (written) communication, able to pace and use time appropriately	Able to write concise, energizing, personable online messages. Able to create 'presence' and 'visibility' in virtual environments.	Able to engage with people online (not the machine or the software), respond to messages appropriately, be appropriately 'visible' online, elicit and manage students' expectations	Able to interact through e-mail and conferencing, and achieve interaction between others, be a role model. Able to gradually increase the number of participants dealt with successfully	Able to value diversity with cultural sensitivity; explore differences and meanings	Able to communicate comfortably without visual cues, able to diagnose and solve problems and opportunities online, use humour online, use and work with

			online, without huge amounts of extra personal time	emotion online, handle conflict constructively	
Content expertise D	Knowledge and experience to share, willingness to add own contributions	Able to encourage sound contributions from others, know of useful online resources for their topic	Able to trigger debates by posing intriguing questions. Know when to intervene, when to hold back	Carry authority by awarding marks fairly to students for their participation, contributions and learning outcomes	Able to enliven conferences through use of multi-media and electronic resources, able to give creative feedback and build on participants' ideas	Know about valuable resources (eg on the Web) and use them as sparks in e-tivities
Personal characteristics E	Determination and motivation to become an e-moderator	Able to establish an online identity as e-moderator	Able to adapt to new teaching contexts, methods, audiences and roles	Show sensitivity to online relationships and communication	Show a positive attitude, commitment and enthusiasm for online learning	Know how to create *and sustain* a useful, relevant online learning community

(which curb excesses in the drivers). Especially important for e-moderating are self-awareness, interpersonal sensitivity and the ability to influence. There is evidence that people who display higher levels of emotional competence have greater success in relations with others (on and offline) and superior perform-ance. In particular emotional intelligence is related to leadership competencies, so we always look for some evidence of emotional intelligence when we recruit e-moderators (Dulewicz and Higgs, 2002).

E-moderators do not need to be subject experts as such, but instead have the ability to 'recognize communication styles and learning patterns from other cultures' (Simons, 2002: 126). Peter Knight's summary of the move towards online facilitation is instructive:'It is ironic that what some take to be dehuman-ising technology may actually need teachers to be more empathetic and considerate' (Knight, 2002: 122). At the recruitment stage you need to look for people with at least sympathy with this view.

Who might you work with?

You may like to consider the mode of recruiting for e-moderators, if you are able to choose them from scratch or are lucky enough to be able to make choices. The Human Resources Manager from All Things in Moderation Ltd writes:

As the main bulk of work for an e-moderator is carried out online, then it seems illogical to test a candidate's suitability in a traditional face-to-face interview. Online interviews can minimize the discrimination sometimes associated with selecting face to face. The cost of travelling to a specific place is saved for both the candidate and interviewer. The candidate can choose the best time to reply to the questions, reducing their stress levels and therefore providing better answers for the recruiter to assess.

Whatever mode of recruitment is chosen, it is important that a good job descrip-tion and person specification are sent to the candidate in advance.

I think it is best to undertake online recruiting for e-moderators wherever possible, as it demonstrates straight away if the candidates are confident with the technology and online written communication. Selecting through Internet-based means allows us to recruit e-moderators throughout the world. We have found that online interviews identify:

1. *Written communication styles* (for example, you can identify their confidence, effectiveness, patience and enthusiasm, which can be different to their verbal communication).
2. *Time management skills* (how will the candidates combine e-moderating duties with their other work/home commitments? Did they provide the answers by the deadline?)

3. *Understanding and answering questions concisely* (do they save time, are they likely to give students a chance? Can they control, engage in and pace a discussion?)
4. *The candidates' comfort in using e-mails and the Internet* (essential for running an online course or practical exercises).
5. *Their flexibility* (are they willing to adapt to a new interview context and working environment?)

The issues I have found important are:

a) How many questions do you want to ask and how much information do you want to receive (interviewee and interviewer workload!)?
b) Should they reply on e-mail or as an attachment? (If an attachment, then this shows they are able to use a word processor – is this important?)
c) How long should they have to answer (same day, three days, one week)? This should relate to the requirements of the job – how often will they need to log on?
d) Will they be e-moderating on a course that is entirely online or will there be some face-to-face or verbal contact with students? (If the teaching/training is blended, then it may be necessary to include a traditional face-to-face interview or phone call.)

Of course, it's possible that someone other than the candidate could answer the questions! However, if you ensure that the online interviews are part of a larger recruitment and selection process, this is unlikely. A well-designed (online) induction should follow successful selection for the job.
Emily

Most e-moderator recruits come from face-to-face teaching where they may have relied quite heavily on personal charisma to stimulate and hold their students' interest. It is a big change to make when switching to online. Even those recruits who are used to developing distance learning materials need to explore how online materials can underpin and extend their teaching. If they are used to being considered an 'expert' in their subject, they may find the levelling effect and informality of conferencing very challenging to start with. It may be best to encourage such staff to undertake 'question and answer' or information exchange conferences until they become more comfortable with the characteristics of online discussion groups.

Stepping down from the 'spotlight' and into the virtual world can be hard. However, lecturers and trainers used to being successful leaders in classroom situations have the basic skills and knowledge to become e-moderators, including introducing topics, engaging participants, and running plenary and feedback discussions (Broadbent, 2002). They may feel more comfortable with 'blended' learning or a mixture of technologies until they have the opportunity to experience the specialness of online working.

Conversely, students used to the paradigm of teacher as the instructor may expect a great deal of input from the e-moderator. This can be very time-consuming and unsatisfactory for both. The e-moderator must explain his or her role at the start, to reduce the chances of unreasonable expectations arising.

Qantas College Online case study

Tony Fiddes is Manager of Qantas College Development. He describes how he set up online training in Qantas Airlines, a large corporation with offices and plant worldwide. He describes the creation of e-moderators from a group of skilled and experienced face-to-face trainers.

Our experience with Qantas College Online to date has shown that creating successful online learning includes course design, administrative and management support, but the role of the online e-moderator is critical.

Qantas College Online (QCO) was established in 1996 to provide greater access to training for all staff within Qantas Airways. QCO uses the Internet to deliver a broad range of corporate development and training programs. Qantas chose the Internet as the delivery platform for the Online College as it enables staff to access training from anywhere around the world at anytime. Through QCO staff have access to:

- course, competency and qualifications information;
- course enrolment;
- interactive online course materials;
- support from tutors;
- e-mail, asynchronous noticeboards, synchronous chat;
- library services.

Asynchronous discussion conferences (noticeboards) are built into each course to encourage reflection and interaction. Tutorials are available through synchronous online chat facilities.

The role of the tutors as e-moderators is now becoming clearer and performance indicators have been established. These are all discharged through the online environment. QCO expects e-moderators to carry out the following duties:

- welcome and encourage participants to progress through the course:
- send a welcoming e-mail within 48 hours of participant enrolment;
- monitor the progress of participants online to ensure that they are making reasonable progress through the course;
- provide online feedback on progress to participants;
- provide feedback to learners on learning activities in a timely manner by acknowledging receipt of participants' work within 48 hours;
- provide appropriate feedback on participants' submitted work within 7 days;
- convene and facilitate online tutorial sessions at times agreed with Qantas College;

- moderate noticeboards discussions by monitoring active noticeboard discussions at least once a week;
- provide input to noticeboards as appropriate;
- assess participants against learning outcomes by ensuring that the participant has met all assessment criteria associated with the learning outcomes;
- maintain participant records by keeping notes of participant interactions using tools provided in QCO to track learner participation, identify those learners who need further assistance and maintain assessment records;
- update status of participants using tools provided in QCO.

Key issues for e-moderators

A number of issues come up time and time again for e-moderating. Understanding these may make the difference between a happy and successful e-moderating experience and a miserable one. These issues include the appropriate numbers of participants in a conference, the use of time online, coming to grips with the asynchronicity and complexity of conference messages and the development of professional online communities. What follows is a brief exploration of these, which I hope will help those of you soon to encounter these in the real online situation.

Group size

What is the right number of participants in a computer conference for it to be successful? Is there a critical mass, in the physical sciences sense, so that with too few participants success eludes even the best e-moderator? The right kind of number for any conference depends fundamentally on its purpose. Six participants and an e-moderator, for example, may lead to all contributing and a collaborative outcome for an online activity. Or one thousand participants could pose questions to an online expert, and all read the answers. They might then join in smaller groups – perhaps of 20 each – to put their own views.

We know that starting off well with good welcoming messages helps very much. After that, part of the e-moderator's role is to try and orchestrate appropriate participation for the purpose. It is always necessary to try and keep track of what is happening to ensure participants do not disappear for reasons that can be changed! Most software systems offer features such as "message history" to help you track numbers and participation. Good e-moderating always includes summarizing and feedback. These are difficult to do with more than 20 active participants.

We have found that one of the best ways of building up the right numbers for a conference is to work with the energy that naturally builds up online (for whatever reason). You can certainly expect increased online activities to be associated with offline purposes, such as assessed assignments, the start of a new section on a course, periods just before face-to-face meetings or the run up to the exam. There may be unexpected reasons for increased online activity (eg a relevant news event or even a problem such as delayed arrival of course materials) and e-moderators can turn this to their advantage. When a conference or online activity naturally starts to wane, it is best to close it and start something fresh.

One key issue in e-moderating in synchronous environments is that smaller numbers of participants than for asynchronous groups work better.

Here's Lesley Shield from the OU's Department of Languages.

We've had a lot of debate in our department about the optimum size for synchronous audiographics groups, partly based on experience and partly on costs. Our face-to-face groups run with around 20–25 students. Because of the e-moderation issues involved with virtual groups, these have to run with fewer members so that the e-tutor can manage the activity. Our pilot studies in 1997–9 suggested 8–10 (maybe 12) students was a good number for various different reasons:

a) ENVIRONMENT RELATED: because of the electronic environment, the protocols and turn-taking are different from face-to-face; for example, there may be unbroken silences because of the lack of body language, and interaction tends to take longer than in the physical environment. This means that a group of 10 students allows each learner more opportunity for active participation than would a larger group, and it also allows the e-tutor to identify and support any student who seems less confident.

b) ACTIVITY RELATED: because students have to split into small groups, work together and come back to plenary, the group size of 10 is large enough to promote discussion even in the small groups.

c) PRACTICAL: that if one or two – or even three or four – didn't show up (our tutorials aren't compulsory) there would still be sufficient for the tutorial to be useful. With fewer than 8–10, there's a risk of non-viability.

It is, however, very expensive to run groups of 8 or even 10 students, so 15 was chosen as a workable number! So we'd say that the optimum number is rather dependent on different variables such as cost, type of activity, and so on but that we agree with 10 as an optimum in ideal circumstances.

Asynchronicity

For trainee e-moderators, coming to grips with asynchronicity in online can prove very demanding because of the complexity of large conferences. The management tutors (see Chapter 4) certainly had some problems when they were being trained. Participants could 'post' contributions to one conference then immediately read messages from others, or vice versa. A participant might read all his or her unread messages in several conferences and then post several responses and perhaps some topics to start new themes. In any conference, this reading and posting of messages by a number of individuals can make the sequencing difficult to follow.

The nature of asynchronicity makes it harder for e-moderators to create positive group experiences and the excitement, rhythm, engagement and focus that we know as 'flow' (Csikzentmihalyi, 2003), compared with face-to-face groups. It is not impossible, though! Key issues are the ability to create clear goals and appropriate challenges, through a vision of the learning outcomes and very short focused steps, good timely feedback and appropriate motivation.

Experienced e-moderator and trainer of e-moderators David Shepherd wrote to me:

When training e-moderators to create online activities (which we call e-tivities), we have noticed that they have a tendency to ask a whole series of complex questions in one message. Such a strategy may work well in face-to-face situations, where the facilitator can pick up on any response and manage the discussion by moving on to the questions in turn. But online, all participants could (in theory at least) respond to all questions, asynchronously, in any order.

Four questions, for example, will present participants with the decision on whether to respond with one message for all four questions or to provide four separate messages over time – one for each question. In a group of many participants some will decide on one of these strategies and others on another – resulting in a complex mix of messages for the e-moderator to cope with. Summarizing and responding become a real challenge, and many of the participants will lose track of the discussions and 'flow'.

By setting out four e-tivities from the onset (one for each question or task), the e-moderator anticipates the difficulty, provides the participants with clear guidance on where to post each message, and how to respond to others. The participant is given a clear process to follow and the e-moderator can see that it will take some time for the participant to work through the four tasks. Weaving and summarizing are easier to achieve effectively. Result? Happier participants who respond, and are more motivated to contribute.

In order to learn from online conferences, participants need to be able to select, organize, elaborate and explore new knowledge and understanding in relationship to existing knowledge. Much of this can be supported by appropriate interactive and supportive design of conferences (Salmon, 2002a) but also by

the appropriate interventions by the e-moderator, including excellent threading and summaries and the removal of irrelevant messages (Schwan, Straub *et
al.*, 2002). One strategy is to reduce the number of messages; another is to
ensure very good reply structures.

> One of the difficulties with this excellent FirstClass is that there are so
> many icons; it's like having a myriad of friends and not knowing who
> you've spoken to, who you've left a message with or who is expecting a
> reply. Any bright ideas – friends?
> Cheers, A :-) AB

This participant uses an emoticon to demonstrate that he is not being too
serious about this problem.

  Since all the texts are available for any participant (or researcher) to view
online, the sequencing of messages, when viewed after a discussion is completed, looks rather more ordered than during the build-up. Yet trying to
understand them afterwards is rather like following the moves of a chess or
bridge game, after it is over. When participants start using online, this apparent
confusion causes a wide range of responses. CMC can elicit quite uncomfortable, confused reactions from participants and severe anxiety in a few. Although
many people are now familiar with e-mail they are not used to the complexity
of many-to-many conferencing online, with its huge range of potential posting
times and variety of response and counter-response. E-moderators can help, as
one noted in his reflections:

> This is a very difficult but rewarding area. More effort is needed to keep
> even paced and also even-tempered at times. A conversation can be spread
> over several days without all the intervening gestures and interruptions of
> real conversation. This can lead to great misunderstanding. Thus to be
> reflective and not 'dash' off replies is important. To seek an even written
> style would hopefully bring some peace to bear, but the delay in reply
> which may be the result sometimes, of other commitments, can be
> annoying for colleagues. A welcoming and encouraging tone is vital, as
> being on the end of a computer, sometimes without a useful telephone
> conversation, can be very lonely.
>   An e-moderator can ensure that all participants are familiar with the
> best the software has to offer and help them to be comfortable in the
> online environment to start with. A key e-moderating role is to build a

clear structure by breaking conferences, if they get too busy, into sub-topics or sub-groups, and by regularly archiving and 'weaving' in summaries. PB

Time

Nearly every participant, new or experienced, teacher or learner, worries about how much time it takes to be online. You will find the concept of time is emotive and value-laden for both e-moderators and participants (Salmon, 2002a). The key issue is that the advantages of 'any time/any place' learning and teaching mean that time is not bounded and contained as it is when attending a lecture or a face-to-face training session. Although a face-to-face tutorial may last two hours, it has a clear start and finish time and is rarely interrupted by anything else. The participants are either there or they are not, and if they are, they cannot be doing much else. Online is not like that. It has a reputation for 'eating time'. Genuine fears and concerns do exist, and must be addressed.

'Finding the time' is a continuous theme. Many participants report 'lack of time' as a key reason for non-participation in online conferencing. However, something more fundamental is probably happening (Tsui, 2002). Time is a social construct, and not something that can be 'managed'. We are so used to living our lives in cycles, and working online disrupts our carefully constructed if tentative feeling of control of our lives. This is not a plea for clocks on the home page! It is worth structuring your course to provide participants with rhythm, enticement, flow and pace to their online study. The technology should also offer quick and easy ways of completing weaving, summaries, archiving and effective presentation of plenary results for e-moderators. Most Virtual Learning Environments (VLEs) don't do this at present.

Asynchronous Internet time is quite different from the cycles and seasons that we are used to in our every day life. Time and place normally provide an 'embedding and situating space for human activity. Human orientation, human interaction and human cognition are all processes deeply and extricably tied in with the time and context in which they take place. . . . An understanding comfortable enough to enhance a person's inclination to act and interact' (Sorensen, 2002: 193). Therefore, interacting with others online and without being in the same place and the same time requires a change in perspective. Working online involves shifting time about and changing patterns of how you work with colleagues and participants. Ways of e-moderating need rethinking, almost a reinvention, to accommodate issues of remote asynchronous Internet time.

'There is no denying how useful clock time can be, but it is clear that it is entangled in our everyday lives . . . with the time of consciousness and memory' (Lippincott, Eco *et al*, 2000: 11–12).

Research on our online courses, during 2000 to 2002, revealed that the participants' experience of online time is one of the most important factors in determining their rate of participation and completion of Internet-based courses. Both learners and e-moderators have difficulty in grasping hold of Internet time. Strong feelings can be evoked, and confusion occur. Without understanding of Internet time, in asynchronous courses, important aspects of personal pacing are quickly lost, together with motivation, satisfaction and self-determination. The design and support to create feelings of tying time into collaborative activity and of being in a 'shared space' are two of the most important e-moderating tasks. One participant put it this way:

> I need to become capable of thinking 'cyber-clock-wise' – I don't know how to explain this, but learning traditionally is a different kind of mental process, not only as far as your role and motivation are concerned, but as far as 'mental data management' is concerned: realizing you are in an asynchronous environment, your classroom is somewhere out there, people are spread all over the planet, and things are happening simultaneously you're involved in multiple actions . . . It's not something Mr Stone Age Man was born with, but it's fun after you've done a bit of evolution. ;-) FF

> Once upon a time . . . before I was an e-moderator...my alarm clock had only one setting . . . now it has many! RA

Time takes on a new dimension online. Working asynchronously involves a radical rethink – not only of learning or teaching time, but also of other aspects of life. Most people find this very difficult indeed to start with. Failing to get to grips with Internet time can result in the feeling of falling into a 'deep well' (and certainly failure to complete the course, discussion or programme). By providing a clear indication of an expectation of active contribution and by pacing and structuring the online activity, we can help participants to make the adjustments to their lives and dramatically increase completion rates in e-learning.

We have found that the first few weeks of being online is a critical time for group forming and confidence building. One e-moderator said:

Currently I'm e-moderating an online course with 15 participants so I go in twice a day. Once around midday and then again after 8 pm. I know when I need to join in – after around 20 posts (not before!). In other words I based my approach on the participants' postings, not on the clock time. This strategy wouldn't work for everyone but I like to monitor the activity closely in the first three weeks for indicators of technical/social/ and psychological well-being. BB

We find that online courses, even those that are well structured, tend to result in more time spent thinking about time itself, and the choices there are to make. Some participants try to control for their time from the start, as the first participant below demonstrates:

Will it take me longer to do more but lightly, or do less but more depth? I've spent 15 minutes thinking about this! AH

I did not pace myself terribly well, wanted to go everywhere and read everything (can't bear to miss out) and found that rest of my life was in fair disarray by week 4! HS

Participants simply will not all log in on the day and time that the course plan intends! A few will come a little early and may race ahead. Some will come late. At least a week is needed for everyone to be ready for the more productive work.

Participants in online learning are involved in a variety of communities of learning and practice at the same time, and have a myriad of other responsibilities. Some of these may be similar in values and beliefs and norms of behaviour to those of the course groups and some may not. You need to build enticement, inclusiveness and pacing to make your experience stand out.

We now provide a regular time beat that provides a framework which starts and finishes at predictable times, and actions that occur regularly, such as the e-moderator's summaries (Salmon, 2002a). In addition, we promote interest and motivation through underlying rhythm. Engaging in authentic tasks and working with others can provide this idea of rhythm. 'Overfilling' an e-tivity with many online resources is the enemy of active engagement online. Such pacing needs to appear in the e-tivities because participants will not meet often 'by chance' online to coordinate for themselves.

Train everyone involved in Netspeak! For example, long messages take time to read and respond to (but may be more worthwhile than short ones). Summarizing, archiving and weaving are the key skills for the e-moderator. They save participants time, and enable participation in new ways. Furthermore, the more successful an e-moderator is, the more likely he or she will be overwhelmed by success in terms of many student messages – our own little Catch-22!

It is important to specify the amount of time and what you expect e-moderators and participants to do and by when and not to leave this open-ended. It is of course important to design for the numbers involved in a conference, and be realistic about how much an e-moderator can do. Online novice learners and e-moderators will need much longer to do everything than experienced participants. Ensure that you use the most trained – and probably the most expensive – people (eg academics, faculty, experienced e-moderators) to do what they do best. Use less trained and experienced people, perhaps cheaper, for other tasks (eg use alumni as social hosts, or to run helplines shared with other schools). When choosing media and activities, make sure the time online is used for what it's good for rather than to force-fit activities online. At the same time, reduce offline activities for participants by as much as you are providing online activities for them, so that looking after both sets does not overwhelm e-moderators. Be explicit about who is going to do what online, how much time you expect them to devote to it and what their payment rate will be. Ask them to do one or two important online activities in a time-bounded way, within a time limit, until they gain experience in managing their own online time. Develop and share a process of working together in e-moderating teams and in providing cover and breaks from online commitments. Develop and publish for all to see 'online office hours' and tell participants how much time e-moderators are being paid for so that there's a reasonable level of expectation about the frequency of online visits.

Networking

Online, as you know, there are three kinds of key players – the participants (students, learners, trainees), the academics (perhaps represented by resource material) and the e-moderators. Researchers, theorists and others can be brought in occasionally, too. It is exciting for participants to have access to expert views, though they may 'go quiet' and let the expert dominate, therefore it is best to keep such sessions down to a week or two. Craft knowledge can be passed on through anecdotes and stories without one individual 'holding the floor'. Some younger or less experienced participants may need to be explicitly drawn in and valued.

By learning through well e-moderated conferencing, each participant can construct his or her understanding according to previous experience and may make this explicit and available for others through the conference messages. The new information can be 'encoded' and learnt by other individuals through linking it to their previous knowledge. The emphasis that constructivism places on creating challenging learning environments, means that continued efforts need to go into training e-moderators and inducting students and to ensure that they understand the importance of online knowledge construction.

With our present state of understanding how to develop and disseminate knowledge online, e-moderators need credibility in the field of study. When professional knowledge is shared in face-to-face meetings, it has been easy to recognize others as 'one of us'. The e-moderator should therefore establish his or her credentials as a like-minded and experienced professional – and probably needs to work a little harder at this online than in a face-to-face group. E-moderators will also need to develop good working relationships with librarians – who are themselves rapidly transforming themselves into ICT resource providers.

Teacher education offers an example of building online learning communities with an impact on professional practice, going well beyond what is possible in specific training events (Selinger and Pearson, 1999; Leach and Moon, 1999). By working in such a community, participants can extend their networking beyond the institution in which they work. They can also work with others from different educational traditions. Selinger shows us that this aids their attempt to seek out and understand new ideas and opinions. Teacher trainees explore new ways of tackling everyday problems and report the results to the online community. The e-moderator's role in such a rich and professional environment is both rewarding and demanding (Selinger and Pearson, 1999). Nursing and medical education offer us a range of similar examples of developing online practice (Leung, 2002).

In a global and technological corporate environment, large-scale electronic networking is proving very beneficial. Shell Technology Exploration and Production is undertaking a major move towards learner and business–centred employee development. Shell has created three core Internet networks, which reflect key areas of the business. Some 2,500 employees log in and take part every week. The conferencing is carefully structured and e-moderated (Loknes, 2000).

E-moderating with synchronous network platforms

In the United States, and in some other parts of the world, distance learning often means learning in a location many miles away from the classroom where the teacher is. Many universities and colleges have installed video conferencing equipment that enables them to deliver the teaching to the distant locations.

This is synchronous classroom teaching, but has little to do with asynchronous networking. In everyday life, synchronous communication is becoming increasingly important.

However, synchronous conferencing can be set up on the Internet. The most basic kind is the text-based chat session that anyone can join. The software shows each participant who else is online at that time, and messages can be addressed to one, some or all of those 'present'. These messages appear almost instantaneously on the screens of all participants, inviting immediate responses. Beyond the mere text, users with the right hardware and software can add sound and vision, though these add complexity too because everyone can't speak at once. The learning environment becomes more like that of a telephone conference call, or even a videoconferencing session.

These technologies allow for real-time communication: users are online together at the same time and speaking or writing to one another immediately. Synchronous 'events' need planning and an e-moderator may be badly needed to avert chaos. They can add a sense of presence and immediacy that is attractive to participants, some of whom find they can engage and get to know others. Many find that being online together is fun, so long as the experience is short, say half an hour or less.

Synchronous applications of ICT are sometimes combined with other media for educational purposes in order to get the motivating impact of e-event but with the potential for some deeper learning. For example, a Webcast, which is like a TV broadcast but delivered through the Internet, can be combined with incoming synchronous messages from all 'viewers' of the broadcast. This enables the presenter to immediately pick up and respond to questions and comments (Pullen, 1998; Scott and Eisenstadt, 1998).

The role of the e-moderator in online synchronous discussion reflects some of the qualities of the asynchronous e-moderator, especially to focus the conference at the beginning, keep it roughly on track and summarize it. Achieving full participation by the students through ensuring everyone 'takes a turn' is also an important e-moderating role. The software may offer special rights to the e-moderator, who can use the technology to control turn taking.

If you are involved in this kind of e-moderating, the usual 'rules' apply. You need to be familiar and comfortable with the applications and aware of their strengths and weaknesses as learning tools. Participants soon spot a teacher who is unfamiliar with the equipment. As always, good preparation for the event is essential. You need to allow time to get ready for the online session and for follow up. Critical success factors are good clear structure to the session, the quality of the visual materials, the clarity of the objectives and roles of the participants and ensuring everyone participates. If your participants can see you, you may need to brush up on your presentation skills! You should also plan to follow up the synchronous online event with a record or action plan, perhaps using e-mail, asynchronous conferencing or post.

The use of synchronous conferencing through the Internet offers partici-pants the feeling of immediate contact, motivation and some fun, which is especially valuable if they are studying largely alone and at a distance, or where there's a need for them to experience a wide range of learning opportunities. Synchronous Internet audio conferencing has been used productively by the OU on foreign language programmes, where it offers benefits to distance learners to develop, helps them to develop oral and aural skills in the target language and to converse spontaneously (Rodine, Kotter and Shield, 1999).

Following a number of research and development projects, OU MBA students are using Internet audio-based synchronous conferencing. They use a software tool called Lyceum conceived and prototyped at the OU's Knowledge Media Institute (KMI) and implemented by a team at the OU's Centre for Educational Software. Lyceum supports Internet audio, dynamic onscreen whiteboard, concept mapper, and image grabber. Voice quality is nearly as good as telephony. See Scott and Eisenstadt (1998) and http://kmi.open.ac.uk/knowledgeweb for overview of Lyceum and examples of synchronous technologies.

Lyceum was relaunched in autumn 2002 in a new version in which the original licensed voice codec was rewritten. As the software is now entirely the intellectual property of the Open University, it can be used more widely, and shared with partners. In 2003 65 groups across the Open University, involving some 2,500 user accounts, were using or evaluating the software for both learning and administration. Professor Paul Quintas of the Open University Business School writes about the experience of an MBA course using Lyceum from 1999:

We rolled out a synchronous audio conferencing tool to nearly 1000 MBA students on *B823 Managing Knowledge* course. Participants are located globally – we have students in Australia, Asia and South Africa as well as throughout Europe. The onscreen tools provide many advantages over telephone conferencing such as participants being able to see who is talking, or who is waiting to speak. Learning teams can jointly develop on-screen shared diagrams or concept maps, and discuss these in real time. Lyceum supports small group structured activities (three or four students), tutorials (e-moderator plus up to 12 students) plus a burgeoning number of informal uses, eg groups of students running their own self-help groups on a drop-in basis. During online tutorials e-moderators can control the screen display of all the students' personal computers and talk through presentation slides. A great deal of work has gone into the design and e-moderation of the online tutorials, building on the experience of good face-to-face facilitators. Synchronous conferencing has huge potential for distance learning because it provides the advantages of real-time discus-sions and group interactions without the need for specialized telecom-munications channels or for participants to co-locate.

Dr Steve Little, the current course team chair of B823, Managing Knowledge, reflects on four presentations and the use of Lyceum for synchronous online tutorials:

> When we first used Lyceum, our online tutorial sessions were prepared and scheduled by the course team and run by the tutors. These were supplemented by ad-hoc Lyceum sessions organized by the students, such as for exam preparation. Later we made Lyceum optional, in support of scheduled face-to-face meetings and other informal groups. In 2003, B823 is in its fourth presentation. 700 to 850 students work remotely using Lyceum on assignments, in small teams, and in online tutorials, with reflection on the process as a core learning objective. In addition, the tutor community employs Lyceum for itself while preparing for the Residential Schools (Little, Fowle and Quintas, 2003).

Interest continues in the OU in synchronous environments. For example Marc Eisenstadt of the Knowledge Media Institute tells us:

> We're now starting to roll out BuddySpace to a group of OU language students; it interoperates with all the 'big name' messengers (ICQ, MSN Messenger, Yahoo Messenger), and more importantly provides features like automatic roster and buddylists, construction of tutor group members and geo-location information for those who want it ('dots on maps' in effect, so you can see who's on . . . all in the interests of community spirit, 'feelgood' factor!) (http://kmi.open.ac.uk/projects/buddyspace).

On another front, the pace of technological change in the huge and competitive market for mobile Internet connectivity is rapidly accelerating. Phone numbers will in future identify an individual rather than a device or geographical location and phone numbers may last for the life of an individual person. Public telephone networks, originally created for voice transmission, will transform to carry data (text, sound and video), mostly based on Internet technologies. Low orbit wireless satellite access to all corners of the world, together with falling prices for computer and communication technologies, will give much wider access and networking on a truly global scale. In countries with poor fixed-line telephone systems, mobile connectivity through cellular systems will provide access to many more people who will 'leap-frog' over others, technologically, by missing out interim stages. How interesting and valuable it will be to have such wide perspectives made available in our online conferencing!

Supporting distance language learners through synchronous conferencing

Regine Hampel, Mirjam Hauck and Lesley Shield from the Department of Languages at the Open University, UK, explain that although they know the benefits of asynchronous conferencing, they choose to use synchronous or real-time conferencing, for the benefits of the dimension of spontaneity and the requirement for participants to 'think on their feet'. (As Lyceum is now used on live courses as an integral part of those courses, we felt 'use' rather than 'experiment' was the more appropriate word.) They use audiographic rather than text conferencing because they believe this to be more appropriate for language learning, where oral communication is a central component of the experience.

Real-time applications support language learners in developing their fluency in the foreign language. Participants use the language to communicate while receiving immediate feedback on their performance from their fellow learners and e-tutors. Real-time communication can range from 'corridor chat' (participants use, for example, instant messaging tools, to announce their online presence to their peers, and perhaps text chat to exchange brief messages) to webcasting (online, live lectures to large numbers of participants), but synchronous conferencing seems to be most effectively employed to support limited numbers of participants taking part in carefully structured learning activities with well-defined learning outcomes.

The purpose of the task may define the role of the e-moderator For language learning, for example, this is usually to foster learner interaction comparable to 'real-life' communication, and the e-moderator may either choose to intervene only minimally or decide to pass on the 'moderation duties' to one of the learners or ask the learners to take turns moderating the event. Synchronous conferencing does not easily accommodate large numbers in the same conference; the level of e-moderation required to ensure such events produce comprehensible output tends to reduce the amount of participant spontaneity, as the moderator must carefully orchestrate the order in which participants contribute, ensuring that the threads of the discussion are intelligible. Participants work more effectively in smaller groups. From 8 to 15 participants appears to be the optimum number, which can be divided into subgroups working on activities whose outcomes are then presented in a plenary session.

In 2002, the Department of Languages in the Faculty of Education and Language Studies at the Open University (OU) in the UK began – in line with the OU's Learning and Teaching Strategy – a progressive move towards delivering all language tutorials online using Lyceum, an Internet-based audiographics conferencing tool developed by the OU.

Despite participants being in different geographical locations, the Lyceum conferencing tool enables students and tutors simultaneously to hear and talk to each other. Apart from the voice facility, Lyceum offers a shared whiteboard (for writing and drawing and for importing and manipulating images), a shared concept map (suitable for brainstorming exercises and word association tasks as well as any other vocabulary-building activities) and a shared document module (for collaborative writing activities). Voice conferencing can also be supplemented by text chat, which provides limited space for additional written input.

A Level 2 German course focusing on the development of reading and writing skills was among the first OU courses to offer tutorials solely online. Research suggested that familiarity with the tools from the outset enhances the learning experience, so since neither tutors nor students were familiar with Lyceum, technology-focused training provided by the OU's technical support team was arranged for all participants (stage one from the five-stage model).

Tutors also attend training sessions led by faculty members with experience of synchronous online pedagogy. The pedagogical training introduces tutors to managing groups of learners they cannot see, and gives them the opportunity to participate in some of the activities in which they later ask learners to take part. This allows them to experience the virtual environment from a learner's perspective.

Online tutorials focus on one main activity (stage three to stage four) but start with linguistically undemanding warm-up exercises in order to help participants overcome their initial inhibitions, get to know each other and to foster collaboration (stage two). The activities are designed to support the development of linguistic skills through communicative interaction and collaborative learning, and gradually introduce students to the shared whiteboard, concept map and shared document modules (stage one). The activity design takes into account the multimodal nature of the technology, and encourages students and tutors to use different tools to suit their particular learning style as well as the task (stage three).

The activities revolve around students' participation in role-plays or other pre-arranged learning tasks requiring collaborative interaction. Students are also encouraged to use authentic Web material in order to collect information. According to their evaluation of their experiences, however, the most exciting aspects for students are their intense interactions with peers and their involvement in collaborative tasks.

As a result of the successful implementation of e-tutorials via Lyceum, virtual summer schools are now offered to those students who cannot attend obligatory residential schools. The first of these, a virtual German school, ran in the autumn of 2002 and proved to be an extremely rewarding experience for both the e-tutor and the students involved. The e-tutor was extremely enthused by the students' motivation and engagement in the virtual school. The students appreciated the opportunity to practise their oral skills in time for the oral exams in early October. Their interactions with the e-tutor made them feel that they were equally as well prepared for exams as those who were able to attend the week of total immersion in the target language at residential school in August.

Abacus Virtual College case study

Gerry Prendergast is Training Director of Abacus Virtual College, which provides large-scale online training courses in the United Kingdom using FirstClass. He gives an example of using online for his Tutorial Asynchronous Workshop, an attempt to capture the reflection associated with asynchronous learning plus the motivation and commitment more easily achieved with synchronous activities. Gerry shows us the importance of careful but flexible planning. You will note the e-moderator's sensitivity to feelings and how this awareness relates to the rates of participation. Gerry's role as the e-moderator (and reflector) is explained as the process unfolds.

Course participants cannot always attend our scheduled face-to-face sessions. Recently, I discovered that none of my group could travel to a central location in order to attend their course final face-to-face day. I decided to try to achieve an 'end of process' event using FirstClass. Its time delays give participants a greater chance to give reflective responses and help to reduce the connection time and costs. I canvassed the participants to ensure that everyone could participate, at least for part of the session. I planned the event prior to the day, just as I would for a face-to-face learning session. A few days prior to the event, I posted the schedule online.

On the day, the activity started a little slowly, with participants first logging in, between 8.36 am and 10.10 am. I started with the following activity, at 8.51 am:

> Hi All,
>
> Welcome to the online module 5!
>   The first area I want to look at is your original hopes explored as this course started!
>   What I would ask each of you to do is to:
>
> Think about what your original hopes were
>
> Then
>
> Contribute: Which of them were realized/not realized and your feelings about these now?
> Post your message
> Log back in 5 minutes later and comment on anything that someone else has said.
> Gerry P

Initially, the participants spent some time acknowledging their presence on the system and socializing with their colleagues ('Good to see you online', 'What is the weather like in?'). I had not planned for the socializing but I realized it was important. This took almost an hour. The first of the answers to my question (shown above) was posted at 9.43 am. The next contribution was posted at 9.49 am. A number of other contributions then followed.

At 9.48 am I posted a second activity (a review of the participants' fears as stated at the start of the course). We now had two separate items under discussion running at once. This is very difficult to undertake in a face-to-face session but worked online. During the day, I found that I was able effectively to run up to three different discussions simultaneously.

The pace of participants posting contributions quickened considerably, as the morning went on. I decided to introduce short breaks, as contributors reported online fatigue. Some participants used this 'down' time to catch up and post more contributions. As the e-moderator, I used the time to review the progress made and to consider what I could hope to achieve after we resumed.

The participants started to log in again during the early afternoon and we again had an intense period of asynchronous discussion. By 3.15 pm I was feeling extremely tired and I became aware that others felt the same. I posted the following message:

> Has anyone else noticed how our style has become a lot more relaxed since we came online early this morning? I think it has a lot to do with us getting tired – it really takes it out of you communicating with five others online all morning.

Among the responses was the following:

> Me too, I thought we were logging in at set times, I have to admit my eyes are struggling as is my brain!

At this stage, the average number of contributions posted by each participant was just over 46. Many of these were two or three line responses, but a substantial number were over 10 lines long and contributed some excellent learning points to the group. At 3.31 pm I called a halt to the proceedings and ensured that a summarizer was appointed.

The results were extremely successful as everyone had fully participated, enjoyed and benefited from the experience and focused on the tasks. The event generated great camaraderie and teamwork and even some online humour.

Open University Centre for Modern Languages case study

Marie-Noëlle Lamy, Lecturer in French at the OU's Centre for Modern Languages, gives us a fascinating insight into two contrasting e-moderating techniques. By the way, Marie-Noëlle warns us that the French versions of the messages are unedited, and therefore contain mistakes.

In language learning, chatting can be a legitimate learning outcome. If the 'chat' is not only in the language but also about language, the benefits of the interaction are heightened. Facilitating language awareness online thus offers the e-moderator a chance to let social needs work in favour of subject knowledge rather than as a distraction.

Open University students of French as a Foreign Language used a bulletin board to take part in 'conversations' about vocabulary learning. The e-moderators used strategies involving different degrees of online visibility. Some were at times highly interventionist, pushing students to develop their subject knowledge, be more reflective, and find ways around their problems of learning in isolation without access to sources of expertise or information. To achieve these aims, however, they relied to some extent on traditional teacher-centred techniques, such as directing, instructing and asking questions to which they already knew the answer, in an explicitly tutorial way. For example, a learner sets off the enquiry and, in the absence of a dictionary or other information, states an erroneous hypothesis:

> Je n'ai aucune d'idée ce qui veut dire 'dicible'. Peut-être la phrase 'au-delà du dicible' veut dire 'the back of beyond'?
> Amitiés

The English translation is:

> I have no idea what 'dicible' means. Maybe the phrase 'au-delà du dicible' means 'the back of beyond'?
> Greetings

There is solidarity but no help from a second learner; indeed, he confirms the error!

> Il y a toute une gamme des choses d'intérêt pour moi parmi votre coup d'essai. Je n'ai trouvé pas 'dicible', mais j'aime la traduction 'the back of beyond'.
> A bientôt

The English translation is:

> There is a range of interesting things as far as I'm concerned in your 'first attempt'. I couldn't find 'dicible', but I like the translation 'the back of beyond'.
>   See you soon

Here is the e-moderator's response to both learners:

> Pensées sur le travail de C-met d'E-h
> Merci, vous deux, car avec de courts messages, vous avez posé des questions importantes. D'abord, prenons le problème des informations qui ne sont pas dans le dictionnaire. Dicible n'y est pas. Mais réfléchissons: nous avons tous dans la tête des connaissances qui peuvent nous servir. Par exemple: dicible est de la famille de dictée, diction, et même bénédicité. Quel est le sens qui est en commun à tous ces mots? Pouvons-nous par conséquent déduire le sens de: au-delà du dicible? QUI VA REPONDRE?

The English translation is:

> Thoughts on the work of C-m and E-h
> Thank you to both of you, because, in your short messages, you have asked important questions. First, let's take the problem of when the dictionary just doesn't have the information you're looking for. 'Dicible' isn't in there. But let's think: we all have at the back of our minds some knowledge which can help us. For example 'dicible' (expressible) is related to 'dictée' (dictation), diction (diction) and even bénédicité (benediction, blessing). What is the meaning that all these words have in common? WHO WILL ANSWER?

The two students were able to respond to this prodding, and their messages, posted on the same day, showed how they had both surmounted the original difficulty. First came a new idea from the original enquirer (this time a good interpretation of the French).

> Bien entendu! 'dic' veut dire 'speak' (du latin, si je m'en souviens), mais 'speakable'??!! Donc, je pense que peut-etre la phrase 'elle aimait la solitude au-delà du dicible' veut dir 'she loved solitude more than words can say'. Est-ce que j'ai raison?

Or, in English:

> Of course! 'dic' means 'speak' (from Latin if I remember right), but 'speakable'??!! So I think that maybe the phrase 'elle aimait la solitude au-delà du dicible' means 'she loved solitude more than words can say'. Am I right?

A further contribution from the second learner:

> Moi aussi C-M! Je suis d'accord.
> (Enfin, un éclair de génie ('flash of inspiration', je l'ai trouvé dans le CD). J'ai cherché les exemples de la famille dic, et en commun est le sens de 'parler' ou 'parler à quelqu'un'. Bien, 'au delà du dicible' devient 'beyond saying, or more than could be said', afin de dire que Barbara vécût la campagne parce qu'elle aimait la solitude plus qu'on va dire.

In English:

> Me too, C-M! I agree.
>   At last, a flash of inspiration (I found that phrase in the CD). I looked for examples of the DIC word family, and in common they have the meaning of 'speak' or 'talk to someone'. OK, so then 'au delà du dicible' becomes 'beyond saying, or more than could be said', to mean that Barbara lived in the countryside because she loved being alone more than we will be able to say.

In total, this exchange was a success in that students identified a problem that interested them and used their existing knowledge of language by way of a generalized strategy for coping with lack of information. They arrived at a solution which satisfied them. However, it remained close to a traditional teacher–learner dialogue, and students were not inspired by it to contribute wider, more naturalistic language.

In contrast, other e-moderators preferred to intervene as little as possible, and to let students become 'teachers' for their peers. Here, a student requested help with the meaning of *obligation dramaturgique*, a phrase which she had found in a newspaper article, but which she was unable to discover in any dictionary. The first person to come to her aid (D) alerted her to the importance of 'context' and offered two possible solutions:

> Je suggère que cette phrase veut dire 'le besoin d'être vu de faire quelque chose ou le besoin de faire un récit mimé d'un rôle' mais on désirerait d'avoir plus d'information en ce qui concerne le contexte de cette phrase. Est-ce que ma suggestion saisit la signification de votre phrase dans son contexte? D.

In English:

> I suggest that that phrase (obligation dramaturgique) means 'the need to be seen doing something, or the need to tell a story in mime,' but it would be good to have more information about the context of that phrase. Does my suggestion capture the meaning of your phrase in its context? D.

After a clarification by the original enquirer, a second student, MK, offered a different approach: he used an analogy derived from personal experience to illustrate the phrase and offered a translation.

> J'aime bien la vie publique et il y a vingt-sept ans que j'étais fonctionnaire pour un conseil régional. La phrase 'une obligation dramaturgique', dans le context que tu as expliqué, fait comprendre à moi la phrase, 'a ritual dance'. C'est une phrase que tous les fonctionnaires utilisent entre eux-mêmes quand les conseillers discutent et jouent des roles adversariales comme dans une pièce de théâtre. Ils montrent les émotions artificiels, ils simulent être en colère quand en réalité c'est simplement la système de débat contradictoire. Pour le grand public c'est excitant, pour les fonctionnaires c'est très très ennuyant. MK.

Here is the English translation:

> I enjoy getting involved in public life and twenty-seven years ago I worked on a local council. In the context which you gave, the phrase 'obligation dramaturgique' suggested to me the phrase 'a ritual dance'. It's an expression which council officers all use amongst themselves to refer to the way councillors discuss things, taking up adversarial roles, as in a theatre play. They display artificial emotion and simulate anger when actually all that's going on is the normal course of a contradictory debate. For the public at large it's exciting, for council officers it's very very boring. MK.

E-moderator 'invisibility' certainly has its place in language learning online, at specific stages of the communication. These students learned something from each other about an item of French vocabulary. However, unlike the pair who discussed 'dicible' with their teacher, these ones did not gain access to generalizable learning skills. The challenge is to marry the two approaches, and devise an e-moderating style which moves learners in and out of two contrasting learning situations one in which there are precise instructions for production of the outcome, and one in which productions are part of the socio-cognitive life of the online group.

Celebrate!

We need to mobilize and deploy the brains and commitment of teachers and trainers of all kinds in the service of e-moderating. We also need to raise the profile of e-moderators, and recognize and reward their valuable work. E-moderating is somewhat less visible (sometimes almost invisible if done well) and therefore special efforts need to go into celebrating good practice! I hope the exploration of roles and qualities in this chapter of use to you and will enable you to recruit and train for very productive online teaching and learning.

For developing e-moderators you can look at the following Resources for practitioners:

1 Time p 151
9 E-moderating with synchronous conferencing p 168

To turn the ideas from this chapter into practice look at the following Resources for practitioners:

6 E-moderation principles p 162
8 Knowledge sharing and construction p 166
14 Boosting participation p 184

Chapter 4

Training e-moderators

This chapter is about the process of creating e-moderators through training online in all their roles. I shall use as my main example the online training programme developed in the OU Business School.

Plan to train

Any significant initiative aimed at changing teaching methods or the introduction of technology into teaching and learning should include effective e-moderator support and training, otherwise its outcomes are likely to be meagre and unsuccessful. Even where technological infrastructure and support are strong, and when worthwhile learning applications are developed, without staff development nothing is likely to happen beyond pilot schemes. In the medium term, the costs of training and support for users can be higher than the provision of the technology; therefore it is worthwhile giving the training of e-moderators due consideration and adequate planning. Even in well-supported and well-developed distance environments, students' expectations of their e-moderators may be higher than the real experience (Margolis, 2003). There is still much to be done!

If you are feeling enthusiastic about developing online learning, please be aware that a fair bit of rethinking of course methodologies, and of training and support for e-moderators, is needed for success. There are examples where, despite early adoption of online, courses reverted to old technologies. This is often due to the lack of support and development of teaching staff, or failure to manage the necessary organizational changes appropriately, or an inability to train sufficient e-moderators for expansion and development. E-moderating is not a set of skills any of us is born with, nor one that we have learnt vicariously through observing teachers while we ourselves were learning. As yet there are few online mentors to guide us through step by step. Maybe in the future, adults will draw on their childhood online experiences and try to emulate the examples of good e-moderators who changed the direction of their lives! But, meanwhile, e-moderators must be trained.

Because the pace of change is fast, few of us can allow for long apprentice-ship through learning, supporting and then teaching in the online environ-ment. It is likely that pressures will build up – either because student numbers are large or you want to be sure of early success – and gradual change may prove too slow. Critically, you must know what you are training for, and, as in any planning of learning activities, what competencies or outcomes you are seeking. Figure 2.1 in Chapter 2 gives you a suggested list on which you can build, bearing in mind your discipline, your students and your context.

Training must take into account the contentious issue of how much time e-moderators can be expected to work online. The time required depends on what they are doing, of course, but you can be absolutely certain that if they are untrained they will take longer and do it less well. As I have said, teaching online needs careful planning and preparation, otherwise the stories will continue of e-moderators being overloaded, underpaid and burnt out by the work.

I've noticed a wide variety of reactions from colleagues in universities and colleges around the world to the introduction of virtual learning environments and other new technologies, ranging from wild enthusiasm from some to strategic undermining by others. Most faculty members are still looking for contractual positions regarding their use of information and communication technologies, so the major moves towards online in many different contexts rely on good will and the support available to reskill. Barriers and opportunities include complex intrinsic and extrinsic factors (Leonard and Guba, 2001).

At present many of the most enthusiastic and successful e-moderators are those 'gypsy scholars' working in a portfolio way, and those who have experi-enced and seen the benefits of leading and constructing knowledge with virtual learning groups. They typically have acquired their skills and understanding in the idiosyncratic online world itself, learning to teach online through the medium.

Most teachers and trainers, especially those in higher education, learnt to teach largely through apprenticeship in their disciplines. Their practice consists of complex sets of values, attitudes and behaviours, many of them largely 'taken as read'. Now there are many people admirably trying to offer them the chance to be 'trained in new technologies for teaching and learning'. However, such attempts to address the reskilling of academic staff through half-day workshops in WebCT, Blackboard and the like clearly are hardly likely to do more than scratch the surface, and they may also convince faculty that teaching online is about learning to use a computer programme. Indeed several studies confirm that 'no amount of hands-on. . . . training can replace the practical application of technology to the teaching and learning process' (Bennett and Marsh, 2002: 17).

Focusing training on use of the features of the technological system is unlikely to do more than enable the slightest dent in the long apprenticeship in practical and theoretical knowledge or competence in the teaching profession, much of which is acquired rather mysteriously, or at least informally. Another strong tendency has been to teach a great deal about teaching theory and hence 'put off' large numbers of potential e-moderators who want practical guides. The innovators and the early adopters persist with more or less good grace, although some 'burn out' or become demoralized in the attempt. For some of the others, the battle is lost early on, and they can become convinced that satisfactory knowledge transmission and construction has to happen face to face. However, if early in the process trainees are enabled to be active online participants for themselves, they see the benefits and are motivated to acquire the skills (Tsui and Ki, 2002).

They then need a 'very safe online environment' where they feel free to express their ideas and concerns, challenge and ask questions (Tsui and Ki, 2002: 40). E-moderators trained in this way perceive the work involved in teaching online very differently Their positive perception is reflected in the way they relate to students online, and ultimately in their self-value and professionalism. Providing such training is a non-trivial task (Richards, 2002). Essentially I am arguing here that there is a new form of literacy, based around the acquisition of e-moderating skills, that goes well beyond training in the platform. To create e-moderators we need to scale up the acquisition of such skills, and if we are to do so, potential e-moderators must be placed in real but virtual situations as early as possible (Bennett and Marsh, 2002).

Downgrading the human role and upgrading the technological impact by suggesting that we now need to consider the 'human factors' misses the key point. What we know of learning is that if we want people to change what they actually do, we need to offer experiences that shuttle backwards and forwards between what they already know, and what they are prepared to develop, between specific details and their implications in wider contexts, and between practice and reflection (Harvey and Knight, 1996).

First, teachers and trainers, new and experienced and at all levels of education, need to acquire new skills in creating, managing and promoting students in participation in interactive conferencing online. These skills are more important but harder to acquire than, for example, posting PowerPoint slides online. Second, key attention needs to be given to enable them to gain confidence and professionalism and continue to develop (Barker, 2002; Bennett and Marsh, 2002; Tsui and Ki, 2002). The mechanism for acquiring the skills initially and continuing to develop should be the medium itself, and it depends on the support of experienced facilitators: the people I call e-convenors, the e-moderators of the e-moderators, the trainers of the trainers.

Just one word about the importance of stable, reliable and appropriate technologies in the support, training and development of faculty and tutors, at least beyond the natural innovators. Just as with infants, sensitization to a potential allergen early in their development may lead to major and sometimes incurable problems later on. Such is the impact of foisting a poor platform or a weakly supported technology on an unsuspecting audience. At the slightest indication of trouble later, they'll be convinced that 'e-learning doesn't work'!

When I wrote the first edition of this book, I argued that e-moderating training was about changes to pedagogy. Since then it has become fashionable to assert that teaching, not technology, is the 'solution' to working online. I guess that's progress! However, it's too simplistic. To train effective and efficient e-moderators, we need to create training that provides an online environment where the sense of emotional identity, the shifting of time, the experience of the context with all its foibles can all be experienced. Most trainee e-moderators are happiest undertaking their online training with others from their disciplines, and hence are able to make strong practical links between theory, practice and skills. It is important to try to model (rather than teach) the desired skills, offer real practical experience and many opportunities for challenge, collaboration and reflection (Richards, 2002).

Training of e-moderators in the OUBS

Here I offer an example of large-scale well-researched training in e-moderating. I describe the steps that I took, with my colleague Ken Giles, in developing and implementing an online training programme for e-moderators in the Open University Business School, 1996–99. Each stage in the model that I explained in Chapter 2 provided a 'scaffold' or guide for training up e-moderators from novice to expert status in and through computer modulated conferencing (CMC). I hope that this account of our experience will be of value to you if you are facing similar training requirements whether on a small or large scale, in whatever discipline.

When we built the first online training programme during the winter of 1995–6 in the OUBS we were faced with a fairly major task. Human and financial resources were limited. We wanted to use the five-stage model described in Chapter 2 as a basis. We expected up to 200 trainees, spread over most of Western Europe – it turned out that 187 registered for the first round of training. They were appointed to work as part-time tutors for the OUBS from home and most had full-time management or academic jobs outside the OU. We could assume that they had basic computer literacy although a few had more advanced skills. E-moderating online was but one aspect among many of the teaching strategy and of their role as tutors for the MBA courses. Online had to be meaningful and worthwhile for both the students and their e-moderators if it was to be judged a success.

We wanted to indicate to our trainees that online was essentially a distance medium of communication and to demonstrate that the training objectives can be achieved at a distance. We therefore considered that the training programme should use CMC itself and be accessed from tutors' own machines, probably at home. The tutors' first need was to be able to log in using their particular configuration of hardware from their home base, rather than using someone else's configuration via a different access point. The tutors truly needed to experience, much as their own students would, the pitfalls and the potential of online if they were to e-moderate effectively. A further very real reason for using online for the training was that to offer intensive face-to-face training would have stretched our human resources and provision of training facilities to the limit. Furthermore we wanted the training to focus on pedagogical knowledge, built up through personal and collective reflection on practice, rather than on acquiring a technical grasp of the hardware and software.

We were reluctant to ground the training in any form of text-based instructional materials, although this is common throughout the OU, because of the risk of these materials being divorced from the construction of the online knowledge and skills. However, it rapidly became obvious that a booklet, showing exactly what the screen should look like at each point in the procedure, was essential and we produced one for the second and subsequent versions of the training. To prepare the booklet, we had to create the online programme first, then print exact copies of the screens and key messages. This booklet supports those who like a paper manual. It also enables them to work offline if they wish, and they don't need to print pages for themselves.

Our training programme had to accommodate people with a wide range of prior skills and knowledge. The programme needed to be intrinsically motivating and lead to competent practice. The task was therefore to develop a programme that, while providing the development of essential basic skills (such as confidence and competence in using the software), represented as closely as possible the realities of teaching and learning online.

We decided the following:

- An average tutor would be expected to devote some ten hours to the CMC training programme.

- The design would be based on the five-stage model previously developed.
- A core of online e-moderators (online trainers of the online trainers) would be selected and trained to e-moderate the individual training conferences within the programme.
- Evaluation and action research would be based on tracking the trainees through the stages in the programme by a series of online conferences and questionnaires of a quantitative and qualitative nature and through monitoring the work of the trainees online after the training finished and the tutors commenced working with students.
- A small fee and a sum for telephone expenses, and a certificate of completion, would be provided that the trainees could claim on completion of their exit questionnaires.

Training programme design

We planned for a wide range of prior knowledge and/or experience of online among the trainees. Each would have his or her own 'map' of the topic. The programme needed to include training in declarative knowledge – what is this icon?, procedural knowledge – how do I send a message? as well as more strategic knowledge – what can I do with my e-moderating skills? However, we planned that trainees would acquire these various kinds of knowledge in an integrated way. The online training programme would not only be about acquiring new skills but would also help trainees to explore their attitudes to online working and its meaning for their own teaching.

We took a number of decisions at this stage about our own approach to online training. The programme was designed to create a series of 'microworlds' in which the trainees could interact with each other, with the e-moderators of the training conference (who we called convenors) and with the software, before progressing to the next stage. We hoped that our trainees would gradually build up their knowledge and software skills, particularly in the use of computer conferencing for management learning. We made them aware of the goals all the way through the training. They were advised of appropriate ways of undertaking the tasks but could also construct their own approach. We tried to enable them to use the software as a matter of routine while we raised their awareness of the teaching and learning aspects. The importance ascribed in constructivism to the building of relationships between new and existing knowledge (Bruner, 1986) led us to a careful choice of icons and titles for conferences, and the use of familiar metaphors for explaining aspects of online working.

Helping trainees to control their frustration is a key aspect of learning to use online. We tried to achieve a balance between a trainee struggling with too much complexity and being given enough involvement in the task. We attempted to give more help when trainees got into difficulties and less as they gained proficiency. In practice some trainees needed almost no help and others huge amounts. It did not prove possible to predict who needed extra help until they asked for it. So it was important to provide a continuously available source of help.

Evaluation

Engaging in reflective and interactive online activities, especially those leading to explaining, justifying and evaluating problem solutions, is a very important learning process. In 1983, Schön pointed out that people change their everyday practice by having reflective conversations, they frame their understanding of a situation in the light of experience, and they try out actions and then reinterpret or reframe the situation in the light of the consequences of that action. Schön also argued that through reflection a practitioner could surface and critique understandings that have grown up around a specialized practice and make sense of a situation for him or herself. We think this applies to online training too.

We wished to find ways of enabling reflection on online practice to happen within the training programme, at each of the five levels. We therefore decided to introduce a set of simple motivational goals, by requiring our trainees to reflect 'deliberately' on learning at each stage. They were encouraged to take part, to post at least one message at each of the five levels, to contribute to the 'reflections' conferences, to complete their exit questionnaires – and only then to ask for their certificate of completion, training payments and expenses.

The training programme was developed and updated year by year. By 1999, over 400 trainees had taken part, with nearly all commenting on their experience of the training through the reflections conferences and exit questionnaires. We also monitored the work of the e-moderators with their students and made adjustments to the training. The examples that follow are from version five, the 1999 version of the online training in OUBS. The model has since been used on a global basis for training e-moderators. There is a worked example in *E-tivities* (Salmon, 2002a, ch. 3).

OUBS training programme

We base the five levels of the online training on the five-stage model described in Chapter 2, Figure 2.1. At every level, the simplest possible set of instructions

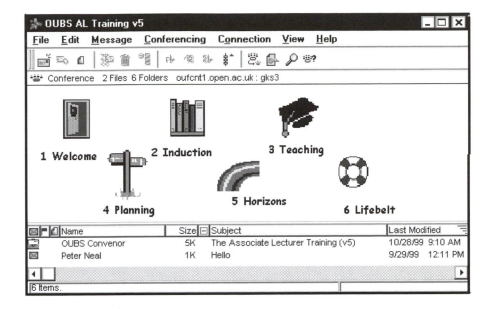

Figure 4.1   *Desktop screen of online training in OUBS*

accompanies activities in the online environment. The printed booklet accompanying the training programme offers a list of conferences to aid navigation, copies of what the screen should look like to the trainee at various stages and a print-out of key online instructions, eg how to post a CV (résumé), how to send messages.

When a trainee logs on, she or he sees five icons, representing the five levels of the training programme. In addition, Lifebelt (or help) icon is available which contains virus prevention software, downloadable manuals, FAQs about the software, Code of Practice for use of the system, helpdesk phone numbers and even a 'lifeguard' to e-mail if necessary.

This is our first message to trainees:

WELCOME!

Each stage will offer you skills with a range of activities designed to enable you to practise those skills. For the early stages the programme will give you quite a lot of help, but for the final stages it will only give limited guidance. By the end of the programme you should have the skills required to work with your students in a productive way.

It is strongly recommended that you work through one stage before moving on to the next. Please visit the 'Reflections' conference at each level before closing that level and moving on to the next. We will use these for evaluating the training and research into conferencing.

Aims and objectives of this training programme

The aims of the programme are to:

- provide you with the technical skills to access and use the FirstClass system and to undertake a range of tasks online;
- provide you with the experience and confidence to use the FirstClass system as a key resource in teaching and learning online as an AL;
- enable you to become an active member of the OUBS online community, participating in and contributing to School, programme and course conferences.

The introductory message for each of the five stages in the training explains the purpose of that stage. Now click on the Welcome icon and announce your arrival! OUBS Convenor

Level one: Welcome

The purpose of this level is to ensure that trainees can find a conference, find, read and send messages, discover who else is taking part and give a little information about themselves.

The new trainee's first task is to visit the 'arrivals' conference, where they find instructions on posting a simple message to announce their arrival. Most trainees succeed in achieving this task on their first, or sometimes their second, log-in. However, their relief or jubilation at having 'made it' is often obvious:

I was preparing to sneak in by the back door but feel so much better having spotted several other 'started before but life got in the way' messages. JI

I have arrived but not sure if I have landed – if you know what I mean! PP

Present but probably not correct! DB

Ho there – my first action is to print everything because I can't remember
anything but the fact that I can't remember anything and have to do
something creative to cope – like printing a whole load of instructions.
RM

These efforts are rewarded by a personal 'congratulations and welcome' message
from the online trainer (whom we call convenor in this context). At this stage
the convenor will also point the new trainee to any sources of help and attempt
to assuage any worries or grievances. Many trainees remember the importance
of their individual welcome into the online environment when questioned
months or even years later, so we feel it is always worthwhile.

At Level one we also invite trainees to explore the difference between e-mail
and conferencing. Increasingly, trainee e-moderators are presenting with fairly
well developed e-mail skills. It is important to explain the differences to build on
their prior knowledge and expertise. Finally we explain how to look at the
résumés of other participants in the training, and invite them to post their
own. We emphasize the important of posting a few details about oneself early
in the training, since we have found that every participant feels more comfortable if right from the start, they have a little knowledge about people they are
working with.

Finally, the last task at Level one is to post a message to reflect on their
experiences so far. Here is our invitation message:

Reflections on Level one

Please ensure that you have completed all the tasks at this level. Then send
a message to this conference reflecting on:

The key learning points from your initial experiences in the training.
After you have completed your reflections message, please close all the
windows from Level 1, and click onto Level 2 Induction' (the bookshelf
icon). OUBS Convenor

Most participants respond, establishing, we think, a small amount of reflection
from the start of their journey into conference e-moderation. Here are some
examples of their messages:

Things often look simple, and can also be simplified, but below the surface there's a lot more than meets the eye. TD

Hey, this isn't so bad. I thought it would be much more complicated given my not so literate computer skills! AL

My overwhelming sense of achievement at leaving this message is diminished by the entirely predictable instability of virtual communications. I feel like I've been trying to send smoke signals in a force 9 wind. DB

Good first session as people's online personalities emerge. It takes longer than I would have expected to read the threads/postings – would not dream of not trying to at least scan them all in case I missed a particularly good one. ;-) Perceive myself to be 'falling behind' which is providing a frisson of worry – at what point does 'asynchronous' become 'forget it'? 8-) A useful insight into what students may feel at times – the gamekeeper turned poacher. PD

I've found the first session a bit strange. It has brought forth an array of responses, attitudes and approaches from colleagues. As my usual teaching style is probably relatively structured, I've been surprised at how an apparently 'structured' set of e-tivities can lead to what (at first blush) seemed such an unstructured set of responses. PR

Level two: Induction

Level two, equivalent to stage two in the model, enables trainees to learn about protocols and how to relate to others through this medium, and to acquire useful software skills.

Trainees work through exercises aimed at analyzing a mock discussion among students who are conferencing about a television programme. The 'participants' are making all the classic mistakes (lack of titles to messages, advertising, messages in the wrong conference, failure to re-title messages when replying and changing topics, 'parental responses' rather than collegiate and attempts at domination of the discussion). The discussion has a 'real' (virtual) feel about it. Trainees are invited to view each message and consider how well or otherwise it contributes to the discussion. Feedback suggests that this is a very successful exercise for trainee e-moderators.

One trainee found this exercise particularly helpful:

> I think this exercise is an excellent one for its richness. It has a provocative title to get you into it, but sorting out the 'good' from the 'bad' proves a little too difficult for me. I would rather view it as an interesting insight into the different motivations these students may have for using online conferencing. On the other hand almost all the participants could be prompted to keep brushing up their netiquette! Great learning, thanks. ML

In addition, trainees are invited to explore appropriate communication styles online by sending a 'postcard'. We have found that this simple metaphor enables trainees to practise giving straightforward information in short messages. It also results in some sharing of information about themselves and some fun!

Here is our message:

> *Send us a postcard, please!*
>
> It takes time to develop a style of your own online – usually somewhere between writing and speaking. It needs to be brief – more than one screenful is rarely appropriate, but informative without being indecipherable or offensive to anyone who might read it. This is not meant to put you off in any way!
>
> Some people suggest that writing conference messages is a bit like writing a postcard. This is your chance to try it!
>
> Use this conference to send a message to your colleague of maximum one screenful. This could give some information about you, or perhaps seek information from others. OUBS Convenor

The postcard messages offer fascinating insights into our trainees, who typically mention their location and often why they're working online instead of doing something else!

> As I sit here on a Friday evening in dark decided wintry Brussels I can imagine the perfect golfing day – warm and sunny with a little breeze.

Never mind for those of you who know Brussels you will know this scene is sadly a very rare actual occurrence – but it has the benefit that you are not often distracted in reality! 'Au revoir' and 'bon weekend'. Best regards. KD

The beauty of this postcard for me is that I don't have to hunt around for a stamp! Usually I forget to buy them. Here in Hampton (West London) it's a glorious sunny morning – postcard weather even. Just off to the Tate Gallery for a cultural fix and then a look at the Millennium Wheel on the South Bank – I've seen it in the horizontal position and now I want to see the vertical version. Regards PB

Not sure 'I wish you were here' in my study staring at a VDU. Life is for living - can you be living focused at a screen, yes I know 'virtual reality' is supposed to be the answer. Can you really experience life by accessing a screen? EP

Fellow holiday-makers, I am sitting here in rainy Dublin, the Celtic tiger looks more like a drowned rat and I am faced with the familiar dilemma of what spurious candyfloss I can use to fill the blank space of a post card. Missing you already AN

Trainees visit the reflection conference at Level two before they move on, which asks:

What key learning points from your progress on the training so far would you pass on to your students?

Here is an example response:

Amazingly enough it's all beginning to fall into place. My confidence in using FirstClass (which I have never used before) is increasing rapidly and I'm not so scared of pressing the wrong button. I have learnt a lot about setting up conferences and keeping them going etc. I find that the contributions from others online, both experienced and new ones, is really useful as there is a wealth of experience out there. This would be my advice to my students – try it – it's amazing! Thanks. FH

Level three: Teaching

Level three, equivalent to stage three in the model, is concerned with giving and receiving information. We have found that trainees like to gain and share information around their professional task of teaching online. We also focus on exercises that show them how to set up their own online conferences. We include an essential practice area, and we offer exercises and discussions on the role of the e-moderator including practice in opening conferences and the 'weaving' of conference messages together. Trainees are invited to post examples of their own opening messages and to comment on those of their fellow trainees. Among the most important skills to be learnt at this stage are summarizing, archiving and weaving. See Resources for practitioners.

Trainees visit the reflections conference before exiting Level three, and again we ask them:

> What key learning points from your progress on the training so far would you pass on to colleagues from a teaching perspective?

By this stage, some excitement and trepidation about conferencing 'for real' is occurring, but there is also evidence of some real learning. Here are some examples of Level three reflections. One participant details his new insights into e-moderating:

> **Lurking**
> I agree that lurking (still looking for a more neutral term) needs investigating as colleagues suggest but note that you can check who has read a message by going to 'History'. This may allow you to identify those who are not picking up the messages (e.g. In a tutorial group) which might justify a phone call. The person may have technical problems, or may be looking in the wrong place. Still lurking is better than not participating at all!
>
> **Weaving**
> HP certainly sums it up well for me: you do have the option of setting up another sub-conference so those who want to wander off can do so in parallel with the main topic in hand. Summarizing the main points so far that are on track and adding a few pertinent questions would also help. I

guess one of the best preparations for a flagging discussion is to keep a few things up your sleeve, so that if/when things flag you have something new/interesting to add in to give it a boost.

Summarizing
I will need to be more encouraging about the contributions individually, select a title that would stand out more to enable late comers to catch up without having to read all the 'red flags' and end with a question if I were 'going live'. Wouldn't you agree. . . ? J. :-) JS

Other trainees compare e-moderating to facilitating face-to-face groups:

For me, opening, weaving, e-modding are, in many ways, just like getting a discussion going in a face-to-face setting. The skills required are the same, only the medium is a little different. Someone once told me that an online discussion group is much like having a party in a dark living room. No one can see one another, but everyone hears what is being said. There are those who whisper in the corners (go off-conference, 1-to-1 e-mail) where others can't hear, but for the most part, one can only make sense of what is going on by paying good attention. This may be a dying art – and there are times I believe that. Enjoy EM

I think conferencing can be a valuable learning tool – capturing immediate reactions and ideas, which are often, very stimulating and which often get lost in assignments and face-to-face seminars – a virtual learning organization! AA

Level four: Knowledge construction

Level four is equivalent to stage four of the model. We have found that stimulating trainees to discuss how they will use online with their students works best at this level. We provide a discussion forum so that trainees can 'meet' and 'discuss' issues with those from their own course or programme. We also attach some texts for them to consider. This gives practice in downloading attached documents as well as giving them ideas to explore. As always a reflections conference is provided at this level to encourage them to consider their progress. They are asked this time:

How do you feel about working with Computer Mediated Conferencing (CMC) with your students, based on your experience of the training so far?

Trainees recognize that they need to get real experience in working with students:

I feel confident enough to get started, but am fully aware I will continue to learn, and probably learn a lot, through actual doing. BF

I feel quite comfortable with this. I used the old CoSy conferencing in my student days and absolutely loved it. It was really helpful in my studies and a very useful contact with other students (especially those on the same course but not necessarily in my tutor group), and other tutors other than my own. It gave me a far broader view than I would ever have achieved otherwise. I hope I can pass this enthusiasm on to my students, and get as many of them as possible involved in using computer conferencing as part of their studies. I guess central to this will be my role in providing the right environment in the conference for lively and useful discussion and support for novice users, so that they can see a real advantage in using it. JB

I've derived great benefit from reading everybody else's reflections. It has truly widened my appreciation not only of the potential of the medium but also of its role in teaching and learning online. I'm ready and raring to do it for real but realize that I will need to 'stand back' and encourage the knowledge flow. JH

I've found computer conferencing an easy and effective method of engaging in debate as a student. Having completed this training I am about to find out what it is like on the other side of the modem as a tutor! I'm determined to build a sense of community with my group and perhaps encourage those who are less willing to contribute face-to-face to do so over the electronic system. (I wonder, however, just how intimidating it is for those who are not as computer literate as I am?) I'll have to ask my group. JP

Level five: Development

This level is equivalent to stage five of the model. Here we explore the use of the Web in teaching, both to build up to trainees' confidence and enable them to consider how they might embed Web resources in their own e-moderating. Trainees share their favourite search engines and sites for their discipline.

The exit questionnaire provides simple feedback to us about the trainees' experience of the whole programme and has enabled us to make incremental adjustments and improvements over the years. Quantitative and qualitative feedback from the exit questionnaire helps us to confirm and develop the exercises and approaches throughout the five levels. Trainees very consistently confirm that the five-stage model of training works for them. Creating motivation at Level one is probably the most complex challenge along with the encouragement of trainees to keep working through each of the levels until they reach Level five. However, from Level two onwards, confidence grows in almost every trainee and many are very appreciative of learning or reinforcing online communication skills and information exchange at Levels two and three. Several comment that these are basic life and business skills that are not otherwise taught in this way. At Level four, trainees really appreciate the focus on e-moderating and considerable anticipation is generated. By Level five, nearly all trainees are very keen indeed to try out their new skills on their participants!

The vast majority of trainees appreciate the highly structured, staged approach to training and learning software and e-moderating skills in an integrated way. A small minority, however, continues to ask for a software 'manual'. They often express this as an 'idiot's' guide to the system. Regrettably, it is not easy for us to simplify an interactive and complex system sufficiently for these people. We encourage such groups to download the instructions that they seek. Another small minority is happy with the training programme taking place entirely online, but wish to take their own route through the training exercises and conferences. We allow for this, of course, although we do find that a lower percentage of this group completes the programme.

Most concerns are somewhat alleviated by the time trainees complete the programme and most consider investment in their training 'good value' for the use of their previous time. However, those worries that remain are typically about the use of their time when working online with students, suggesting that expectations, reward and recognition in the use of e-moderating time must always be given careful consideration.

I have two fears: 1) my students not using it very much; and 2) it will be used a lot by my students and it will take up too much time! MD

Some students may be accessing conferences through an employer's system at no phone cost to them. Could this encourage excessive inputs and unreasonable demands on the e-moderator's time? PB

And a word of caution. It all gets so engrossing that it is easy to forget the phone bill or that it is way past bedtime again! People at the office will be wondering why I always seem so tired. NH

Most trainees feel they have achieved and accomplished personal development by Level five and are very pleased to have completed the programme. Completing trainees frequently say they believe such a training programme should be compulsory for e-moderators before they are 'let loose' on student conferences. They express very tangible progress compared to their first tentative messages at Level one. Some are by then already working with their students online. Some are very enthusiastic. We encourage staff to reflect on their whole range of feelings at the end of the process, and to recognize who or what has contributed most to their learning. Most participants express a mixture of relief and regret.

Mixed feelings here because the e-moderators course is ending. . . .
    Happy because the light is finally emerging, the feeling of managing to pull through and survive the 6 weeks course is beyond speech. . .
    Thankful . . . so used to reading many of your postings: fun one, serious one, deep and profound one, encouraging one, refreshing. . . . I am learning soooooooooo much from all of you! What a powerful collective learning process I witness! When paths cross, life changes. . .
    Excited . . . to share with the colleagues the good news of an e-tivity and the gold mine in it for learning.
    Carefulness . . . mindful of the pitfalls and possible traps for implementing an e-tivity for engineering modules.
    Regret . . . I didn't respond to many of your questions and comments; some I have not thought through, some make me smile and delighted, some I simply can't find the messages again after being interrupted, . . . If only time allowed. . .

Christine, Ken, and Len . . . Thanks for showing me how to be a good e-moderator.

I have enjoyed and learnt very much from the course. LC

Now, what am i to do with my life
When i need not log-on to my e-tivities?
But, should i accidentally do so
(post a message or respond to one)
Will I find that there's no soul there
to acknowledge, encourage, and say a kind word or two?
What's life i wonder. . .
In post-e-tivity!
NE

Many thanks all.
Have enjoyed the ride.
Special thanks to you e convenors Keith, Larry & Carole.
Have learnt much by doing the work!.
And especially seeing how you model the skills. Great job!
MD

This is the future. I have seen it and it works (sometimes). BA

Using online reminds me of the time I learnt to drive a car, I was very proud I could drive, but now I am much more interested in the places I can visit in the car. I have a feeling this is going to be similar. HF

Summaries act well as closures to an online learning experience. E-moderators can offer encouragement to participants to continue to implement their new knowledge and understandings along with their farewell messages:

E-moderation - the next step

Congratulations to all of you who have completed this 5 week e-moderation course.

While you have all learnt much along your personal learning journeys, this course is only the first step. In your discussions, you have already identified some of the aspects of your work that could be modified to support better both yourselves and your students.

Some things that may need to be reviewed include:

1. *Induction* – how will your students know what is expected of them?
2. *Assessment* – how are you going to ensure your assessment processes are valid and reliable, fair and authentic and that you are not absolutely overwhelmed with work?
3. *Collaboration* – how will you 'sell' this concept to your students? When will you use collaborative learning activities to achieve maximum impact?
4. *Motivation* – how will you design your programme to ensure all students participate where required?
5. *Organizational support* – how will you promote the changes in the way you wish to work to your senior managers, policy makers and funding sources? Sometimes a new way of working challenges the accepted practices in an educational institute. Engage a 'champion' who will press your case for change at appropriate occasions.
6. *Collegial support* – how will you maintain your interest and enthusiasm for this new way of working? You need friends and supporters to share new ideas and to test new approaches. Think about how you can maintain the enthusiasm and momentum that this course has already generated.

Best wishes, good luck and farewell , your e-convenor Christine

Dr Gillian Roberts of the Caledonian Business School in Glasgow tells us of her work with colleagues to introduce a virtual learning environment (VLE) and promote its successful use by teaching staff. Gillian is a Fellow in Communication and Information Technologies in Learning and Teaching. The Business School is based in a large city centre environment, where most students live close to the university. The traditions of teaching and learning were those of face to face until recently. Her story starts with the pilot of the VLE and continues to 2003. She tells me it's still work in progress!

Developing use of a VLE at Caledonian Business School

Our starting point was the strategic commitment of Caledonian Business School to use a VLE (Blackboard). In 2000 we targeted first year modules with large numbers (800+) students. Evaluations showed that 80 per cent of students wanted to continue using Blackboard. As a result, we extended the use of the VLE to include all undergraduate and postgraduate teaching. Blackboard was adopted by the university and found to be user-friendly and empowering for non-IT literate staff. Many staff wanted to use VLE in their teaching, after they had tried Blackboard.

When our academic staff first used Blackboard in 2001, we asked them for their reflections about their capability to exploit the benefits of a new Web-based teaching and learning environment. They indicated that their approach was to transfer what they would have been done in a classroom into an online environment. They knew this didn't work too well.

> I think we were trying to marry traditional and online teaching without a good understanding . . . we were launched straight in to do it. We needed development time.
>
> We are still using traditional teaching methods. I don't think we are familiar enough with the online environment yet to actually change the way that we teach or incorporate the full benefits of having the technology.
>
> It's the same as we do now, isn't it? If we are going to do it next year and we want to use Blackboard more and make it more of an online facility – and I think it's quite exciting - but I'm just lacking in knowledge to take it that one step forward now.
>
> We really need to approach this completely differently. I am still thinking lectures first and then tasks and everything else later on, whereas to use the system effectively does require a completely different approach. I certainly don't feel I've got enough experience or have got enough know-how to actually say 'well, this is what I would like to do differently'.
>
> We don't really know the possibilities it offers. We don't know its full potential. If we knew what it could do, then we could be a bit more creative in developing things.

As a result, we wanted lecturers, at both undergraduate and postgraduate levels, to be able to widen and deepen their use of the VLE. We developed an e-learning staff development strategy. There are three prongs to our approach:

a)   Staff undertake a half-day, lab-based workshop for using Blackboard.

b) Prospective online teaching staff experience e-learning and develop online skills and understanding for themselves through taking a five-week online e-moderating course in Blackboard to develop their e-moderating skills. The course is based on Gilly Salmon's five-stage model.

c) We identify specific modules and programmes for online development. Subject groups work with a multidisciplinary team of e-learning experts (technical, pedagogical, informational, etc.) and engage in short, intensive events, (two to three days), to 'get their course online'. This methodology is known as Carpe Diem – seize the day!

Linking staff development to our strategy for e-learning has given a direction, focus and a timescale for online learning at the Business School. We have completed the first part with most lecturers and are now experiencing the transformation processes of stages b and c.

Staff going through the online staff development course find that their understanding develops very rapidly as their reflections demonstrate:

First-hand experience by us of learning online is a great foundation for any course we design. Not having learnt online or been an e-moderator before I had no preconceptions as to what is a fast or slow pace. An interesting and informative experience! Application of our learning to our work situation is now the challenge. I'm off to try this virtual stuff for *real*. MO

I started designing e-tivities myself recently, I thought that this was a very good way to approach putting courses online. Now, however, I know that's only the start. I need to keep all my participants 'on board', create rhythm and melody. Phew! KB

I think I've managed to turn myself from a user into a creator and manipulator of this environment. I just didn't understand it at first. I needed to play with it a lot to work it out and develop my game. HP

We undertook the first Carpe Diem event in December 2002 and achieved the outcome of a live online module in e-marketing with 25 students from February 2003. At the end of the module, in April 2003, there were still 25 active students! Feedback from the module leader and tutor involved, Noreen Siddiqui, is very positive. She reports that pioneering the Carpe Diem process and e-moderating the resulting online course were rewarding but also very hard work!

In Spring 2003 two further Carpe Diem events took place. One of these was a major event involving our Certificate in Management programme comprising six modules. This scale of development involves a teaching team of 12 lecturers. All the prospective teachers on these modules also completed the five-week online e-moderating course before the Carpe Diem event took place.

The Carpe Diem process is proving to be an appealing and successful model of achieving significant change in academic staff perceptions of the deeper potential of online learning. In the two-to-three day intensive development session, a teaching team is able to take an existing module descriptor, rethink the teaching, learning and assessment strategy, draft an interactive approach to online learning based on constructivist and socially mediated learning philosophies, and produce it in the VLE. That is, the overall design of the online module is agreed, some specific learning activities and assessments are developed in the VLE which are user tested, learning activities are adapted in the light of testing and at the end of the event, an action plan to complete the module development is agreed.

The teaching teams undertaking a Carpe Diem event are supported by a multi-professional rapid development task force (RDTF). This team then helps the roll-out of the Carpe Diem methodology for use by other teaching teams within the Business School. The team contributes to the conceptualization of the new online module as well offering practical help in actually designing and producing online learning activities and resources. Bringing teaching and support staff into a closer working relationship has proven to be very productive, and is resulting in significant changes in understanding among RDTF members of how their role in, and contribution to, online learning can be developed. A win–win situation for teaching and support staff!

The use of a VLE within Caledonian Business School has now developed a momentum of its own. Of course, not all staff are enthusiastic about using Blackboard. Many have concerns about computer access from home and workload. However, the staff development strategy is working to support and enable staff to move from use of the VLE for subject information transmission towards developing networked online learning communities through their e-moderating skills.

Monitoring the work of trained e-moderators

New and experienced e-moderators benefit from feedback and support in order to develop and professionalize their roles (Weller and Robinson, 2001). There are many benefits in sharing both resources and understanding (Barker, 2002).

The Open University has always had policies and extensive systems to monitor the quality of its tutors' performance. It provides them with feedback and offers development where necessary. Until the advent of large-scale CMC, this monitoring took the form of visits to face-to-face tutorials, day schools and residential schools by full-time academic staff, and the systematic and very large-scale monitoring of correspondence tuition, based on a peer review system. Drawing on the experience and procedures for these, we devised and implemented from February 1996 a system of monitoring of online e-moderation for the Business School. This system involves a series of virtual 'visits' to each conference by peer or colleague tutors who have fully and successfully completed the online training. They provide reports on their view of conferences that they visit and comment whenever they find good practice in e-moderation. They also alert managers to problems or lack of participation. There is a direct correlation between active e-moderation and successful completion of the online training. The monitoring system has been gradually built up and refined over the past few years, and is now extending to other courses and faculties.

An online community of OUBS tutors has also emerged, centred on discussion and information conferences known as the 'SCR' (Senior Common Room). The exchange of good practice, support, collaboration – and the flattening of communications with the full-time course team – are welcome. We did not anticipate the importance and strength of these communications devices at first but they have proved an unexpected bonus. There is little doubt that the training has produced new cohorts of OUBS tutors comfortable with communicating electronically. This has an almost immeasurable impact on the sense of professional community that this generated. I recommend to everyone that they set up an easily accessed but 'e-moderators only' online conference for sharing and exploring good practice.

To gradually build up appropriate and consistent e-moderating practice in your own context, you do need to set up monitoring of your e-moderators' work. You may, like us, wish to base this on a peer review system. It is tempting to revert to visiting face-to-face sessions, where these are feasible, but it is better to review and monitor the work of e-moderators online. I suggest you make sure that the reviewers are fully comfortable and competent themselves as e-moderators, so they don't apply old paradigms of teaching and learning to the new environment! Of course, another important way of determining the success of the work of the e-moderators is to explore the responses of the participants. Chapter 5 provides some ideas for success factors for participants.

This chapter has explained and explored preparing and training for e-moderation. The following Resources for practitioners will help you create training programmes for your e-moderators:

1 Time p 151
3 Weave p 155
5 Presence p 160
7 Housekeeping p 164
9 Synchronous conferencing p 168
12 Evaluating and assessing p 178
13 Training E-moderators p 182
15 Monitoring p 187
24 Myth busters p 210

Chapter 5

E-moderators and the participants' experience

This chapter focuses on understanding the participants' experiences of online. E-moderators could fall into the trap of thinking of online as one experience, whereas each participant will respond according to his or her individual needs. In this chapter I explore, with case studies and examples, the needs of special groups such as novices to computing and people with disabilities as well as attempting to explain some behaviours such as 'lurking'.

Frequently, participants' expectations of online learning are high, but some become disillusioned and disengaged. As more students are taught, with fewer resources, their expectations of online continue to rise. In addition, participants in online programmes are becoming ever more diverse, in terms of their ages, backgrounds, locations and needs (Harris and Higgison, 2003).

There is currently still a low take-up of ICT-based learning. Many 'barriers to entry' studies have concentrated on the obvious reasons, such as time, cost and entry qualifications However, these studies fail to take into account that many people display a persistent tendency to refuse to learn in formal ways (Selwyn, Williams *et al*, 2001). Therefore informal learners should do well online, with its flexibility. Most, however, find online alienating without a human supporter. The support and actions of e-moderators, more than the functions of the technology in use, can truly make the difference between disappointment and highly productive learning. In a situation of widening access and value in diversity in online learning, ensuring inclusiveness has never been more important (Chisholm, Carey *et al*, 2002). I suggest that as an e-moderator you should imagine what it is like to be a novice participant. I mean you should try to put yourself in the shoes (or at least at the keyboards) of your participants. In this way, you will be aware of the barriers that prevent learning, as well as discovering how to include every member of your online group.

Access and participation

Participants' readiness to learn online is the first issue e-moderators need to consider. Rheingold articulates well the novice's fears:

> Fear is an important element in every novice computer user's first attempts to use a new machine or new software: fear of destroying data, fear of hurting the machine, fear of seeming stupid in comparison to other users, or even to the machine itself. (Rheingold, 1995: 10).

It is so easy for us, used to working online, to forget what it's like to be a novice. My colleague at the Open University Business School, Ken Giles, now one of the most experienced e-moderators I know, recalls how he felt when first confronted with working online:

I'm not really fundamentally interested in computers as such. I just want to use the technology in the same way I use a telephone to achieve results that matter to me, that is, I want the system to take care of itself and not require too much precise intervention by me. When I admire ducks swimming on a pond, I'm not much concerned with what's going on under the water. I can still remember vividly what it was like to be a novice! Well, you need keyboarding skills before you can use Windows. My own way in was that I knew where the keyboard letters were because I could type (with two fingers). I didn't know a great deal about Windows (but just about enough to get started). And so had problems initially with things like downloading (I couldn't find where stuff went!), screen sizing, opening and closing windows. The first hurdle was installing the software and getting connected. When you're on your own and not very confident, setting up a remote connection can be a major hurdle. Unfortunately, the nature of the beast is such that a pragmatist like me can't just dive in and have a bash. 'I wonder what will happen if I do this. . .' usually doesn't work! Get one thing wrong in the sequence of steps, even a misplaced dot, and that means trouble – trouble for someone who already feels anxious about the process. Too often, even today, I'm aware I complete information requested in splash screens without really understanding the implications and I get things wrong as a result. Ignorance is not bliss, but

I don't really want to bother with acquiring such understanding. And when you've got over the initial hurdles of getting connected, there's the worry that through ignorance you'll do something silly that will show you up publicly – send a message to the whole world by mistake, or wipe something out that's crucial. And all this with the speed of someone not well trained in keyboarding skills. . . and perhaps concerned about online telephone cost. . . I could go on. . . but you know, it was all worth it in the end. Ken.

The relatively few 'early adopters' are likely to tolerate technology that does not always work and be willing to take risks – they will believe that the benefits outweigh the difficulties (Norman, 1999). However, most participants fall into the 95 per cent category of late or later adopters of the technology. These people will be pragmatic and realistic, looking for convenience and reliability, and their tolerance will be low. Most will not want their learning to be disrupted. Would you?

Putman (1991) in commenting on reflective practice, points out that new users search for rules and recipes early in the learning process. The best way to help them is to offer a start, then 'stand back' and gradually let the user embed the learning in his or own experience.

Prior success or failure can be crucial. Rogers describes a 'test' that adults use when deciding how easy or difficult it will be to learn something new:

how far the subject matter coincides with what the individual believes to be their own abilities. Usually built on prior experience of success/ satisfaction or failure, the perception of personal attributes will to a large extent determine the location of the subject matter in proximity to or remoteness from the self. (Rogers, 1993: 205)

In the early stages of learning to work online, users draw on their previous computing experience if they have any. In most contexts, the percentages of students with difficulties over access or with no computing knowledge are decreasing. This trend is likely to continue. However, students' experience is most often in word processing or spreadsheeting, surfing the Internet for information or in playing multimedia games. As yet, few students are starting to learn through online with much experience of communicating through computers. Training and induction programmes will be important for some years to come.

Even those participants who are very familiar and comfortable with e-mail need some support in understanding the collaborative and collegiate environments offered by conferencing. Some students need help with appreciating the shift in the teaching and learning approach that accompanies increased use of online. In stage one in the five-stage model there is a strong element of deferred gratification. As participants are struggling to get their hardware, software and links set up, the benefits may not be intrinsically obvious to them! Their expectations of what the e-moderator can and will offer are often very high.

Skills that are promoted and developed through online working may well be important study and work skills for the future. Participants need to become literate in online communication: this is going back to writing and reading, involving extensive use of typed text. They need to develop new skills of acquiring and managing information and knowledge obtained in the online environment – and applied elsewhere. Learners need the ability to select items from masses of data to inform their judgements. They need to learn flexibility in using varied resources. They need to function in global communities. They need to maintain their motivation without constantly meeting in learning groups, and without encountering the professor in the corridor. While induction into online working will not meet all these needs at a stroke, it can lay the foundation for the development of such skills.

To learn effectively once a course begins, novices need to feel comfortable in the medium first, during their pre-course induction and training. In learning computing skills, two main types of knowledge are needed. These are 'declarative knowledge' or 'facts' (eg what icons exist on the screen), and 'procedural knowledge' (eg how to undertake tasks with the keyboard or mouse). In learning to undertake a series of tasks, learners need to memorize basic sequences and gradually build up associations with prior knowledge before starting to undertake these procedures almost automatically, as they do when driving a vehicle. Then they can hope to benefit from online networking's collaborative learning potential.

Induction needs to be planned, to take account of novices' need to learn the skills and procedures of the software, and how to operate online successfully and productively. This induction requires a staged but extensive process, to be undertaken online rather than through more traditional teaching or training.

Student orientation at Monash

Here is Sandra Luxton again from Monash. She found that support for students is as important as it is for staff. Monash has run student online orientation for some years.

Student hesitation and unfamiliarity with the medium slow down their initial involvement in their online courses or in some cases, cause them to withdraw. We developed a two week pre-semester orientation module to assimilate students into our interactive learning environment whilst inducting them into the tools of WebCT on which their learning later heavily relies. The orientation module addresses the first two stages of the five-stage model. The latter three levels take more prominence after the marketing course commences. Graphics and screen colour, icon design and navigation menus are replicated from the marketing degree subjects which the students move to after completion of the orientation module, thus providing a feeling of familiarity with the learning space when making this transition.

An experienced e-moderator from the staff engages the students in a number of useful e-tivities including posting a message to the WebCT forum, submitting an assignment, contributing a URL, accessing online support services and navigating through the online learning areas and resources. Through this process technical issues experienced by our students are resolved. Appropriate online behaviour is modelled by the e-moderator.

Online e-tivities cover aspects of technical or socialization behaviour, often both. The technological objective of the orientation module is primarily to allow students to successfully connect their computers to the university's network. Once this connection is established, they can focus on using and experiencing the WebCT environment. We also offer a number of 'hints and tips' in response to technical difficulties that they typically encounter. The social objective of the module is to facilitate students' interaction with each other in an environment where everyone is 'in the same boat'. We find that the absence of any grading or assessment of performance in the orientation encourages active participation with minimal risk.

The programme commences with the e-moderator posting an encouraging introductory message. Here is an extract.

> Hello, and welcome to online study! I'm Andrew, and I'll be spending the next couple of weeks online with you, introducing you to our online system, WebCT. During this time, we'll get to know each other, and explore the WebCT technology. This will ensure that you are off to a flying start when you commence study in your online units on date . . .
>
> You are currently in the 'Discussion Forum' section of WebCT. This is where you will post new messages to the group, and read other people's messages.
>
> Every few days I'll add messages like this one, with instructions and small tasks for you to complete, to help you become familiar with WebCT.
>
> Let's spend the next few days just getting to know each other!
>
> Let me introduce myself a bit more. . .
>
> Now – over to you! Your first task is to introduce yourself to the group. And feel free to reply to other postings too, if you'd like to. Then, later this week we'll start on some of the WebCT activities.
>
> You're all in the same boat here – just starting out on WebCT – so share your experiences with us. It's not too difficult once you get used to

it, and it really is a great way to study. We know you will be able to fit it in around your working and everyday life.

Best wishes, Andrew

Students usually respond in a comfortable way. Here are some extracts of typical responses.

Hello to Andrew and everyone else who is participating in this Online Orientation Program. My name is Karen. This summer semester I am going to complete my first online subject – Marketing Theory and Practice. So this is all very new to me – scary but exciting at the same time! . . .

Hi Everyone
My name is Frances and after a few initial hiccups logging on to WebCT, I have now been able to successfully log on – YAY!! . . .

Hi all, My name is Prasad and this is my first try at studying online, so all this is a little new to me. I did a Business degree a few years ago and have decided to come back to do my Masters to update my skills. I am employed by * Bank as one of their mobile financial advisers.

Hi everyone, I'm Sally. Studying 1st year of Masters of Marketing part time. Working crazy hours in my job at the moment so I think online study will be more convenient. Any ways short message because the weather is too nice to be on the computer all day. Bye for now.

Gradually the students start to explore the technology and undertake some basic application to marketing education such as finding a related journal article in our online library. Students vary in their commitment to taking part just as they do in the face-to-face environment, as the following extracts indicate. You will also see how much the students start to 'open up' and share with their groups.

Hi Andrew,
I'm a little behind in my online activities. I have been away and am now catching up on all the postings in the Discussion Forum and the activities that you have set. I hope it is not too late for me to be doing these. I have attached a journal article titled 'Branding on the Internet'. I found this whilst searching under relationship marketing. I found this activity scary! I'm still getting used to studying online and get a little freaked out when I have to do something new! Silly I know. Anyway, I hope that I got it right. Cheers Karen

Hi all,
I was fascinated to read up on the concept of: The Value of Perfect Information. It talks about whether or not certain decisions are worth supporting, or taking the risk on. The key here seems to be based on the assumption that new products have a 20% success rate, and how factoring in your losses can determine whether the venture is worthwhile. My understanding of this is that by allocating resources to research, you are minimizing your risk, or loss potential. Even if your product still fails, the cost to determine this (based on the 20% success rate of new products) is 80% less than if no research had been conducted at all.
    Does that make any sense? Regards, Dave

Fewer of the students who take part in online orientation need to contact Administration for assistance. Teaching staff report only minimal calls from students prior to the start of semester and that the nature of the questions is usually academic.

Our research finds that students who participate in our orientation module are more active learners in their online study due to fewer access problems and reduced fear of the online system. E-moderators report that they are able to focus more quickly on subject content because the students are well prepared. Students like being able to 'meet' their classmates via the online orientation programme, and often bond into their own support group before commencing their actual semester's work. In addition, students' confidence in the medium increases their activity on WebCT later in the study period. An upward spiral!

Learning styles and approaches

All e-moderators need to develop a clear sense of their 'audience', as well as the purposes of groups whose work they are facilitating in the online environment. When e-moderating online it is easy to have a standard image in your mind of 'the students', but the best e-moderators manage to keep a sense of the composite needs of the group, along with those of a variety of individuals.

Online learning must be tailored to appeal to all learning styles to avoid the need for offering a variety of learning methods. Teachers in the classroom respond to differing styles through working with individuals. Similarly, e-moderators should be responsive to individuals' needs online, rather than assuming that the only way to deal with individuals is to revert to meeting face to face.

In face-to-face groups, most communication involves talking and listening so those students who learn aurally are well accommodated. However, online platforms operate through reading and writing. It is likely therefore that it will appeal to those more comfortable with the written word. This places at a disadvantage those for whom writing (or typing) is a problem, or who are working in something other than their first language. In the OU Business School, we accommodate large numbers of students working online who are using English but it is not their first language. Typically they prefer to read and compose offline and take their time. They also need reassurance that minor mistakes are made by everyone in conference messages and so long as the sense is clear, this is unimportant.

Honey and Mumford (1986) suggest that students use a mixture of active, practical, theoretical and reflective learning. Activists, as they call their first category, tend to learn best when they are dealing with new problems and experiences. These learners need to have a range of different activities to keep them engaged, and the ability to 'hold the floor' (or in this context, the conference) and to be able to 'bounce ideas' off of others, all of which working online caters for extremely well. Pragmatists, on the other hand, need to be able to see an obvious link between what they are learning and problems or opportunities with which they are engaged in their work. They must become fully engaged in the learning process. They tend to want an immediate opportunity to try out what they have learnt in order to evaluate its practical use and value. In designing for online work, pragmatists can be catered for through online activities. Honey and Mumford's theorists need sufficient time to explore the links between ideas and situations. As the asynchronous nature of online builds in a time delay and, with structure and encouragement, the exploration can occur. The high level of peer interaction online should appeal to theorists, although they are likely to be the first to cry, 'it's all rubbish' if topics are not dealt with in depth. Good structure and archiving are important, so they can work in appropriate conferences with serious topics. E-moderators should, as always, encourage questioning, probing and exploring.

Honey and Mumford's reflectors probably benefit most from being online. They engage with the learning task with time to think deeply about the concepts and activities, and to give considered responses that synchronicity and conventional classrooms rarely allow. Experienced e-moderators such as Gerry Prendergast from Abacus Virtual College suggested to me that activists and pragmatists frequently behave online as if they were extrovert personalities, while the theorists and reflectors have more introverted styles.

Brooke Broadbent offers us advice on working online based on Kolb's learning styles. These include the 'convergers' who like to think rationally and will appreciate good online documentation and the 'divergers' who like creative approaches such as role play. 'Assimilators' will be those willing to undertake Web searches on behalf of the group and explore and explain differing perspectives. 'Accommodators' will promote the relationships and community and engage others (Broadbent, 2002). Aspects of Kolb's cycle found missing from many online courses are those of the opportunity to reflect and evaluate individual learning experiences, and opportunities to work with others, especially a tutor (Friedman, Watts et al, 2002).

Howard Hill's research uses the Myers Briggs Type Indicator (MBTI), a personality model. Of the e-learning population 45 per cent seek direct praise for their learning efforts, and 52 per cent enjoy discussing ideas, of which 18 per cent want strong debate. Thirty-three per cent want to take the lead, 23 per cent want to develop others, while 45 per cent want harmony and 26 per cent need role models. This is another example of the need for diversity of approaches, and a challenge for e-moderators (Hill, 2003).

E-moderators need to keep these various styles in mind and plan their work accordingly. In particular, a clear mixture of engagement in immediately relevant activities, and the opportunity to reflect on messages or eventually contribute some, are both important. Activities can either be entirely online, begun face-to-face and extended online, or prepared for online and continued face-to-face. An array of tasks can be provided and groups can be split into smaller learning sets. Such variations are likely to meet a wide variety of learning styles and preferences.

Widening access

Many educational organizations hope that online offers a new approach and a widening of access to non-traditional customers and clients. Many teachers have had the vision that new ICT-based courses will empower individuals and groups (Viera, 2002). However, there is still a low uptake of ICT opportunities (Selwyn, Williams *et al*, 2001). Many 'barriers to entry' studies have concentrated on the obvious such as time available, cost and entry qualifications. Students used to encountering 'passive' learning methods such as lectures may display resentment of the substantial cognitive energy required for involvement in networked learning. However, we can observe many millions of people on the Web learning informally from and with others, teaching themselves the technology with minimal training (Montieth and Smith, 2001).

A fresh approach to 'investment' is required in online learning by participants and e-moderators alike, widening the vision of 'learning to learn' (Waeytens, Lens *et al*, 2002). For example, the journey from stage three to stage four of the model, from passivity to activity, is in itself not easy but it is especially worthwhile (Green, 2002). The role of the human supporter, the e-moderator, is of critical influence in promotion widening of access through networked computers.

Assessment processes

For the foreseeable future, most participants will want to achieve qualifications, accreditation or awards, so assessment in some form or other will be necessary. Indeed, many course designers find that assessment is the engine that drives and motivates students (Brown, Bull and Race, 1999) (Moon and Hawkridge 2003). Most learners crave teachers' responses to their coursework and their examinations. Learners see the quality and quantity of feedback on their work as an important part of their relationships with their professors and educational provider. Where the use of online is integral to a course or programme, the assessment should in some way reflect the skills participants are using and developing to learn (Macdonald, Weller *et al*, 2002; Weller, 2002a).

As you have seen throughout this book, the use of e-moderated online learning directly addresses the broadening acceptance and understanding of learning as a socially mediated and constructed process (Billett, 1996) and of knowledge as personal and not 'fixed' (Hendry, 1996). However, many assessment procedures are still based on the transmission model of information. This means that unless issues of evaluation and assessment are tackled as the use of online for learning increases, the gap between how students learn and how they are assessed may widen. Some students already comment on the irony of spending most of their learning time communicating through their computer, but taking their examination in a formal setting with only a pen and paper for company. As e-moderators become more comfortable with their online teaching roles, I think they will start to look closely at online assessment and evaluation, and will not wish their time and their students' time to be constrained by old assessment methods. Highly networked organizations such as professional associations are already waking up to the huge potential of 'any time, any place' assessment.

We need to move towards 'aligning' our assessment with our online teaching approaches. Biggs's framework (1999) suggests a form of matching between learning outcomes, assessment, teaching methods and activities. My colleagues at the OU with experience in large-scale online assessment agree:

> The interactivity offered by online conferencing and the submission of assignments in electronic form offer new and exciting potential for the assessment of networked courses . . . It is important that the assessment should reflect course aims and objectives and . . . provide a corresponding level of affordance and flexibility in content to that provided by the course itself . . . the assessment must reflect the values the course is trying to teach. (Macdonald, Weller *et al*, 2002: 17)

You may want to try assessing along the steps of the five-stage model to see whether the learning and development of your participants are showing progress. This kind of assessment has been tried at Caledonian Business School:

We see several pockets of developing assessment practice based on sound constructivist approaches and utilizing research-based models. Where module teams attempt explicit implementation of the five-stage model of online learning, they often then wish to assess along similar lines. For example, in one honours marketing module students are allocated 20 per cent of their coursework mark for their ability to facilitate, as well as contribute to, online discussions on each other's seminar papers. The assessment criteria issued to students show the clear influence of the model:
Assessment criteria:

1. Motivation and online socialization skills demonstrated through regular and frequent contributions.
2. Knowledge and understanding demonstrated through sharing of relevant information.
3. Ability to draw out, compare and reflect on applications of knowledge in a variety of contexts, demonstrated by the quality of message contributions.
4. Ability to evaluate and synthesize others' contributions on the discussion board, and post messages accordingly, hence demonstrating personal development and learning.

Gillian Roberts

Online learning offers more opportunities for students to write for themselves to benefit their own learning and also for each other (rather than 'writing for the tutor'). Through networking students can make their writing easily available for review and assessment. As a start, suggest to participants that they should use conference messages in their assignments and that they will be given credit for their ability to use and integrated messages in their work. You might like to try a peer review process of students' written work, even if their essays, assignments or exercises are afterwards handed in for marking by a teacher/ assessor. If you try such a process, ensure that the criteria for judgements are made explicit from the start and based on learning outcomes. Digital portfolios can be tools for both learning and assessment (Tolsby, 2002).

Networked and multimedia technology offers new possibilities for online assessment. The OU and a number of other universities, such as the Dutch OU and Monash in Melbourne, have introduced opportunities for students to submit their assignments electronically and for tutors to mark, comment and return them online. However, this is only the first step in what might become a revolution in assessment processes. More universities will innovate in online assessment, usually based on campus networks using commercial software. Several pioneers are already addressing important concerns (O'Reilly and Morgan, 1999). These include issues of access and security, plagiarism and cheating (is this work really my student's?), the time and costs of setting up (efficiency gains), dealing with bias, fairness and anxiety, and test design and implementation of systems (Brown, Bull and Race, 1999). It is likely that students, as customers, will drive this sensitive but important area further towards online provision in the future. A corollary will be the need for the valid assessment of the performance of large numbers of learners at low cost.

Disabilities and online working

In the United Kingdom more than 4 per cent of students have an acknow-ledged disability and true numbers are probably closer to 10 per cent (Newell, 1999). At the OU, 7,000 students declare a disability and 1,000 of these prefer other than print materials. In some countries, legislation requires at least minimum access to courseware for disabled learners. What can online do for them? Is it accessible?

Online messages appear to others as an individual's thoughts, without them knowing much at all about the writer's age, race, appearance, gender and disability (Gold, 1998). Users with a disability appreciate that they can go online more or less at any time and in any place, obviating the need for travel and physical access. Instead, they are valued for their thoughts and contributions. The challenge for you as an e-moderator is to be aware of the issues involved. Valuing every contribution is essential. Doing so is likely to engender the best possible response from anyone who is disadvantaged, whatever the reason.

Online can be an open door for those with restricted mobility or difficulty in accessing buildings. Online provides an opportunity to 'travel', meet and learn with others with comparative ease, but only if accessible materials and processes are on offer. Technology can help or hinder, of course. Keyboard or speech commands can be provided for those unable to use a mouse. Electronic text can be designed so that it converts to Braille. With forethought, Web pages can be designed to be more effective for certain disabilities although the increased emphasis on graphics has created new challenges, especially for smaller providers of software packages.

A visually impaired tutor took part in the online e-moderator training (see Chapter 4) and appeared on my first list of 'lurkers' to follow up by telephone. I discovered he was waiting for special software to be installed and was mean-while having the messages read to him. He soon secured software that produced an audio version of FirstClass and took part later in the training with very few problems. He proved to be an effective and active e-moderator on OU Business School conferences. The learning point for me here was that I should not assume lurking necessarily meant laziness – participating might take longer for some people with visual impairment, but they can still gain and contribute.

Blind participants can adapt online software through Braille printouts of messages or through using speech synthesis. They cannot use a mouse so need to become adept at keyboard commands. An experienced intermediary is needed to train and support blind users to the point of competence and independence. When changes are made to the system, blind participants must be notified early so that they can arrange for specific adaptations and training, in advance. Manuals and instructions need to be recorded onto audio tape by experienced readers able to describe flow chart diagrams and the like, in words.

In constructing conferences, consider the font and style and how they might look on a variety of screens and to different people. This will help those with partial visual impairment, but will also be of benefit to all users. Even where course texts are provided as print, it can be helpful also to provide them electronically, so that visually impaired users can manipulate fonts, sizes and styles to suit their personal needs. The Open University puts some of its courses onto CD-ROM so that they can be played with a speech synthesizer, or displayed as larger print: the CD-ROMs carry a voice-recording too.

A deaf colleague wrote to me on e-mail of his encounters with online networking:

> Conferencing was for me a hugely liberating experience. I started working in industry in 1973, when the 'managerial communications' model was through using the telephone. My then MD was someone of good heart and intentions who thought I would never be able to 'be a manager' because I was excluded from the information community of the company. Not his terms but that's what he meant. So I was placed into special projects, away in an alcove, where I could work on my own.
>
> I arrived at the OU in 1986 just as the CoSy conferencing system was getting implemented. It was a secret known to a few – I heard about it by grapevine over the photocopier. I joined and nothing was the same again.
>
> Liberation came for me in several linked forms. Firstly was the sense of 'connectedness' – the world expanded beyond my desk. I didn't have to get up and physically see someone in order to make contact. The relief from a sense of embattled isolation was immense. Second was the increased meaning in communications because I could find out more about the context of what was going on. Not just answer a specific question but get a sense of why some things were seen as problems or opportunities. That meant having a 'relatively' relaxed sense of the 'social' or off-topic communications that frame the on-topic discussions. This is quite important in giving a sense of communicative competence.

Third is another aspect of communicative competence. The ability to 'say'. This can be difficult for deaf people as communication face-to-face needs an awareness of the social turn-taking codes of communications and these can be very subtle. Hesitate and you are excluded. So conferencing can unleash the power of 'speech' for a deaf person. It did a lot for my confidence in other situations too.

Here is where an e-moderator can play a part, by fostering an appropriate online communication code so that all can find a way to take turns.

A factor that didn't apply for me but does for other deaf people (especially for those whose first language is signing) is that literacy can be a problem. English can be very much the second language for some people and written English a particular trial. So conferencing isn't necessarily a panacea for the deaf . . . Maybe some awareness by e-moderators of strange and sudden pitfalls with written language can help.

Finally conferencing – and associated e-mail facilities – put the initiative with a deaf person. Not being dependent on others to initiate or negotiate contacts is once again a liberating experience. Freedom can be rather frightening, so for me the e-moderator's role in creating 'safe spaces' is very important.

(Bevan, 1999)

Online educational counselling for learners with long-term health problems can be provided using online for social and study support within the environment of a peer group area accessible only to specified participants. Margaret Debenham suggests recruiting two e-moderators. One (from the student group) looks after chat, medical and technical discussion issues, leaving the educational counsellor as e-moderator of an educational support topic. Margaret tells us that online fosters communication with the participants, which is both 'intimate and distancing', as well as promoting a considered dialogue between counsellor and student. In her study, the participants demonstrated increased motivation towards their studies and the majority preferred support online to the support through the telephone (Debenham et al., 1999).

University of Maryland University College case study

Claudine SchWeber of the University of Maryland University College, outside Washington, DC, who has experience of e-moderating in innovative ways, sees e-moderating as 'guiding a discussion and fostering interaction among students rather than between students and instructors.' This can be a challenge, because as Dr SchWeber points out, the tendency in a question and answer session online, much like some onsite classes, is for the students to respond to the instructor rather than to each other. The Maryland experience suggests the importance of purposeful and explorative nature of collaborative working online. The best activity was through an online case analysis where students commented, reacted and referred to each other's work. This case study shows how potentially contentious and emotive issues can be surfaced and explored productively online through supportive groups.

The key e-moderating activity in this example was setting up appropriate and challenging questions to ask online and the gradual sequencing and release of appropriate material. The case dealt with an engineering company's branch located in the West Indies, far away from the headquarters somewhere in Europe. It involved issues of management and supervision, superior and subordinate relations, race, age, perception, organizational culture, feedback, trust, diversity, new and experienced staff, home country and expatriate relations – and a surprise ending. What a great way of gradually introducing material into an asynchronous environment! They started out with four guiding questions on which students were asked to comment by a given date:

1. What are the perceptual issues? How did these impact the situation and affect the outcome?
2. What are the cultural/diversity issues? How did these affect the relationship between B and R, and R to the rest of the unit?
3. What are the performance appraisal and retention issues? What motivational and job satisfaction issues played a role here? How might B have handled the situation if he knew about relevant management theory?
4. What are the trust, communication, and feedback issues here? What strategies did the men ignore? What might have been done? Then, the question that brought it home: assume Y has been fired and you have been brought in to replace him. What might you do in the next two weeks? Why?

Even before the due date, the class became intensively involved in the questions and in what they might do as a replacement for Y. Some of the students were originally from countries outside of the United States and from ethnic and racial minorities. Their reaction to the expatriates and locals situation in the case was intense, highly engaged and from their personal perspective, as these excerpts show:

Trust was an issue from the very beginning. As I am a (member of) minority myself, I am glad that X left the company. I wish he had done it sooner. I did see it coming though. What gives anyone the right to imply that they know a race of people without ever walking in that race's shoes?

Our views, while similar in affront (for the most part), differ when it comes to agreeing with R's decision. Under the circumstances it would be difficult not to share his anger. I still believe, however, that he blew it.

On your question 'What gives anyone the right to imply that they know a race of people without ever walking in that race shoes' – how do you feel about X's written comments 'bashing' (others)? And, you made several comments about the expatriates, suggesting they all behaved like Y. The case study gives no evidence of this.

The online discussion, commentary, reaction and referrals went on for about a week, as those who joined in later got involved in some section of the comments. Dr SchWeber pointed out that this had never, ever occurred in a face-to-face class; not with the same intensity, not with that frequency of response to each other (several people made several comments), not in the students' willingness to disagree (as noted above) on controversial topics such as race, nor in their apparent ability to look at the conceptual issues and the theory that might apply.

One dramatic difference from the face-to-face class was that there was an ongoing transcript, so students could join in at any point and comment on points made earlier (which they did), or refer to each other's recommendations. For example, one student said, 'A's recommendation to hire J as a consultant is a good point because. . . '. That kept the dialogue going, somewhat like a ball on an elastic that keeps bouncing back in and going out again. Dr SchWeber eventually met the students and when the case was brought up, everyone was much more subdued and discussion did not take much time. Faculty colleagues who looked in later on the discussion said that they had never seen such a fine and thorough discussion of this particular case.

Corporate training and development

Top management is increasingly realizing that their access to the Internet is critical. In 1991 it was estimated that only 13 per cent of top executives in Japan, 9 per cent in the United Kingdom, 7 per cent in Germany and 3 per cent in France had access to the Internet. Surely every senior manager in these countries now has access? Could this be the new competitive capacity issue?

The research on which this book is based was conducted with distance learning students on a programme leading to a qualification, the MBA. However, in these times of major emphasis on life-long learning, 'learning organizations' and 'corporate universities', the role of online for corporate education is becoming increasingly important (Schreiber and Berge, 1998). Online is especially useful for organizations where many employees are distributed across different geographical locations or travel frequently as the online environment can be used to productively share knowledge and create a joint sense of mission. Much of the advice given in Part 2, Resources for practitioners, especially relating to access, e-moderator training, good online design and the purposeful nature of each and every conference, holds good. However, careful consideration needs to be given by the e-moderator to the structure and form of participation of online groupings and to building of trust in communications, especially if learning groups cross formal organizational boundaries and hierarchies.

If you are considering an online learning site within an executive development programme, you need to be especially sensitive to the sub-cultures within which managers and executives typically operate. Executives are usually comfortable with information as holistic, complex and imprecise and they may especially value learning from peers. They frequently feel isolated and remote in their role and often find themselves in only formal relationships with immediate work groups. They often relate best to peers within their industry but outside their own organization. They are likely to see IT as limiting and distorting and their fear of 'failure' in its use may be very high. In some sectors, senior managers rely on secretarial or administrative support and therefore lack online experience. The audience for your online learning programmes may be transitional due to especially high mobility. The need for early and useful learning outcomes is critical. For these kinds of programmes, e-moderators need to work even harder than usual to integrate the online learning with other activities and to ensure authentic and relevant online activities (Sloman, 2001).

There is a feeling in commercial organizations that the investment that universities are making in IT is lagging behind that of the corporate environment (Robinson *et al.*, 1998). They often, however, assume that a learner, familiar with business processes online, will be as comfortable with learning online. My experience is that this is not the case. In addition, there is still little understanding of how in-company learning systems link effectively with aspiring knowledge management processes and systems and in particular how one feeds the other. Induction programmes into the online learning environment, preferably with good in-company support, are therefore especially critical to success.

Gender and e-moderating

Access by women to networked computers has reached a similar level to that by men. Some authorities believe that women's ways of communicating and working lend themselves particularly happily to communicating online

(Lapham, 1998). Women are generally perceived to be comfortable with communications technologies such as the telephone but, because of the somewhat male-orientated image of computers, may be initially put off online. Telephones ensure a one-to-one conversation, but conferencing involves group behaviour and much depends on the e-moderation of the group. E-moderators need therefore to concentrate on focusing on individuals' contributions to conferences, rather than their offline gender or identity.

Others are concerned that online discussions may be dominated in some of the same ways that occur in face-to-face groups. Spender's (1995) book gives a wide exploration of the issues of women, communications and computers. As she points out:

> One of the starting points for change has to be in the educational arena. For more than a century, women have been engaged in a battle for equal educational rights, and the struggle must now be transferred to the virtual society. We cannot continue to rest. . . because women now achieve comparable results to men in print-based systems and assessments.

> (Spender, 1995: 210)

For e-moderators, it is important to be sensitive to any individual or group that appears to be disadvantaged or not participating online. While it is difficult to police harassment and inappropriate behaviour on public listservers and the like, these cannot be allowed in any kind of educational environment. Harassment of any kind must be stopped immediately online, as it is on campuses and in corporate environments, to ensure equality of learning opportunity for all. In particular, e-moderators should regularly consider the tone of their messages and their online behaviour (and be open to monitoring from their peers), to ensure that no exploitation of their more powerful position occurs, even inadvertently.

In addition, personal communication style has an impact. This exchange, from an e-moderating training course, shows that sensitivity in communication is always needed.

Hi Lurkerperson.

I hope this finds you well. I'm sorry we haven't heard from you yet. We really would welcome your contribution to the discussions that are taking place. Don't you think that it's a little unfair that other students are making the effort and taking the time to contribute and you're not? SO GET YOUR BUTT IN GEAR AND SAY SOMETHING. TR

And the response:

> My goodness, if anyone wrote to me like this I would be horrified, not my language at all. While it could work wonders for some people it would alienate me enormously! Derek's style would motivate me much more, for example, 'I notice that you have not logged into the course yet. If you are having technical difficulties or problems with the software please contact me and I will offer any assistance I can. The course is off to a good start and many of your fellow participants have started to post assignments. Please explore the software, post your work and have fun. Thanks for your participation; I'm looking forward to reading your work.' I liked the positive approach and particularly encouragement to have fun – it seemed so warm and human. Isn't it interesting how cultures, and sometimes sexes, tend to use different approaches to motivating people. Working with people from different parts of the world don't we have to be aware of sensitivities? Many years ago I saw a foreigner to me make an impassioned plea to a British academia audience which failed because the speaker used emotional reasons when the audience expected logical arguments. It made a big impression on me because I realized how I could totally fail to get my messages over to other people if I used the culturally inappropriate style of argument and motivation. SC

E-moderators and lurkers

In the exit questionnaire from the e-moderator training described in Chapter 4, I ask the trainees their level of engagement with the training programme and their maintenance of interest throughout. This question is intended to elicit a crude notion of whether trainees have, by the end of the five-stage programme, become active users and whether the software has facilitated this. However, the question is typically answered in a more sophisticated and expansive way than I originally expected. Although over three-quarters of the trainees report 'active participation' online, half also point out the value of 'passive' participation, ie browsing, 'listening' or lurking. Late starters in the programme are more likely to report 'passive' engagement than early starters (who perhaps had more opportunities to complete the online activities). This suggests that timing (and considerable amounts of time) to get used to communicating online, are very important. The OUBS's participation figures show a very wide range of response to online, from willingness to spend huge amounts of time and mental energy to a need to be online but to 'browse' before actively contributing. We have therefore re-labelled 'lurking' as 'browsing' in an attempt to recognize this need in some individuals and to remove the negative connotations. If, however, the majority of members of a conference are browsing, it is time for a rethink and redesign of the purpose and activities of the conference. There is no doubt that the more active participants become upset with browsers, however. Managing the interface between contributing and browsing is a key e-moderating task.

A face-to-face facilitator is often able to ascertain from body language why a learner is listening rather than contributing. The listeners form the audience and they may be nodding agreement, applauding or sleeping! The e-moderator cannot look at the audience and determine its reaction in the same way.

Online communication involves commitment on the part of the contributor of various kinds, hence the importance of the five-stage scaffold to enable increasing trust, motivation and purposefulness. Silence on the part of participants seems much 'heavier' online than in face-to-face contexts (Mathiasen and Rattleff, 2002). It is important that the e-moderator creates the feeling of 'presence' too, without unnecessary interventions. See Resources for practitioners 5 for ideas (p. 160).

Some browsers visit but leave no trace of their presence other than in the message history. Try to establish why they are browsing, if necessary contacting them by e-mail or telephone.

Are lurkers learning? It looks as though many are, and some are unabashed about this:

> As a confirmed lurker, I have found the conferences stimulating and broadening. It is seldom possible to access views from such a wide range of backgrounds. There are individual contributors whom I will always seek out in particular where I have found their solutions to questions of benefit. NH

From the OUBS conferences, we noticed three main types (Dence, 1996):

1. The freeloader

> It has come to my attention that we have a large number of lurkers and freeloaders in this conference (don't take offence – just my way with words). I am not saying that a lurker is a bad person but I am saying that a lurker is using my contribution and giving me nothing in return. And that makes me feel some grievance. My experience of such things is that

> *what you get out* is in proportion to *what you put in*. So feel free to contribute!! PN

2. The sponge

> In fact, in lurking in this particular area, I am getting good tuition both in the use of the medium and in the vocabulary (jargon, if you like) of an area of knowledge that is new to me and into which I would hesitate to insert a contribution. AB

3. Lurkers with skills or access problems

> I'm lost. Please help me. I just can't remember how to post a reply to the right conference that will get me help. I'm in a loop. I'm really upset about the combative tone of the active people in the course conferences – I'm really not here as a thief you know! GK

Learners generally browse before they are ready to contribute – and, as you have seen from the model in Chapter 2, this happens in different ways and at different paces. Sometimes a participant would have posted a message but does not because what the participant wanted to contribute has already been said by another member of the conference (Rossman, 1999). Often they contribute on a topic or at a level with which they feel comfortable, perhaps in a different conference. However, most participants are put off by a conference that is constantly dominated by one or two individuals (including sometimes the e-moderator!). The names of such over-keen individuals get spotted and other participants fall away. E-moderators need to watch carefully for this happening, as groups often find dominant individuals more difficult to deal with online than they might face-to-face. The solution is to encourage dominant individuals into e-mail or to set up conferences of their own and create increased structure in your learning conferences.

OU Master's course case study

David Hawkridge's example of students' response demonstrates the wide variety of responses and the patterns of communications that develop between widely dispersed participants. David Hawkridge, an e-moderator, writes:

> From February to October each year I tutor 10–20 students who are taking a 600-hour Open University (OU) course called Foundations of Open and Distance Education, offered by the Institute of Educational Technology (http://www-iet.open.ac.uk). My students live in many countries besides the United Kingdom. They receive print, video, audio and CD-ROM course materials, but must also have access to e-mail and the Web. On average, I'm in e-mail contact with each student about once a week. They also send me six assignments via the Web site: I mark them on screen and add comments before returning them electronically, usually two or three days after receiving them. En route, the marks are recorded automatically at the OU, and the marked assignment may be copied for quality control purposes.
>
> The password-protected Web site is essential to the course. It provides a welcome page, online text resources, an assignment submission page and entry to the electronic database of the OU's International Centre for Distance Learning and to a site for alumni. From our welcome page, students and tutors move directly into a bulletin board system (BBS) divided into a plenary discussion area for all and areas for each tutor group. This is where I e-moderate conferences in my own group and help with those in the plenary area.
>
> I've learned a lot over the last three years about how students, most of them new to all this, respond in the different conferences. In the plenary area, there's a noticeboard, an area for discussing course themes and issues, a café and 'ask the experts'. Students read the noticeboard but, no surprise, seldom reply to any of the messages there unless there's a panic about something. By contrast, the course themes and issues generate discussion, often based on activities written into the materials. Here are some threads (conversations) for Activity 2.2, which is about Donald Schön's writings on reflective practitioners. The last two messages are about how to save Web pages onto your own computer, because one student wanted to do that. The e-moderator (me, David) chimed in four times. Notice that no women joined in this time.

> no 82 Activity 2.2 17 Feb 99, Neville-g
> no 89 Reflections on Schön and Eraut 18 Feb 99, David
> no 95 Reflections on Activity 2.2 18 Feb 99, Stephen-m
> no 100 It works for me 18 Feb 99, Neville-g
> no 126 Ahhhhhhh 21 Feb 99, Christopher-h
> no 127 Practising in a 2nd generation institute 21 Feb 99, Christopher-h
> no 136 Reflection-for-action 22 Feb 99, David

no 143 Reflection on reflection 22 Feb 99, James-c
no 172 Group therapy 25 Feb 99, Christopher-h
no 173 Shooting students 26 Feb 99, David
no 237 Over egging the pudding 25 Mar 99, Neville-g
no 242 Web grabbing 26 Mar 99, Christopher-h
no 243 Web Grabber 29 Mar 99, David

In the café everybody introduces themselves – some only in late March – and each message usually gets at least one cheery rejoinder, from a student or a tutor. By mid-1999, with about 40 students on the course, the café had well over 200 messages. Students start threads spontaneously, puzzling about course content and technical problems as well as exchange social pleasantries. Some threads end after a couple of messages, others are much longer.

'Ask the experts' gives students a chance to put questions to a few well-known experts who agree to join the BBS. For a week in May this year, students were in touch with the author of the study guide they were reading at the time. She responded to their detailed questions. I didn't have to moderate that conference at all, merely start it.

Just as in conferencing systems elsewhere, most messages come from about a third of the students, with another third fairly active and the rest very seldom writing anything after the first introductions. As e-moderator, I don't try to stimulate specific students to contribute, although I can see from the system statistics how many times each student has visited the BBS. Lurking abounds, of course, though students rightly object to the term and prefer 'browsing'. Students (and tutors) can read any message anywhere in the BBS for this course.

With my own group, two kinds of conferences develop each year. One, like the course themes and issues in the plenary area, is based on the course content. The other is a series of workshops, one for each assignment. Over the three years, block conferences have generated useful threads, some of them really long. I regard myself as an equal participant in these threads, although I suppose it's true that the students expect me to be more knowledgeable than they are. Last year, quite a lot of discussion occurred in this one. So far this year, there's been only a handful of messages.

Assignment workshops are usually extremely active, but that's because there's a percentage (usually 20) of marks allocated for appropriate use in assignments of quotes from the threads. Not all tutors agree that this is a good idea, though it does stimulate the conferencing. The problem lies in devising sound criteria for allocating the 20 per cent.

I take the initiative in the workshops by posting a longish message containing hints about how to approach the assignment, which is always an essay of 2,000 or 4,000 words. Students comment on what I've said, and as moderator I don't usually enter the thread much, leaving it to them to discuss the assignment with each other. I can intervene, of course, if somebody raises a knotty problem or misunderstands something in the course materials. I do read all the messages.

Here are the threads for the second assignment (TMA02), spread over 20 days. This time the women joined in, and so did I:

no 59 TMA Workshop for TMA02 04 Mar 99, David
no 60 reply to TMA02 04 Mar 99, Hilary-g
no 61 Activity 4.1 – Closed?? 05 Mar 99, Christopher-h
no 62 Technology and openness 08 Mar 99, Stephen-m
no 63 Reply 08 Mar 99, Melanie-j
no 76 Hi from Big Brother! 13 Mar 99, Nigel
no 64 Technologies 08 Mar 99, Hilary-g
no 85 Passing control to students 15 Mar 99, Beverley-p
no 86 Sorry for the intrusion! 15 Mar 99, Beverley-p
no 102 No apology needed, Beverley 20 Mar 99, David
no 65 Independent learning? 08 Mar 99, Hilary-g
no 66 Right on, Hilary and everyone else! 09 Mar 99, David
no 67 Beautifully refreshing Activity 4.8 09 Mar 99, Christopher-h
no 68 Johnson 1990 P80 S4 B1 10 Mar 99, Neville-g
no 69 Johnson again 10 Mar 99, Neville-g
no 71 The written word 10 Mar 99, Stephen-m
no 77 Selling OL 13 Mar 99, David
no 80 OL vs. DE 15 Mar 99, Neville-g
no 81 To continue the argument 15 Mar 99, Melanie-j
no 70 Activity 4.1 10 Mar 99, Neville-g
no 73 Johnson's Second Point 11 Mar 99, Melanie-j
no 75 Johnson!! 13 Mar 99, David
no 78 More Activity 4.8 14 Mar 99, Christopher-h
no 79 TMA02: straight to the point 14 Mar 99, Bustami-k
no 90 To continue the discussion 16 Mar 99, Melanie-j
no 91 Error in TMA02: straight to the point. 16 Mar 99, Bustami-k
no 94 Brownie Point Earner 17 Mar 99, Neville-g
no 97 Help 17 Mar 99, Neville-g
no 98 Help -2 17 Mar 99, Neville-g
no 99 Meaning? 19 Mar 99, David
no 108 Commenting on comments 23 Mar 99, Neville-g
no 109 Chunking the messages 24 Mar 99, David
no 111 HTML 3/26/99, Christopher-h
no 92 Defining learners' needs – who and how? 17 Mar 99, Bustami-k
no 95 Assistance 17 Mar 99, Neville-g
no 96 Assistance 2nd try 17 Mar 99, Neville-g
no 93 Who meets the needs? 17 Mar 99, Melanie-j
no 100 Defining our terms 19 Mar 99, Stephen-m
no 101 Learners' sacrifices 19 Mar 99, Bustami-k
no 103 Society 21-Mar-99, Christopher-h
no 104 The Rolling Stones 21 Mar 99, Christopher-h
no 110 On the ball, Nora! 24 Mar 99, David

It's amazing, but I've never seen a real case of flaming anywhere in our BBS. The nearest to it was one year when two students, one Greek, the other British, were discussing at length the philosophical foundations of truth. One finally accused the other, hotly, of being unprincipled, even amoral. The other just laughed (yes, online) and said he had better get on with his assignment! I wish I could quote the messages to you, but of course the copyright in them rests with the students concerned. They both finished the course with good marks, though I did notice that the first one changed from being a very active contributor to a browser.

E-moderating does take time, and I don't think we know enough yet about how to do it both well and quickly. I watch my fellow tutors by reading their group conferences from time to time: their style is not the same as mine, but they seem to do a good job. One responds at length and in detail, but less often than I do. One has a great sense of humour. One is incredibly laid back and seems to be appreciated by many of his students. I'll keep an eye on their e-moderating and pick up some tips.

Participant induction

Steeples and her colleagues suggest that a face-to-face meeting is appropriate for induction, especially for small groups, because of the bonding that occurs and because early problems can be ironed out on the spot (Steeples, Vincent and Chapman, 1997). Such a meeting is not always feasible, however, or may be simply too expensive, as it is for the Open University's Business School (see Chapter 4).

We found in the OUBS that it is possible to use many of the messages from e-moderator training for the student induction. Issues such as communication styles are included, as well as key software skills. At levels four and five, conferences are offered to enable the students to go online and to prepare them for study. At level four, the emphasis is on setting and sharing personal object-ives and study skills and at level five discussing key management topics (see Figure 5.1).

The induction conferences remain available to students in a non-interactive form during the year. They are visited or revisited by other students and as a reminder by some of those who have already taken part.

Following the first online induction conferences for OU MBA students, informal feedback from the students' conferences was positive and contributed to the largest ever use of CMC in the OUBS in 1997. Participation rates and purposefulness have gradually built up since then. See Gray and Salmon (1999) for responses in a large-scale course.

Students with little experience of technological applications before a course begins may find it all but impossible to undertake the course itself as well as getting to grips with problems of the technology. They face many of the same issues that trainee e-moderators face, for example, 'red flag' overload (in

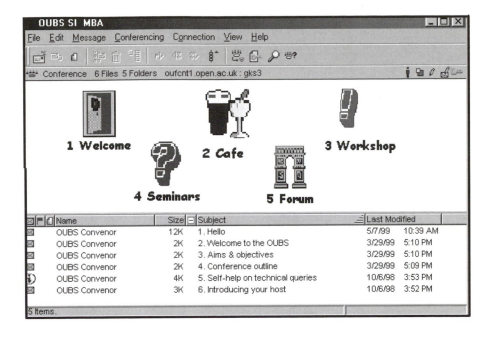

Figure 5.1 *Desktop screen of student induction in OUBS*

FirstClass unread messages are shown with a red flag). With up to 100 students over a short period of time in each conference, e-moderating may be needed almost daily.

Exit questionnaires and follow-up e-mails collected student feedback after their induction into the world of FirstClass in the OU Business School. On the whole, student responses to online induction are very positive:

Brilliant. . . EVC

. . . an excellent tool. DF

I think it will make all the difference. EV

Conferencing is of great help to students be they in an English city or miles away from anywhere somewhere else in the world. When you hit a low there is always someone there to pick you up and dust you off. You can bounce ideas off people. It is easy dip into a conference for a few minutes each day or week. I have never been involved in face-to-face

> self-study groups but these must take a lot more organizing and time for the event itself. PS
>
> It gave me the initial confidence boost I think most people require when entering the unknown. DG

Others were convinced during the induction and went on to become active course conference participants:

> Despite my limited participation due to time constraint, I found that ideas and issues raised developed fast and feedback is almost immediate. Online discussions have a life and a genre of their own! The outcome of such conferences is interesting and useful. NM

The most commonly expressed doubts and concerns about online for learning are about time (set against the rest of the course's demands) and how to strike a balance between studying, working and domestic life.

> It is useful but gets clogged with messages that don't add *value for me*. I wasted a lot of time on it initially and felt inadequate when I couldn't keep up with all of the new messages, but I do find I get some useful info. I tend to set a time limit and stick to it. RA

And finally an e-moderator's advice to participants:

> Don't assume that those people already on the system are experts – some may well be only one step ahead of you! Ask the obvious questions – (others may have the same problem and be grateful to you). RB

Scaffolding participants' engagement

Participants continue to display the need to gradually learn to engage with each other and the online e-tivities. Here is Gillian Roberts again from Caledonian

Business School. She shows us some student reflections from one of the online courses developed through the Carpe Diem process described on pages 101–2.

2001 . . .

At first, we used Blackboard mainly for 'announcements' and the posting of course documents, PowerPoint slides and lecture notes. At that time, students offered positive support for their access to subject resources and the benefits of convenience and time saving this provided:

> For me having the course content online is important. Knowing what I have to learn so I don't revise the wrong things for the exam. And it was handy having the announcements on it as well. Instead of having to run up and down and look at notice boards all the time! Plus the lecture notes were very, very useful.
>
> The courseware was set out really well. A lot of lecturers spent time actually putting their lecture notes on so you had a set of overheads and you had a set of actual lectures.
>
> I just think that the fact they have that feature with the lecture notes is beneficial. If we didn't have Blackboard, then we would probably all be asking for a bit more time with our lecturers. Apart from that, it saves you getting copies if you happen to miss a class or if you do want to read ahead, the information is there so I think it's quite good, it is beneficial, it saves time.

2003 where we've got to now . . .

While we were pleased that students were using the VLE, we wanted to go on and deploy more constructivist and engaging approaches. Staff were trained, supported and encouraged to use e-tivity-based approaches, scaffolded by the five-stage model.

We recently collected students' reflections at three points in a 12-week module based on these principles and developed through the Carpe Diem method. The module topic was e-marketing. Opportunities to provide reflective feedback were designed into the online course at different stages. At the start of the module students were asked to post one positive and one negative feeling they had about embarking on an online course. As you will see, they had a strong sense of the advantages and disadvantages for them from the start.

First reflections

I think it might be hard to learn as we will have to discipline ourselves to go online in our own time. My main fear is that my computer totally fails me, as you can probably tell I am a technophobe. But one positive thing is that I will be able to work in a much more flexible way which is really good as I can focus on my dissertation when I want to.

One of my fears is that i may lack motivation to work on my own as i will not be spoon fed information. One positive aspect is that I can work at a pace that suits me. My fear is that I may feel lost and not know what to say. A positive aspect is that it is new and interesting and everyone else will feel much the same as me.

My initial fear is that I will fall behind in the work due to there being no formal lectures etc to attend. I have internet access at home and so there is no need for me to come into Uni for this module at all! As for a positive aspect, it'll improve my understanding of the usefulness of the internet for learning, and save me a fortune in petrol and parking!

This is the first chance I've had to explore the module. I didn't know what to expect until I managed to log in and read Unit 1 this evening. It was good to read some of the responses. It was encouraging that others in the course were expressing their feelings.

My fear is although I like using computers a lot and learning from them, I'm not really sure what to expect from the course. I certainly wouldn't be able to do this in the uni at this time of night, so it's definitely an advantage that the course is flexible! I've not attended an interactive course such as this before, so I think it will be a new and enjoyable experience from which I can learn.

I really like the fact that there are discussion boards like this because i really feel like im getting to know more people and everyone sounds really friendly and in the same boat – with lectures you don't often get to talk to everyone in your class because everyone tends to keep to themselves or to the people they know but this way – i think everyone feels comfortable with talking on the discussion board.

I agree that this method of communication allows us to interact better in some ways. In a lecture, you might hear people's responses but you often aren't able to put a name to that person. I was wondering if those of us who are ahead and comfortable with the module, would be willing to use lab times to arrange to meet up with those who are struggling?

Half-way

After a few weeks, the students were still engaged and learning about self-management, motivation and the spectre of time, as well as e-marketing.

Yay! Just finished unit 3! Think I rushed through this unit as I fell so far behind with both unit 2 and 3. This module is a lot harder than I first thought it would be and find myself struggling quite a lot of the time to motivate myself to actually sit down and do the work. Have now made up a new timetable for myself so hopefully this will make me manage my time better not just for e-marketing but for all my other modules as well.

Aspects I like are having the opportunity to work at my own pace (even if it is snail like). This isn't my regular course and I don't really know anyone so there isn't the awkwardness of going to lectures and not having a clue who anyone is!

Finding it quite easy to communicate within our group, hope the others feel this way too. Mind you it is nice to put a face to the e-mail so we have met at least once and will be again. Have enjoyed going through the web pages, but I always love doing that, just need to read up on my SWOT etc.

Finally reached the half-way point, I never thought I would get this far when I first started out. I have been so used to face-to-face teaching that I have found it very hard to adjust, however, I am getting there slowly but surely. I have found myself lagging behind and felt I would have achieved more if I had Internet access at home. Never mind on my way to unit 4!!!

I have finally finished this unit (a week late, I know!) and am ready to make a start on unit 4. This module is a lot more work than I thought it would be, but I think it will be good practice for 4th year (I hear you get left your own then!) The aspect that I like and dislike at the same time is not having lectures and working at my own pace. These are both advantages and disadvantages.

I feel as if I am learning a lot from this module and am actually taking it in more because I am hearing other people's views on the discussion board, then trying to think of something different to add myself. Also if you are in a seminar environment then sometimes people can be too shy to speak. I think discussion boards are good in this respect.

The end in sight . . .

In the last week of the module, students were asked to reflect on their penultimate unit and on their views individually and in groups. As you can see, they seem somewhat shocked at some activities that they felt were not obvious to them at the beginning – something we will avoid in future. Most have found producing a product as a virtual group very demanding. However, no one dropped out and some recognized the great value of their learning experience.

I think i paced myself quite well in this unit, and it was useful that the activities were placed up on a weekly basis. However, like many other people i was surprised when more activities kept popping up!

On the whole I feel that our time on this module has been a positive experience that will stand us in good stead when we enter employment in the 'real' world.

Motivation to keep up with the work is certainly the main issue that needs to be addressed by students studying via these means. With no formal classes, lectures etc it is very easy to forget to do the work or to put it off and then have a large amount of work to do at the last minute. Discipline is key I think.

Working as a group to produce reports is a fairly taxing process in the real world, never mind doing it online. However, the tools available allowed us to share documents and drafts very easily which was a bonus. As it turned out we managed to complete the report with no major problems.

It takes a lot of self-motivation to get the work done as there is no lecturer telling you to get your bum in gear. It's good because in the 'REAL World' we have to be self-motivated no-one is going to hold your hand and tell you what to do next. The group work was a major hurdle as no-one is on-line at the same time perhaps due to technical difficulties, other commitments so it was hard to organize, but it got done in the end.

It's been a strange experience. You work individually, but get a sense of what others think and feel in more depth than you would in a classroom situation. I think this is because everyone is free to discuss their thoughts and feelings without the influence of others, and that everyone gets a chance to contribute, so even shy people who wouldn't benefit in a classroom situation can benefit online.

I did feel part of a group as people did respond to questions put by other students. I think that it was good because students even, shy ones were able to put forward their own opinion when perhaps in a real classroom they would feel inhibited.

I hope this chapter has convinced you of the importance for all e-moderators to understand (rather than 'see') the variety of issues and needs that each participant will bring to his or her online conference. Induction for all is important, at least for the foreseeable future.

The following Resources for practitioners provide summaries and some practical ideas:

Chapter 6

E-moderating: the key to the future of online teaching and learning

I hope in this chapter to raise your awareness of the need for imaginative e-moderation to embrace a range of new directions. The most successful educators of the future will not be those who keep up with the race to put content on the Web or on CD-ROMs, but those who can predict and act on the less obvious, weaker signals coming from the environment, and then work out how to enable productive, happy e-moderating for learning (Salmon, 2000). I consider here what these opportunities might be. I believe that even a rough and ready chart is better than no map at all. I highlight a few key areas that will have an impact on the work of e-moderators: the changing education environment and the nature of future online participants and communities. I risk a view of the up-and-coming technologies, and throw out a challenge to those responsible for providing us with the tools of our trade, the platform creators and manufacturers. Each area has a developing body of literature for you to explore. I hope I shall stimulate you to create your own map of the future for e-moderating in your own context.

Scenarios

When the first edition of this book was published and we greeted the new millennium, futurists predicted four key discontinuities that we would experience in this century. They relate to time and space, mind and body, real and virtual experiences and humans and technologies (Martell, 2000; Burn and Loch, 2001). As I write in 2003, their influence on educational institutions is still incalculable but we can be sure there is a serious shake-up going on (Clarke, 2002; Edwards, Ranson *et al*, 2002; Slevin, 2003; Remenyi, 2002; Ben-Jacob *et al*, 2000).

Using scenarios helps us to explore the increasingly puzzling and uncertain world in which we live and work, learn and teach. A scenario is a descriptive forecast of a landscape that an organization or institution might find itself in. Scenarios are not about forecasting the future but about looking at the possibilities – what we might think of as holding 'strategic conversations' (van der Heijden, 1996).

Scenario planning helps us to make sense of the choices we face. It started in large organizations to help them understand their external environments, but scenarios can also be useful tools for all of us when we face uncertainty and complexity and grapple with what's happening within our own practice and disciplines. They help us to tap into our own judgements and explore our own visions as key resources to help us to prepare for uncharted territories. In this way we can avoid a simple 'solutions' approach and the risks of trivializing potentially significant decisions.

Scenarios usually include commercial, sociological, technical, economic, political, regulatory, ecological and other domains that make up the external environment of the business world. I've tried to consider elements close to our hearts such as learners' needs and expectations, assessment, research, teaching philosophies and learning technologies, and the role of e-moderators. I hope to promote our strategic conversations and ultimately enable us to work within the reality of what actually happens more happily and successfully. To accomplish our purpose, come with me on a starship voyage to a new planetary system as we boldly go . . .

Scenario 1: Planet Contenteous

Landing on Contenteous, where Content is king, you find technology as your gateway and delivery system for e-learning. Contenteous dwellers attach high importance to targeted virtual learning environments (VLEs), content management systems, integrated learning management systems, multimedia, industry standards, DVDs, digital and cable television and high-capacity bandwidth.

Historically, the early years of the century on Contenteous are known as 'the Dog's Breakfast era'. The telephone, cable, wireless and satellite companies competed to deliver as much information as any e-moderator and online learner could use. The war between open source and off-the-shelf solutions was finally resolved in favour of commercial interests, resulting in their considerable continued investment in e-learning. Combinations of technologies and widely used high-bandwidth access helped a little to move learners from watching and listening to slightly more interaction. Nowadays, rivalry between solutions providers is still strong, though two or three market leaders are emerging.

The predominant pedagogy on Contenteous is that of the transmission model of teaching, where information is transferred from experts to novices. Content and 'push' are king and queen. There is a strong role for the observation of physical, location-based events (called Big Brother learning) using the latest technologies. Initially Big Brother learning was used for clinical practice, but it is now being deployed across a wide range of disciplines. Economies of scale and efficiency are reached through reduced interaction between teachers and learners compared with the lecture and question mode of teaching. Everyone is talking about the new plug-in that immediately senses who has written an article, for whom, when and what the commercial interests involved might be. Customers make choices on where to study from media profiles, online resource availability and league tables of various kinds.

Diagnostic tests, delivered early in the learning process, determine which content is needed by which student. Assessment of students' learning is based on reproduction, comprehension and critique. Frequent automated testing is delivered in very small chunks through complex and structured questions. A popular feature is fast, sophisticated automated feedback on achievements and assignments, which also guides students' future learning directions.

The e-moderating role on Contenteous is a combination of e-librarian, e-lecturer and e-mentor. E-moderators are recruited especially for their content expertise, their advice on developing multimedia programmes and for building online libraries and pathways through resources.

E-moderators need to captivate big audiences. The Internet and digital television spawn their own e-lecturing stars, and the most successful assume 'rock star' status. However, support for these elite few requires a very high level of research to go on in the background. Of course there are still a few lecturers campaigning actually to be with their students, rather than look at them on monitors. Some have joined the medical doctors' campaign for real patients. But they are fewer each year. We will remember them.

Recruitment of e-moderators for Contenteous is from those at home with broadcasting and presenting, in love with the media, media wise and 'savvy', and with personal qualities indicating media 'presence'. Screen tests are set up for e-moderators. The select few are very good 'communicators' and happy to work with commercial media organizations and businesses. Training for Contenteous e-moderators includes professional grooming for those showing particular aptitude. They receive media presentation and communication skills (putting yourself and your content across to the audience) and understanding of and insight into their audiences. They can earn big money.

Scenario 2: Planet Instantia

The pedagogy on Planet Instantia is usually called e-learning. Instantians use sophisticated learning object approaches, with information technology seen as a basic tool. Computer-based courses are offered from desks at work or in learning centres. Learners work and learn almost simultaneously, since every technological object is integrated with everything else. Flexibility and instantaneousness are the keywords.

The costs of travel, training facilities and trainers are slashed compared with those on Earth. The role of ambient intelligence in devices is seen as key on this planet. Every device that is connected to electricity is also connected to the Internet, known as always on and always everywhere. Simply everything and everyone has an e-address. Hence educational providers are able to think both creatively and in a very integrated way about learning devices.

Individual learners assess the value of the learning experience, asking, 'Is this learning just for me, just in time, just for now and just enough (known as Tagmania)?' With the impact of the skills at work shortage and the rise in importance of corporate universities, professionals only join an organization that has its own special university. Bonus systems are linked to success at learning and application. The inclusion of e-career development is standard in salary packages.

The key feature of assessment on this planet is authenticity. Employers consider whether learning provision helps to recruit the right people for the organization. They also evaluate the speed and effectiveness of the learning provision by considering the extent to which organizational performances improve. Assessment tasks are always related to specific work or professional needs, and are deeply embedded in the learning activities. Gaming technologies are used to create 'real life' scenarios that combine learning and assessment in seamless environments. There is a high level of tracking of outcomes, which are automatically transferred to employees' development accounts.

This planet has sometimes been accused of navel rather than star-gazing since the inhabitants spend much of their time exploring the core of the planet rather than considering its environment. Telescopes are no longer in use, for example. Seismology and geophysics have replaced astronomy. However, with the increase in effective links between e-learning, performance and knowledge management, an improved systemic approach has been achieved and the advocates of lifelong learning have begun to see the benefits of including Instantia in their universes.

On Instantia, e-moderators support autonomous learning (although many learners exist magically with little human contact to sustain them). Real e-moderators or virtual prepared responses (simulacra) are available 24 hours a day, both synchronously and asynchronously. E-moderators focus on skills development in employees (to enable them to learn in this way) and on ways of fostering the adoption of a strong in-house knowledge culture.

E-moderating talents are part of the package of competencies expected of human resource (HR) professionals on Instantia. They are recruited from within an organization's HR function, and are considered professionals. They come from a corporate training tradition. They are also skilled in needs assessment, and the tracking and measurement of learning outcomes (so act as a kind of learning accountant). Their professional training includes working in networks and information exchanges, and in developing professional practice. Their loyalty is to their profession, organization or community of practice rather than to the learner.

Scenario 3: Planet Nomadic

At first on Planet Nomadic the impact of smaller, faster and wireless technologies went well beyond kids with mobile phones, and they were adopted by the most forward-looking universities. Consider teaching and learning in a world where democracy is promoted by net-based voting and where everyone carries one Gb of digital storage in their shirt pockets! Radio chips replaced barcodes on manufactured objects, and wireless Internet nodes became ubiquitous in pubs, cafes and hotels and all places of retail and entertainment. Learning devices were once carried, then worn and are now often embedded subcutaneously.

Some people think that part of our sense of identity is based on not only who we are, but where we are and knowing our precise place in the world (Harvey, 2001: 784). Global positioning systems (GPS) using a network of satellites can fix someone's location on the planet to within a few metres. These devices first transformed exploration and the emergency services on Nomadic but as soon as everything in the physical world became tracked, tagged, barcoded and mapped, teaching and learning opportunities emerged. Location technology fixed learners in the physical world, while inviting them to operate in the virtual world. By connecting learners in a network of people with a physical sense of place, this finally took away the sense of isolation, although for a time during the first decade of the century, invisibility became a lifestyle choice.

On Nomadic there is less stability, less structure, less fixed time for work and leisure, retirement and education than on Earth, along with significantly more nodes for accessing learning. Planet Nomadic provides portable learning for mobile lifestyles. Learning on the Planet Nomadic is time-independent and individual. The learners are seen as electronic explorers and adventurers. The technology that originally merged GPS with telephony, to keep people safe and comfortable during walking weekends in Wales or Montana, now offers them access to their learning resources after the post-hike supper.

The explosion of opportunities for travelling learning resulted in hype and myth about mobility, similar to that about e-learning in the closing days of the 20th century. However, once the pedagogy was worked out and e-moderators had been trained, real benefits emerged. Learning is now truly any time, any place. Textual, visual and audible information becomes available as learners move closer to their e-moderators. Individuals choose based on their cognitive preferences and styles. Pacing and timing for distance learners are easier than on Earth, as learners carry 'place and pace' keepers with them.

There are few physical classrooms left. Terrestrial universities and corporate training facilities have disappeared; new e-universities have inherited the planet. Students calculate the cost of their courses based on airtime and connection, rather than attendance at class, or purchase of books, as on Earth.

English has become standard for learning. The *New Oxford Very Concise Internet Dictionary* is the all time best e-seller. (The Campaign for Full English Grammar gave up in 2007.) However, mobile learning is also popular to support modern language development. (Visit the country, live in the culture and access your course at the same time.)

Technologies are highly portable, individual, adaptable and intuitive to use (Sharples, 2000). Mobile technologies are seen as essential communication and learning tools, rather than as disruptive, as at the turn of the century. Main technologies in use are tablets, personal digital assistants (PDAs) and palm tops, fourth generation mobile phones, GPS, unfolding keyboards, blow-up screens, wireless and personal networks, low orbit satellites, national and international communications networks, infrared connections and e-books. All students have tablets or palm tops and text and voice mobiles. Styli are commoner than pens. Breakthroughs occurred when safety was achieved in the use of mobile phones, and decreasing size matched increasing functionality and capability. Costs of handsets and devices are very low. PDAs were worn in underwear for the first manned mission to Mars. Indeed, the latest fashions and jewellery always include a suitable pocket and strap for the PDA.

The war between the PC or the television as a focus for home entertainment gateways was won some years ago, as set-top boxes for games and learning are now ubiquitous in children's bedrooms. Interactive games are the new chocolate buttons. 'Finish your homework and you can play the game', say parents. A few forward-looking educators combine games and learning, and scoop the e-learning market.

All universities, colleges and schools produce their own very cheap micro-processors, led by the UK Open University's new mission, and these are embedded in everything from shoes to furniture, buildings and regions. Planet Nomadic heralds the move away from generic software applications to providing focused key learning components geared towards an individual learner. Wearable components (WCs) have 'context awareness' and hence interact with the users and their environment. They know when to switch themselves off, and importantly, regularly help to pace the learners, day by day, through their courses.

On Nomadic students design, negotiate or choose their own assessments, often in collaboration with their assessment helpers. Assessment helpers are sometimes real people, peers or alumni, and sometimes programmes based on artificial intelligence. Assessment of learning is in small bites, based largely on projects and outcomes, and achieved incrementally. Every assessment event contributes to updating an individual's learning profile, and hence suggesting future learning needs. Interaction is evaluated using the latest computer mediated tools. The great mobile phone exam scam of 2006 accelerated the demise of several struggling universities, and promoted the use of biotechnology to ensure authentication of students' own work. Biometrics ensure the security of learners' identities. Portfolio learners expect to transfer their learning credits easily from one institution to another. The shift away from memorization towards performance is welcomed by learners, universities and employers.

E-moderators are as mobile as their students are. Many are portfolio e-moderators and work for several educational institutions and providers, all over the world, at any one time. They have not only a highly developed awareness of the ways in which traditions of learning and expectations vary in different cultures, but also the ability to work across disciplines and levels of education. They can break activities and content down into tiny components that can be transmitted and studied in small chunks. They are fully comfortable with using online assessment, and confident in the technologies that ensure the students they are assessing are the same ones they are teaching. They can relate well to students without needing to meet with them, so the issue of plagiarism is less of a concern than on Earth. They focus on promoting the concepts of ownership of the learning process, active learning, independence, the ability to make judgements, self-motivation and high levels of autonomy. They provide and support resource-based learning, working with skilled technicians and e-librarians.

On Nomadic e-moderators self-select if they feel 'the call', having first saturated themselves in the ways of learning on Nomadic. E-moderation is an outgrowth of enthusiasm for the e-mobile lifestyle and a love of helping people to learn. People graduate to e-moderation from being effective e-learners themselves, and there are few professional barriers between being an effective e-learner and becoming an e-moderator. Nomadic e-moderators move in and out of the work as fits their particular professional wishes and the needs of the moment. Training for e-moderators on Nomadic includes experiential learning, observation, apprenticeships, networking and learning on the job, as befits a mobile lifestyle.

Scenario 4: Planet Cafélattia

This planet is the outcome of Dibbell's prediction: 'Someday the Net will be the summation of the world's total computing resources. All computers will link up into chaotic digital soup. Tremendously powerful and. . . . Hard to harness' (Dibbell, 1995).

Communication and mediated networked computers can be used to build upon and amplify human talents for collaborative purposes. On Cafélattia hundreds of millions of people lend their computers for cooperative purposes. The impact can be positive or negative, used for inclusion of those disadvantaged, for learning or destructively (Rheingold, 2002). As a result, new global subcultures blossomed, new industries were born and older industries launched furious counter-attacks. This threw into relief the different needs of learners, and resulted in much increased merging and competing in educational provision. Much energy and money was wasted chasing rainbows.

On Cafélattia instant messaging is used for most communication and everyday transactions, with automatic language translation where necessary. Travelling is an indulgence, not a necessity.

What emerges on Cafélattia is the importance of peer-to-peer technologies for data, documents, music and knowledge sharing across offices, across campuses, from industry to universities, from professional associations to learning providers, and across disciplines and cultures. New information and knowledge are no longer the preserve of academics. Collaboration is commonplace, and integrated into everyday work and learning, but often in unexpected and unplanned ways. The impact of 'smart mob' technology already appears to be both beneficial and destructive, as it is used by some of its earliest adopters to support democracy and by others to coordinate terrorist attacks (Rheingold, 2002).

On Planet Cafélattia, learning is built around learning communities and interaction, extending access beyond the bounds of time and space, but offering the promise of efficiency and widening access. Think of individuals as nodes on a network (Haraway, 1991)! The key technology is the developed, entertaining, effective Internet (beyond the browser!), to allow immediate and satisfying interaction between students and students, and between e-moderators and learners. Technologies are asynchronous and synchronous group systems to support a wide variety of environments for working and learning together. Rather than a place where millions of users all connect to a handful of large sites, the Internet has reclaimed its purpose as a place where everyone talks to everyone else, equal to equal. Peer-to-peer (P to P) technologies have survived their legal challenges and become acceptable. Groupware in use is specially developed for learning purposes, rather than based on messaging or corporate meeting software as on Earth. Both co- and remotely-located learning communities (clicks and mortar) are of key importance. Individuals utilize new forms of community, based on augmented awareness of their proximity to places of interest and each other. This is known as the Outernet highway.

Although media cartels and government agencies sought to create and control online participation in the interests of ownership, in similar ways to the broadcast era of the turn of the millennium, e-moderators and learners maintained their power to create rather than consume. For example, the online 'free learners' movement fought cyberbattles over file sharing, copy protection and regulation of the radio waves. Most individuals are provided with free technology, since they are expected to connect into the global network for distributed computational tasks from time to time.

Learners connect through both low and high bandwidth devices and systems. Hence the technologies are seen only as mediating devices, promoting creativity and collaboration. Cafélattia learning appeals to a very wide range of people, including the increasing numbers and percentages of 'grey learners' who have a great deal to offer to others, a desire to learn through non-traditional means, and who have the time and resources to access networked technologies (Swindell, 2002).

The pedagogy is based on notions of a very strong social context for learning, with the model of acquisition, argumentation and application. Key activities for learners are finding and interacting with like-minded individuals anywhere on the planet (for example by gender, by interest, by profession), and being intellectually extended by dialogue and challenge from others. Learners express themselves freely through speech and text. The roles of reflection (an essential tool of expert learners), professional development and the sharing of tacit knowledge are of critical importance. Learning is contextualized and given authenticity by the learning group and the learning community (rather than by the university, as on Earth). On and offline resources are important, but electronic and structured information support and stimulate the learning group rather than replace the active, participative learning experience.

Assessment is based on complex problem solving and knowledge construction skills. It is learner-driven and negotiated with peers. Assessment is seen as non-restrictive, and an enhancement to and motivation for learning. Hence the level and scope of assessment are largely the product of interaction with other like-minded learners. Group and peer assessment has become the norm.

Equatorial (360 degree) assessment is common. Evaluation of contributions to text, interaction and complex problem solving is all automated.

E-moderators on Cafélattia think globally but are able to turn their ideas into local and contextualized action. They see the technologies as yet another environment for learning rather than as tools. They are experts at mentoring individuals online, and may be seen as companions in the democratic net-worked learning process, rather than teachers as such. They know when to take part, when to provide expert input, when to act as a peer and when to stay silent. They also have very highly developed skills in online group development for learning and in the use of online resources to stimulate groups. They know how to welcome and support learners into the online world and how to build effective online communities. They act as intelligent agents and facilitators. They have the ability to visualize others in their situations. They know how to allow a sense of humour and fun to manifest itself online. They know how to build gradually on the processes of exchanging information, and how to turn this into knowledge sharing and ultimately into knowledge construction.

Recruitment of e-moderators on Cafélattia comes from community workers and people mobilizers. They are teachers who are interested in e-community development. They value people for themselves and for their potential as self-developers. They are natural leaders who emerge 'on the job' as they themselves demonstrate their e-learning prowess and are encouraged by experienced and effective e-moderators to take up the work. Cafélattia e-moderator training is on the job as apprentices and as part of communities of practice. Like their e-learners, they are self-developers as they seek to improve their professional practice. As they dip in and out of e-moderating, so they seek ways to maintain and update their knowledge by drawing on sources of continuing professional development – particularly virtual and experiential ones.

What planet are you on?

It's likely that all the planets will have an element of reality, and there will be a variety of players and processes. Institutionally, we will probably see further combinations of these scenarios, such as universities with corporates or colleges partnering media companies. There are key branding and rebranding issues to consider. If elements of Nomadic come about, for example, where does that leave beautiful campus locations such as Bath in the UK or the Gold Coast of Australia? If Cafélattia gains a hold, where does it lead the high-profile research-based universities such as Oxbridge and Harvard? You may find that different groupings of people in your organization are excited by the possibilities of some planets and horrified by others. For example I've found that managers often favour Contenteous and IT people Nomadic. Academics often like the constructivist Cafélattia and teachers Instantia with its learning object approach. Where do you stand?

However, the patterns of the use of information and communication technologies cannot easily be determined, as the ways learners and explorers will use new forms of online learning offerings are unpredictable. Acceptable use and the meaning given to new technologies are a complex mix of 'distinctive and perplexing forms of rational and non-rational behaviour' (Silverstone and Haddon, 1996: 45). Silverstone and Haddon see the implementation of information and communication technologies as a process of 'taming' wild objects, and adapting them to the routines and rituals of everyday life – a process that has largely yet to happen on a wide scale for teaching and learning. I think that as the e-moderators increase their skills and add the magical human touch, the wildness can be changed in a more ecologically friendly direction!

I hope you will start your own strategic conversations, challenge these scenarios and develop new ones. I hope they will help you to see through the confusion, spot developments before they become trends, see patterns before they fully emerge, and grasp the relevant features of learning technologies that do truly reflect our needs, and those of our students. I hope they will help you find a suitable pathway through inflated claims (vendors?), unrealistic expectations (students and users?) and unformed strategies (politicians?). Furthermore, exploring scenarios for e-learning and e-moderating is best done with other people – from other departments, faculties and universities. Even within our own organizations, dealing with complex scenarios and their future potential must be handled in multi-functional teams. We need to engage fully with the providers of the technologies themselves as well; in this way deeper understanding and dialogue will emerge. I believe you will be convinced that there is a very strong role for e-moderators in all these scenarios, but the way these responsibilities and privileges are discharged may be rather different from yesteryear.

So what will actually happen? To a large extent, it's up to you. Vision it and action it! When you approach each of these planets, check out the atmosphere for yourself before landing. Does it support life for your discipline? Where will the power come from to sustain you on this planet? Are you the first to walk on this planet? And do you want to be? If not, what can you learn from previous explorers? Either way, please make sure your experiences are available for others who follow you, both your successes and your failures. In this way, not only is knowledge built, but also a new explorers' e-moderating community.

Going boldly and successfully into the future inevitably involves organizational change. The gap-closing exercises probably involve many years, so we need tactics as well as strategy along the pathways. One way of helping, as education goes global, cyber and geo-located, would be to recognize a world-wide licence for e-moderating.

So as you can see, it's still teaching, but not as we've known it on Earth. Most of the skills we have already acquired are much needed, but there is more. In this way, the amazing and diverse planets will continue to be open to exploration not only by e-moderators but also by learners who will boldly go . . .

Resources for practitioners to help you further explore ideas are:

23 Virtual learning environment paraple p 207
25 Future scenario p 212

Part 2:

RESOURCES FOR PRACTITIONERS

The following provide a variety of resources for you to try out with your students and e-moderators. All are research based and have their roots in practice, commonly in the OU or OUBS or sometimes from my training courses. None are intended to be definitive, but they provide you with checklists to make your own or to use as the basis of resources for online or offline workshops and discussions.

Resources for practitioners 1

E-moderating skills: taming online time

E-moderators issues

E-moderators tame time more successfully if they have:

- online training for their role;
- well developed skills in weaving and software to help;
- familiarity with writing on screen;
- the ability to work flexibly and integrate working online with their everyday life;
- the reusability of resources and e-tivities;
- the e-moderators' ability to create 'presence'.

Technical issues

These issues help with use of online time:

- everyone's experience with the platform;
- quality and appropriateness of the technology for engagement;
- the levels and availability of technical support;
- the connectedness for use any time and any place;
- efficacy of platform in use for the mode of learning.

Self-support

Self-support of participants depends on:

- deployment of the five-stage scaffold;
- level of excitement of participants;
- participants' socialization and emotion comfort with the online learning.

The impact of success

Full engagement by participants probably means more time for the e-moderators and depends on:

- numbers of participants;
- levels of contribution;
- levels of browsing.

Resources for practitioners 2

E-moderating skills: components of online socialization

Colleagues sometimes feel that they would like to spend less time on stage two, the socialization part of the model, and get on with the 'real learning'! However, time and time again we have found that it is essential to undertake this stage successfully, in the interests of better participation later in the model. This resource tells you a bit more about stage two, and offers some ways of spending less time and effort, under certain circumstances.

There are three main components of stage two. They are establishing a successful online team or group, introducing the knowledge domain and the approaches to the learning, and the induction of the participants into and their use of the online environment itself. For all three, it's insufficient to post information. Participants need to work with these ideas and truly get to know about each other to make them their own.

Component 1: establishing a successful group

E-tivities at this stage need to:

- enable individuals to create and work with their online identities;
- elicit, expose and begin to explore the diversity of cultures and expectations each participant brings to the learning;

- create a climate of, and ways of, everyone contributing actively;
- build an effective virtual team;
- establish an online culture and ways of behaving in this group at this time for this course.

Component 2: knowledge domain

E-tivities should:

- explore the nature and approach online of the overall discipline or domain of knowledge, its wider context and relevance to the participants, and its use and application in the online environment;
- establish how your topic will be handled and what is expected for their learning;
- determine how assessment and learning outcomes will be handled and their relationship to the online opportunities.

Component 3: online environment

Introduction to:

- the way pacing, timings, rhythm will work in this programme, what deadlines are essential, what flexibility there is;
- the nature of asynchronicity and its advantages, such as opportunities for reworking contributions and reflections, and whether any synchronous 'events' will be used, requiring attendance at a particular moment;
- key technical issues, especially enabling participants to get the most from the software without it getting in the way of the learning.

If you are e-moderating a group that is already well established as a team and familiar with the knowledge domain, but new to online, then you can undertake one e-tivity from components 1 and 2, and put most of your effort into stage three, helping the group to work successfully in the online environment.

If you have participants who are used to communicating online and have experienced earlier parts of a relevant learning programme, but are new to each other, then you can focus most of your stage two e-tivities on enabling them to work effectively and virtually together.

If you have a well-established virtual group who are starting out on a new course, a new project or higher level work, then most of your stage two energy can be put into exposing the team to the joys of using online in the service of new objectives or directions.

Resources for practitioners 3

E-moderating skills: how to weave

1. 'Collect' up all the contributions into one message (if your software allows you to do this) or cut and paste them into your word processor.
2. Read through quickly and colour code the key themes.
3. Create a list in the file for each of these, with titles.
4. Identify the unifying themes.
5. Identify the points of disagreement.
6. Summarize by a sentence or bullet point or two for each of the themes, identifying points of agreement and disagreement, perhaps by giving examples, attributed to the originator.
7. Add your positive and reinforcing feedback.
8. Add your criticisms and point out omissions.
9. Add your congratulations.
10. Add your 'meta' (overall) comments or teaching points.
11. If you wish to move on the discussion, ask specific but open-ended questions.
12. Delete all the original data and create simple formatting for ease of reading.
13. Post in the conference with a clear title, invite further comment.

An example message from an online e-democracy coordinators course:

The differences between summarizing and weaving?

Summarizing is rather like reproducing the material in shortened form, picking out the main points. The original meanings are not removed.

Weaving is a more creative task that selects themes and rearranges them into a new statement, making connections that may not have been intended by the writers.

Compare with lots of woollen threads. A summary might say 'there are five red ones, five white ones and five blue ones and two of other colours.' A weave might say 'I have made a small flag out of coloured wool, including some that I had left over from another project!'

So to summarize, the summary shortens, the weave selects and adds to, and the insight may be that the e-moderator weaves when he or she selects some themes from the participants and relates these to things that he or she is aware of.

You can also undertake 'mini-weaves' more like a ribbon rather than a flag!

What about the shorter, quicker, more direct weaving which draws out a theme or implication on the hoof perhaps from a short run of messages – sometimes only three or four? The e-moderator can spot and draw out an implication or make an observation and hold it up for inspection and invite comments.
Ken

Resources for practitioners 4

E-moderating skills: treading on cultural toes

We rarely think about our own culture – the habitual ways in we go about the business of living, learning and teaching in our daily lives in our particular society or discipline. We take it for granted. This resource is an encouragement to find out more about the implicit world of your participants before you begin to e-moderate – especially their ideas about working online and about the other participants – and then to remain alert to signs of different cultural differences and expectations once you have started. Sensitivity and discretion may save you potential online embarrassment. Needless to say, none of the following should be taken as implying any criticism – it's just the way things are!

Styles of address, hierarchy and authority

The Anglo–American style of informality is itself culture-bound and may not be the norm elsewhere. Some societies preserve a greater degree of formality. Cultural norms differ even across Western Europe. If, for instance, you are e-moderating a conference for German participants, you may experience greater formality and hierarchy online than you might expect in an Anglo-American setting. Titles may be used in addressing other participants and use of first names may not be much in evidence. However, academic institutions may be a little less formal than other organizations. In general we suggest that as a wise

precaution you ask participants what they would like to be called, and invite
them to sign their messages accordingly.

Male and female

In some cultures, relationships between male and female are more constrained
than in westernized societies. In some the opinions of females may carry less
weight than those of males, and females may appear inhibited or indeed be
ignored in the presence of males. The e-moderator needs to be alert to
ensuring everyone can contribute, and everyone's views are valued, and model
these responses too.

Asking questions

Asking direct questions can sometimes be problematic. For instance, in traditional Chinese culture asking questions, particularly of teachers and parents, is
not generally encouraged. So being urged by the e-moderator to ask questions
online may not translate naturally into action, and may need active and
continuous – albeit sensitive – prompting and support. As a corollary, in some
cultures, there can be an expectation that the teacher will 'tell' and the student
will learn what the teacher says. A preoccupation with assessment and 'getting
through the work' can follow. All of these may translate into an expectation of
authority by the e-moderator on the part of the participants. It's impossible in
a short time to change this. However, creating an atmosphere of equality and
the e-moderator setting structured opportunities will help.

Critiquing

Being asked to offer a critique of someone else's offering may be seen as being
rude in some cultures. The person whose work is critiqued may feel slighted
and in danger of losing face. Someone of lower status may be inhibited from
offering an opinion other than a complimentary one. In the online environment, we try to enable gradual development and support for all participants, and
then we encourage them to challenge. Some people may need more help than
others in this way of working.

Opening up online

Personal disclosure online as part of socialization into the group, which some
of us may take for granted if we are used to the Anglo-American style, is again

not necessarily the norm in all cultures. And some will be more generally reticent about articulating their thoughts online. Really good e-tivities exploring cultural differences at stage two will help lay the ground for the valuing of all contributions. Make it clear people do not need to disclose personal information, and avoid posting your own information based on marital status or career achievements, since this may otherwise 'set the tone'.

Using names

Asking for preferred names for addressing participants can save great potential embarrassment. If you are used to the Western style of first name and then surname, you need to take especial care. Find out as much as you can from the course sponsor. Take the list of participants' names and annotate it with each preferred name as you learn it. Print off that list and keep it constantly by you whilst you are online. And try to gently insist that people sign their messages with their preferred name.

Genders can easily be confused too. Here's a recent example exchange from one of our e-moderating training courses:

> JC writes:
> Val Richardson proudly added an example with his 6 year old grand-daughter.
>
> VR writes:
> Interesting gender assumption here!!!!! Juan, my name is English and it's Valerie. Val
>
> JC writes:
> Sorry Val! Valery? Cultural misunderstanding. In Spanish sounds closer to Valentin.
>
> PC (the e-moderator) writes:
> Hola Juan
> Maybe I can give some assistance here. Val is a she, I've met her! You can find her introductory message in Week One Announcements Forum.

Resources for practitioners 5

E-moderating skills: presence

Many online participants expect a great deal from their e-moderators, while e-moderators try to encourage online participants to be self-sufficient. Here are some strategies that create a feeling of 'presence' online, without the e-moderator having to be there 24 hours each day!

- Send out a personal e-mail letter to all participants before the course starts, indicating how often they can expect you to visit (usually once a day).
- Greet each participant by a welcome e-mail on his or her first arrival, as well as acknowledging his or her arrival in the conference.
- Ask for each participant to send a personal e-mail to the e-moderator as well as post a message in the conference, early in the course. This helps to check who has arrived and when, and makes it easy to respond individually.
- Mention each participant by name at some point in early summaries. Continue to mention individuals in your messages. This is very motivating and a fine way to acknowledge contributions.
- Run an e-tivity at stage one, exploring how participants expect to fit the conferencing into their daily lives, and self-disclose a little about yours.
- As the conference builds up and you find you have many messages to read on your arrival each day, focus on the last few messages in a thread (rather than reading them chronologically).
- As participants become more self-sufficient and motivated (by stage three), avoid responding to each message but focus on setting up discussions really well and then summarizing after a given length of time, adding your own teaching points then if appropriate.

- Be prepared to put congratulatory message up and then an invitation to further action (such as, 'Very interesting points here, can I invite a summarizer', or maybe, 'please focus on ★★★ aspect now to build on the ideas').

E-tivities (Salmon, 2002a) offers you more ideas for designing for effective and efficient use of e-moderator time.

E-moderating skills: e-moderation principles for productive conferencing

1. Make sure you are in the conference with welcoming messages before the participants arrive.
2. Provide time for participants to become familiar with the conferences in the programme, preferably in advance.
3. Create structures and expectations for conferences.
4. Set clear objectives and clarify expectations for your online groups.
5. Provide enough, but not too much, intervention (not more than one in four messages from you).
6. Build up your conferences through stages of individual welcome, social community building as quickly and effectively as possible, but never leave these stages out.
7. Be flexible, responsive and innovative to conference design and development.
8. Be inclusive of all and value all participants.
9. Be satisfied with one or two key points emerging from the discussion.
10. Find the unifying threads in a discussion, build, weave and re-present ideas constantly (present and be comfortable with conflicting opinions).

11. Accommodate lurkers or browsers, at least for a while as they may have their reasons but e-mail or phone them with support if they persist in non-participation.
12. Be patient and persistent, especially with novice users.
13. Let participants know if you are going to be offline for a while.
14. Model behaviours and ways of communicating online.
15. Be clear how often you are logging on and what participants can expect from you.
16. Work towards Level five behaviours, eg request reflection and comment on the learning occurring online.
17. Pace the conferencing realistically.
18. Change inappropriate titles and headings of messages (with e-mail explanation).
19. Move messages in the wrong conference (with e-mail explanation to the contributor).
20. Deal quietly and privately with anyone dominating the discussion – ask them to reflect before responding.
21. Conclude discussions before they peter out – if a conference flags, delete it (with an online explanation) and start another.
22. Encourage participants to use conference messages as data or for illustration in assignments.
23. Collect participants' views and feedback on your own performance through online mechanisms.

Resources for practitioners 7

E-moderating skills: conference house-keeping

The conferencing environment needs to be looked after, in much the same way as your house, apartment or teaching environment, in order to keep it service-able. These factors are largely 'hygiene' factors, ie will be invisible if they are working well. Without them, many conferences have foundered. Without 'housekeeping' your loftier or more creative teaching and learning online goals are unlikely to be achievable. Many studies have shown that small changes in housekeeping make a considerable difference! Make these protocols clear to your e-moderators:

1. Decide whether conferences and their sub-sets will be set up in advance, or whether you will allow topics and sub-conferences to 'emerge' over time – and housekeep accordingly, so that the conferences operate how partici-pants expect.
2. Allow interesting and relevant topics to 'emerge' from participants at various times, create sub-conferences to support emergent topics, and delete dormant conferences to make virtual space for them.
3. E-moderators need to visit often (agree how often) and notify participants if they are likely to be offline for more than a week or so (lack of appear-ance online mystifies and disturbs other users). Ask a colleague e-moderator to visit your conference whilst you are away.

4. Teams of e-moderators should work together to ensure regular responses to participants and maintenance of conferences.
5. Create and maintain good 'layout' of onscreen access conferences, very easy navigation around them and the quick closing and deleting of inactive conferences to keep the screen as clear as possible.
6. Summarize, delete or archive messages so that no more than around 20 messages in any one conference or sub-conference are active at any one time. This avoids participants being overwhelmed upon visiting a conference after a few days.

Resources for practitioners 8

E-moderating skills: knowledge sharing and construction

It is at Stage 4, knowledge sharing and construction, that online conferencing has the most to offer teaching and learning. To achieve these, e-moderators need to do the following:

1. Get technical questions out of the way before the real start of the course.
2. Make clear what the e-moderator's role is, ie to collect and represent participants' views.
3. Create a setting and an atmosphere where differences as well as similarities are appreciated, and where disagreements are seen as an opportunity to learn.
4. Be an equal participant in the conference.
5. Avoid directive interventions and 'right answer' responses.
6. Encourage and support other participants in the e-moderating role.
7. Stimulate the debate, offer ideas, and offer resources (rather than 'the answers').
8. Provide 'sparks' (comments or stimulating questions that will prompt responses). See *E-tivities* (Salmon, 2002a) for more ideas.
9. Be prepared to collate carefully, weave together and represent the discussion, ie undertake summarizing and modelling activities.
10. Intervene at the right point in time in the debate and appreciate the delicate balance between 'holding back' and intervening.

11. Share your range of experience but avoid overload or overwhelming participants.
12. Make explicit to participants that their contributions are wanted and valued.
13. Be careful to acknowledge and be inclusive of all contributions.
14. Be clear to the group about what additional 'powers' you have as e-moderator, and the circumstances in which you would use them. (Some participants believe that e-moderators sneak around online.)
15. Be very tolerant of natural twists and turns of discussion – it's unlikely to go the way you originally expected!
16. Use software that supports good threading and weaving and searchable archives.
17. Look for evidence of knowledge construction and reward it (rather than expecting specific outcomes).
18. Accept variety and diversity in responses and reward these.
19. Reward task accomplishments rather than test for information recall.
20. Assess co-operative, group, collaborative and team outcomes, rather than individuals' ones, wherever possible.

Resources for practitioners 9

E-moderating skills: e-moderating with synchronous conferencing

In synchronous environments, as in asynchronous ones, the e-moderator is a manager and facilitator of the learning, more than a teacher. In the same way that the role of the e-moderator differs from that of the traditional teacher, there also appear to be a number of other special critical success factors for synchronous conferencing.

- Ensure that a technical helpdesk is provided within the platform during the time you are working online. This means that if participants, or e-moderators, experience problems during an online event, they can receive help and support without interrupting others.
- Manage participants' expectations so that they understand they may occasionally experience connection problems such as unexpected disconnections, 'choppy sound' or a slow screen refresh rate.
- Start with stage one- and two-type e-tivities as a 'warm-up'.
- Use carefully structured e-tivities and publish these on a Web site before the synchronous event.
- Provide ways of students working together in small work teams in different 'rooms'. The e-moderator can 'visit' them and help during this period if necessary.

- Run 'plenaries' with structured reporting from the smaller groups, and follow this up by a discussion. E-moderate these well, ensuring careful turn-taking where appropriate.
- After the structured e-tivities are completed, encourage people to speak if they wish.
- The e-moderator should finish by offering feedback to the group. This may include anonymous feedback where common errors are corrected but not attributed, a summary and teaching comments.
- Encourage continuing work on the topic.
- Provide a summary and teaching comments after the event is over, if appropriate.
- Provide a related Web site with not only details of the activities but also other items such as course news, a course schedule, assessment material, links to additional resources and other relevant information and, of course, if this is appropriate to your learning outcomes, an asynchronous conferencing environment where participants can post in-depth, reflective comments, exchange longer pieces of written work and reflect on the learning/teaching experience as a whole.
- Participants need a way of signalling their desire to speak. Most software provides for this, but protocols may need to be developed if not.
- Provide an alternative channel such as text chat as a 'back channel' that allows participants to communicate whilst not actually speaking.
- Encourage the use of graphic or text-based emoticons.
- Use a platform that allows private conversations between participants, thus permitting e-moderators to offer immediate support or error correction to individuals without drawing the attention of the group to this.
- Let participants know that silences are natural in this environment. In the physical environment it is possible to see when learners are thinking or working silently. In the virtual environment, this is not possible and a period of silence can seem much longer than it really is. As their experience grows, e-moderators become more confident and are able to judge at what point they should moderate the silence and encourage learners to participate actively in the conference.
- No response may mean that a participant has lost the connection or been interrupted, and left the computer. Ask participants to let others know if they need to leave the computer for a short while or for the rest of the session. Preferably use an application that allows an 'away from the keyboard' indication.

Many thanks to Regine Hampel, Mirjam Hauck and Lesley Shield, Department of Languages, Open University, UK for their advice for this resource.

Resources for practitioners 10

Managing e-moderating: using the five-stage model

You will find below a summary of advice relevant to each of the five stages of the model. For each stage, there is advice on technical support you can provide, on helping participants to learn and on e-moderating in particular.

Stage 1: Access and motivation

Technical support

- Provide a helpline for password and access problems.
- Ensure new participants can read and know how to send messages as soon as they are online.
- Give great attention to precise detail in your written and onscreen instructions.
- Clarify the differences between e-mail and conferencing.
- Provide a printed manual for those who prefer one (may be copies of your own screen messages).

Motivating participants

- Recognize that taking part is an act of faith for most participants at this stage.

- Present (sell if necessary) learning online as a new way of learning through networking, emphasizing its importance as a communication and networking tool.
- Specify how online will be used in the course or programme.
- Ensure the 'look and feel' of your system is user-friendly for all comers.
- Try to create fun, making online enticing and enjoyable.
- Assure novices that their fear and anxiety will be overcome by trying out online conferencing.

E-moderating

- Acknowledge high levels of anxiety and lack of confidence in some participants may mean that some 'hand holding' is needed.
- Welcome participants individually.
- Constantly improve and update support materials.
- Keep the conference structure very clear and simple.
- Encourage participants to log on regularly, and do so yourself.

Stage 2: Socialization

Technical support

- Explain carefully how to save time and, if connecting through a phone line, money.
- Provide a 'lifeguard' – a person to e-mail for help online.
- Focus instructions on software facilities where participants can see immediate benefits, eg the address book, file attachment facility and shortcut keystrokes.
- Expect participants to believe there must be 'bugs' in the system since it does not behave how they expect it to, and be prepared to be very patient in providing support, explanation and resolution.
- Suggest to some participants that they should make a print-out from the screen, to have beside them when working through instructions for exercises.
- Navigating around the conferences will be easier if you use meaningful names and icons.
- Look out for those who lack confidence in manipulating Windows and be ready to help them.
- Some participants may need reassurance from you about spelling and typos.
- Don't alter the look of the desktop too often – novices get very worried by frequent changes in it.

- Know the rationale for your choice of platform, and the benefits of it for your participants, because some may make unfavourable comparisons with other more familiar software.

Learning

- Enhance participants' confidence in using online learning by praising their contributions.
- Offer ways for participants to benefit from reading about other people's online experience and problems.
- Explain the importance of acknowledging others online and set an example yourself.
- Point out why it is usually better to keep messages short and purposeful.
- Explain the benefits to participants of their working at their own pace.
- Ensure that ways for individuals to establish their identities online are used, eg explain how to read and post CVs (résumés).

E-moderating

- Check for any participants with relevant disabilities, however minor, and find out how you can help them.
- Use metaphors and straightforward explanation to provide bridges between familiar ways of communicating and online.
- Emphasize transferable skills and links to other experiences.
- Promote awareness of appropriate online communication styles.
- Encourage practice to reinforce developing skills.
- Allow lurking or browsing, without making this a moral issue.
- Offer structured exercises and activities to participants, especially those involved in finding online others with similar interests.
- Help participants with navigation and selection of conferences.
- Help participants to develop their own online identity.
- Allocate an online mentor to newcomers when possible.
- Aim to summarize and archive messages often, so that there are not more than 20 unread messages for any participant in any conference.

Stage 3: Information exchange

Technical support

- Offer advice and 'tips' for developing skills.
- Check that all basic skills are achieved.

- Encourage participants to see that the conferencing technology works and is quite simple to use.
- Provide information, for those who want it, about more sophisticated and advanced uses of software.

Learning

- Provide practical ways of sharing information online.
- Look for and build links with other media and processes in the course.

E-moderating

- Provide relevant and purposeful conferences.
- Deal with requests for information.
- Deal promptly with difficulties among participants, such as dominance, harassment, and perhaps excessive lurking.
- Offer tips and strategies for dealing with information overload.
- Provide a variety of conferences to suit different student needs.
- Set up useful activities and tasks – especially those not so easily or productively undertaken offline.
- Provide links into suitable electronic resources, eg Web sites and CD-ROMs, to use as stimuli for conferences.
- Remind participants of the protocols and guidelines if conferences get too busy or confused.
- Introduce structured e-tivities.

Stage 4: Knowledge construction

Technical support

- Encourage participants to become more technically independent and less handbook-dependent.
- Ensure good use of conference titles and icons.
- Promote benefits of learning online through explaining its technical aspects, eg its ease of use, asynchronicity and lack of dependence on a fixed location for each participant.
- Deal with any persistent technical problems.
- Ensure that all e-moderators have access and the skills for setting up conferences, creating sub-conferences, summarizing messages and creating archives.

Learning

- Pose insightful questions and give participants time to reflect and respond.
- Encourage participants to contribute to the conferences, not merely read them.
- Ensure there is no domination of conferences by one or two individuals.
- Explore every opportunity for online collaboration with others.

E-moderating

- Be prepared to explain and clarify the e-moderating role to participants (especially if they are still expecting 'the answers' from you at this stage).
- Work on developing your skills in e-moderating for knowledge construction.
- Share with other e-moderators insights into how to deal with online 'problem participants' and 'problem groups', in case you encounter them.
- Encourage full contribution and participation by students.
- Know when to stay silent for a few days.
- Be prepared to value every participants' contribution but summarize, summarize, summarize.
- Be ready to hand out specific e-moderating tasks to participants, to give them a chance to experience e-moderating for themselves.
- Close off any unused or unproductive conferences and create new ones.
- Use structured e-tivities.

Stage 5: Development

Technical

- Ensure that links exist from conferences to the Internet, library, etc.
- Ensure that selected participants can be given access to set up and e-moderate their own conferences.

Learning

- Enable participants to offer help to others or to become e-moderators.
- Provide opportunities for reflection on the what and how of learning online.
- Provide opportunities for development and progress.

E-moderating

- Expect and welcome challenges of all kinds (the system, the conferences, the conclusions).
- Ensure that appropriate evaluation, monitoring and reflection on your own practice occur.
- Encourage participants to reflect on their learning by providing conference areas to discuss the impact of online networking for learning.
- Explore comparisons with face-to-face learning.
- Look for those with good online skills and communication styles, and encourage them to support others.

Resources for practitioners 11

Managing e-moderating: keeping e-moderating costs down

Here are some useful tips to help keep e-moderating costs down:

1. Make clear decisions about roles and numbers of e-moderators that you will need and ensure they are trained in advance.
2. Train e-moderators online, rather than face to face.
3. Establish early on how much e-moderators should expect to do, and what are reasonable expectations on the part of students.
4. Keep your e-moderator support to students focused and specify what you expect them to do and when – if necessary, publish total number of hours per week or month available to participants.
5. Ensure that e-moderators can up- and download messages offline if they wish. Teach them how to use the software to best advantage to save connection time.
6. Look into transfer of costs of hardware, software and connection to students, perhaps with grants for those unable to afford the cost, and to e-moderators, who may be able to count them as tools of their trade for tax purposes.

7. Set up good helpdesk and online support systems, and encourage compet-
    ent students to support others, leaving more of your e-moderators' online
    time for learning related e-moderating.
8. Use existing resources and online constructed knowledge as much as
    possible rather than develop materials and/or pay for expensive third-
    party materials use.
9. Develop systems for reuse, where possible, of online conferencing materials.
10. Build up economies of scale as rapidly as possible – choose only systems
    that can be expanded cheaply.
11. Learn about e-tivities.
12. Promote student workgroups.

Resources for practitioners 12

Managing e-moderating: evaluating and assessing participation online

Selecting objectives to evaluate

Betty Collis and Jef Moonen of the University of Twente have extensive experience of implementing the changes to teaching associated with technology. They tell us, 'What we are most interested in regarding learning as a consequence of using technology often can't be measured in the short term or without different approaches to measurement. Measure what can be measured, such as short-term gains in efficiency or increases in flexibility' (Collis and Moonen, 2001: 132).

Networked learning is an important part of the new approach to online teaching; therefore you should consider very carefully the objectives you want to use in evaluating your success with it. These objectives may be different from ones you have used in the past (Duchastel, 1997):

- Be explicit from the start about your instructional strategies and the ideals and values behind your use of online teaching and learning.

- Provide ways for participants to collaborate on authentic and relevant activities through online (e-tivities).
- Encourage students to use conference messages as data or illustration in assignments.
- Look at the processes of learning rather than testing the content transmitted.
- Explore the impact of conferencing on skills such as reflection on practice, meta-cognition and practical outcomes.
- Integrate course activities and assignments with the use of online and look at students' learning as a whole, because you'll have trouble if you try to separate out the influence of online alone.
- Accept diversity of outcomes rather than demanding uniform learning.
- Consider whether knowledge is being created and disseminated rather than information merely communicated.
- Consider how well tasks and outcomes have been achieved.
- Consider the success of teams rather than only that of individuals.
- Encourage and reward cross-boundary, cross-disciplinary achievements and complexity.
- Use the online medium for review and assessment rather than reverting to old ways such as closed book, paper-based examinations.
- Use online feedback questionnaires to get fast and effective feedback.

Evaluating what?

You may want to collect data from your conferences for evaluation purposes. Make sure you respect the privacy of conference messages. Avoid dropping in unannounced, and seek permission if you want to quote a message from the conferences (the copyright belongs to the originator of each message, strictly speaking).

Here is a list of some questions you could explore:

1. How many of your participants log on at least once, read and contribute? It used to be said that a third of conferencing students read and contribute, a third only read messages and a third neither read nor contribute because they never access the conferences. Is this true for you?
2. What helps to motivate participants online, what do they enjoy and benefit from, what encourages them to contribute? Can you develop a control group for comparisons? When you change something online, try to measure the impact, which can be quite large.

3. Do those that do not take part participate less in the course overall or are they choosing alternative means of communication? Do more of those who fail to take part drop out or achieve lower results?
4. Who is relating to whom and in what way? What requests are there for setting up new conferences or other online activities?
5. Do the conferences provide learning to those for whom it was intended? Or are they providing learning only to 'early adopters'? Are the benefits spread across all learners? Do some groups benefit more than others? Check whether there are improvements in student learning, as opposed to enthusiasm about the novelty of working with new media.
6. What are the trade-offs on conferencing? What is not happening that did before?
7. Does the five-stage model (Figure 2.1) hold true for your learners in your online course?
8. Are costs shifted onto the students by working online? Is this worth it for them, and for you?
9. Can you use message history and log-on facilities to spot and support students who are struggling?
10. Are there differences in results between structured and unstructured, well and less well e-moderated conferences?
11. How much time do participants spend online? How does this compare with your traditional ways of learning and interaction? If it is more, or less, is this good or bad?

Aligned assessment

A variety of approaches to assessment of networked learning are now being tried in the Open University. Assessment should continue to indicate the constructivist and collaborative nature of working online (not just 'delivery') and should therefore be 'aligned' with the learning. Here are a variety of researched and tested ideas from Janet Macdonald, Martin Weller and their colleagues (Macdonald, 2003; Macdonald and Twining, 2002; Macdonald, Weller et al, 2002; Weller, 2002). They suggest:

*   Encourage participants to include messages in their assessed tasks from their participation in conferencing. This type of assessment feeds back into online skills development (true alignment!).
*   Keep tasks very simple until participants' ability to collaborate has built up (stage four). Don't expect useful assessments to emerge from e-tivities, until participants' ability to collaborate has built up (stage four).

- Ask participants to work on a joint produced 'product' which forms part of a submitted assessment. Marks may be rewarded in part for individual contributions and in part for the collaborative outcome.
- Give participants a chance to practise and demonstrate information literacy in using Web resources.
- Create some flexibility rather than standardization, in other words an acceptance that in constructivist courses there can be no 'true score'.
- Offer a variety of approaches to an assignment or examination answers, allowing scope for individual development or initiative, and for the most able students to add additional research findings.
- Increase freedom as the programme progresses.
- Ensure that teaching and assignments support information retrieval and skills development as well as assessing for them.
- Use assignments to encourage reflection on the course e-tivities, and encourage participants to use their reflections as part of assessment tasks, perhaps revisiting, reworking or comparing and contrasting aspects of the conferencing.
- Try extended essays or portfolios rather than closed book proctored exams for the end of course assessment.
- If you have electronic submission of assessments, encourage exploitation of the media, for example by submitting assignments in HTML and enabling links to further reading or images, or as a Web page with links and reflection.
- Award marks for both content and presentation if you wish (but avoid participants spending all their time, say, on 'Web design').
- Offer 'templates' for submission of work if appropriate. These make expectations of the students clearer, and marking easier and faster, but reduce creativity.
- Allow participants to continue to present their work for view and comment by others, indicating that only the final submission will be scored (perhaps using an 'unknown' marker at this stage).
- Provide a contingency, less technology-dependent, approach if possible in case the student has severe problems at the last minute.
- Provide very good novice-tested instructions.

By the way, you might be concerned about plagiarism. Martin Weller's experience with large-scale online assessment tells us, 'Tutors reported that verifying the students' work was not difficult, and that the prolonged interaction offered by such networked courses means they come to know their students to a greater extent than on traditional distance learning courses' (Weller, 2002b: 114).

Managing e-moderating: training e-moderators

1. Ensure that the trainee e-moderators experience online learning as learners before they start e-moderating for real.
2. Ensure that they undertake all or most of the programme in the online environment itself – make it a real experience.
3. Keep the focus of the programme on the development of the trainees as e-moderators – the training is about e-moderating rather than about the software or other aspects of their training better dealt with elsewhere.
4. Keep the training as simple as such a focus will allow – don't over-complicate it.
5. Provide an environment suited to trainees with a wide range of prior skills (or none).
6. Check the training programme thoroughly before the programme goes live – use a novice for a final check rather than an expert, but give the trainers an opportunity to familiarize themselves with the programme in advance.
7. Provide the minimum of print-based materials consistent with helping trainees to get started and make sure that those materials match what is on screen.
8. Make clear to the trainees how much time you expect them to spend on the programme.
9. Make sure the training programme is accessible 'any time, any place'.
10. Build in help with the software and the system as much as you can to control frustration.

11. Enable trainees to acquire skills in using the software as they gradually build up their understanding of the online environment.

12. Ensure your trainers of the trainers – your e-moderators of the trainee e-moderators (we call them convenors) – model exemplary e-moderating skills in the training programme.

13. Include strategic knowledge (how will I work with my students?) as well as declarative knowledge and procedural knowledge (availability and capacity of the software and the system).

14. Offer plenty of opportunity for the trainees to explore their attitudes to working online and its meaning for their own teaching.

15. Ensure the trainees have opportunities to interact with each other.

16. Make the trainees aware of the goals of the programme all the way through it.

17. Use familiar metaphors for explaining aspects of online and e-moderating.

18. Try and spot trainees needing more help and offer it promptly (see 'swimmers, wavers and drowners' in Resources for practitioners 20).

19. Build reflection on e-moderating practice into your training programme.

20. Monitor the work of e-moderators and use feedback to improve your training programme.

21. Ensure that ongoing development of trained e-moderators is available and build an online community of e-moderators' conferences after the training programme has been completed.

Managing e-moderating: boosting participation

I'm often asked, 'In what ways can e-moderators make learners participate online?' Well of course you can't make anyone do anything, but you can ensure the online environment is attractive and worthwhile for as many people as possible and reduce known 'turn-offs'. Here is a list of ideas from experienced e-moderators for you to consider. The ideas are divided into 'carrots' (encouragement) or 'sticks' (penalties for not participating).

Carrots

Sell benefits

- Promote the benefits of online at face-to-face meetings with demonstrations if possible.
- Get others to explain how they were once online novices and their satisfaction of achieving online communication skills.
- Ensure the benefits for learning are explained.
- Explain how easy online is.
- Explain the support available online.
- Explain that many people find online reduces panic as assessments and tests come nearer.
- Explain the opportunities for making contacts and friendships online.
- Explain online's role in providing confirmation of one's own ideas.

- Explain that it will help with everyday life skills, eg e-business and e-commerce.

Add value to the learning methods

- Provide online feedback on students' progress.
- Give recognition (public and private) to those successfully contributing online.
- Give opportunities for individuals to explore own ideas and influence others through online networking.
- Ensure that online enhances understanding of course content.

Build contacts and communities

- E-moderate most carefully to ensure inclusion of all, lack of discrimination and celebration of diversity.
- Ensure online enables the building of a community of peers (not only teacher–student contact).
- Ensure conferences give access to the knowledge of others in a distributed network.
- Give access to known experts in the field.
- Provide activities that are not available or possible except online (eg large-scale but easy research).
- Provide specialist contact, eg industry or interest groups.
- Provide conferences that enable individuals to 'keep up' with news about peers and competitors.
- Ensure everyone has a chance to contribute, ie personal visibility.
- Ensure academics, instructors, teaching assistants log on as well as learners.
- Ensure social and friendship building conferences are available.
- Provide ongoing online contact after the course is over.
- Provide for self-help groups and voluntary group working.
- Allow for lurking, give time for participants to develop.
- Keep the purpose of all conferences clear and focused and constantly reiterated throughout online activities or discussions.
- At level 4 (knowledge construction) provide for working through new problems, insist on valuing all contributions and no 'right' answer, creating and making meaning from all contributions, excellent e-moderating, sharing good practice.
- Provide online tutorials and support on course material that has proved difficult or challenging.
- Run online tutorial sessions before assessments or exams (watch them flock in!).

Assessment

- Provide extra marks for participation or percentage of marks of total score.
- Consider peer endorsements based on quality of contributions to discussion (for further ideas see Resources for practitioners 12).
- Monitor and publish longer-term performance, especially if working online leads to success on the course, linked to online participation of students.

Sticks (try to convert sticks into carrots)

Sticks to use

- Make other ways of achieving the same learning or assessment more difficult to undertake.
- Insist on online participation having a direct relationship to assessment, ie assessed components of course cannot be completed without online participation.
- Provide some key pieces of information online, ie only way of accessing.
- Enforce compulsory group working by making completion of projects impossible otherwise.
- Post relevant and useful information online for short periods only (ie an incentive to log on at a particular time).
- Set very clear and structured deadlines for submission of online work.

Sticks to avoid

- Discrimination of all kinds;
- Technical and access difficulties (for participants and e-moderators);
- Attacks from active contributors on lurkers;
- Lack of academic recognition or credit given for work online;
- Bullying of any kind (including by e-moderators);
- Exclusion from the course because of lack of online participation.

Resources for practitioners 15

Managing e-moderating: monitoring e-moderating

You may find it useful to use something like the form overleaf, if you decide to build up monitoring systems for quality assurance in e-moderating. Appoint monitors from experienced e-moderators who can take a collegiate and development approach to supporting and developing others and can themselves learn from the experience.

The form can be completed online or in hard copy by the monitor after a visit to a conference.

E-Moderators monitoring report

<table>
<tr><td>**To:**   Name of e-moderator</td><td>Date: ....</td></tr>
<tr><td>**From:**   Name of Monitor</td><td>Copied to: ....</td></tr>
</table>

I visited your conference(s) called *(names of conference(s))*

On *(dates and times)*

Here is my reaction to your online activities (as an eavesdropper). Please see my comments as a starting point for a debate. Please contact me by e-mail if you would like to discuss any of them.

Aspects of your e-moderating that seemed to be working well:

eg
I observed that your opening questions were successful because. . .

I noticed that your activity ** went very well because. . .

I thought your review of (assignment, activity, technique) worked really well because . . .

Aspects that I'd like you to reflect on:

eg
Have you tried...

One technique I find helpful is. . .

I noticed that Participant X may need extra help because. . .

Maybe it's time to close off Conference Y because. . .

Here is my personal view on your online activities:

Approach to:	Great	OK	Needs improvement	Comments
Housekeeping				
Use of Time				
Creativity/flexibility				
Content/resources				
Diversity				
Participation				

Best wishes (name of monitor)

E-Moderator's response to monitor:

Resources for practitioners 16

Managing e-moderating: communicating online

Good online communication cannot simply be directed or taught. Try using these ideas to discuss, change and build on. Eventually when there is some shared agreement, adopt your agreed approach to online communication as a protocol and inform newcomers of the approach from the start.

When to e-mail, when to conference (try this metaphor)

Imagine a conventional pigeonhole system. There is an individual wooden box affixed to the wall for every person in the group, usually with a noticeboard above or nearby too. Now, I have a slip of paper containing information for you. So I pop it in your pigeonhole. However, that information may need to be seen by several people, so I can make copies, and put them in their pigeonhole too. Sometimes, though, the whole group needs to see the information. I can post the message on the noticeboard where everyone can see it in their own time.

Conferencing allows you to do the same thing, only online. You can send a message directly to my individual mailbox, so that only I can see it. It's more secure than if you had put it in a sealed envelope in my physical pigeonhole. Or you can send it to several people at once. Or you can post your message in the conference so that everyone joined to that conference could see it.

The advantage of the pigeonholes and noticeboards being online is that you can use the same method to reply. Everyone else's pigeonhole and noticeboard are right there on your screen.

Use e-mail when:

- You have a message for one or several people that you don't want everyone else to see or they don't need to see.
- The convention is to address messages directly to people who need to take action or who need to reply to you and to copy the messages for information to people who you believe need to know about the content – but think first before sending an unnecessary message!

Use conferencing when:

- the message is intended for everyone in a particular group;
- you expect that everyone will have the right to reply;
- there is benefit from everyone in the group seeing replies.

E-communication may be unsuitable when:

- Conveying something upsetting to someone else – choose face-to-face or other synchronous communications.
- To discredit someone by sending e-mail copies to people you consider 'should know' about some problem or misdemeanour. This reflects badly on the sender.
- To perpetuate 'recycling' of a problem or issue without closure or decision. E-mails and conferencing can be very good at exposing and exploring issues. However, someone needs to move to taking and articulating decisions or actions before long.

Online 'netiquette' for e-mails

E-mail conventions:

- Never copy on an e-mail to anyone not on the original list, nor into a conference, without asking and receiving the permission of the originator of the message.
- Be very careful with titles. Choose a short effective title for your e-mail.
- If you reply to someone and change the subject, change the title too.
- Keep to one topic per e-mail with a relevant title. It's far better to send several short e-mails with different titles than one long one covering many subjects.
- If you need to make a number of points in an e-mail, label them 1,2,3. . . This way, it's easy to reply.

- If you reply to just one part of someone else's e-mail, copy and paste their words into the start of your e-mail, so it's clear the sections to which you are referring.
- You can build 'groups' of people to e-mail for your convenience. Use these cautiously and only when your message truly concerns everyone in that group. If you have frequent messages of that kind, setting up a conference may work better.
- If you receive an e-mail message which has been addressed to a number of people, think carefully before replying to all of them when you may only need to make the comment to the originator of the message, or one or two other people. Some people get very annoyed about many minor e-mails circulating around large groups.
- If you receive a message that contains a 'reply all' to a large group including you, and which you consider irrelevant, simply delete it. Treat it as junk mail. Avoid replying to 'all' again in your anger and perpetuating the problem.
- Delete, before opening, all emails that are 'junk' or strange – they may be caused by, or conveying, a virus.

Online 'netiquette' for group conferencing

Enter a CV (résumé) so that others know a little about you. Include:

- something about your background, jobs and interests;
- any particular expertise and support you can offer to others;
- your geographical location.

About computer conferencing conventions:

- Take advantage of training and support to get the most from the computer conferencing software. Then you'll be able to discuss issues rather than ask how to find conferences or send messages. However, you will find people on conferences very willing to help you with anything – just ask.
- The main principles of computer mediated communication are the same as those of any conversation or dialogue but with a little more emphasis of coming to shared understandings.
- Wide participation without being able to see people offers distinct advantages of any time/any place. It means, however, that you need to be even more considerate than usual in the way you communicate and relate to others online because all communication is text-based and displayed.

- There are delays before response, and with more than a few individuals joined to a conference, considerable complexity results, therefore you need to follow some protocols and conventions.

Communication principles:

- Writing styles tend to be informal.
- Conferences are more public than e-mail, so you need to be careful what you say to or about others.
- Thank, acknowledge and support people freely.
- Acknowledge before differing.
- Speak from your own (or an acknowledged) perspective.

Keeping online communication flowing:

- Lift and quote from the messages of others before replying.
- Use 'emoticons' to convey emotions, eg ☺ to convey a joke.
- Avoid putting words into capital letters – they are considered to be equivalent to shouting.
- Ensure that you place new messages in the appropriate conference.
- Put your test messages in a test conference.
- Put a short effective title for your message.
- When replying to someone else's message, use the same title if the subject remains the same as before, otherwise start a new thread with a new title.
- Keep all messages short – never more than one screenful.
- Use several messages for different topics (this aids replying).
- If you have something longer to say, attach it as a document.

Attaching documents to an e-mail or in a conference message:

- To send or share anything longer than one screenful in a message, it is best to attach a document.
- Make sure the title is clear and there are one or two lines of description in the message so that your recipients can decide whether, and how soon, they need to download the document.
- Make sure that your recipients have suitable software to download and open your document (you may need to make an *.rtf version to be certain).
- Always check a document for viruses, using up-to-date virus checking software, before you send it to others.

See Crystal (2001) for more about text-based online communication.

Online participants: encouraging self-managing groups

E-moderating large groups can be time-consuming, and participants benefit from becoming self-managing, at least by stage four. The basic framework of small groups is similar to the face-to-face version, for example:

- Invite larger groups into smaller work teams. Give them good time to complete an e-tivity and then report back to the larger group.
- Offer clarification about the task, the timescale and the form of presentation if necessary.
- Leave them to get on with the task, only intervening if they fail to post their contribution to the plenary on time.
- Start a discussion on the results of the plenary contributions but do not dominate it. Summarize yourself or ask an experienced participant to do this.

However, there are some special characteristics that will help groups to self-manage online:

- *Ask individuals to confirm when they have joined in*. A simple joining activity in the thread will leave a trace to indicate that participants have arrived. A cross-check against a list of participants will reveal who is late. Designate a participant from each work team to follow up less visible contributors.

- *State the purpose of the task.* The task will motivate the participants. Offer clarification if necessary but allow opportunities for flexible interpretations.
- *Describe how groups will be formed.* An element of self-selection helps to maintain interest, but ensure that the method is simply described and incapable of being misunderstood.
- *Set up a thread for each group and let the group know where to locate the thread.* If you don't they'll only ask you!
- *Describe the form and type of content that the group should produce and where they should post it.* Aim to be prescriptive without being too restrictive. Indicate the main issues that must be addressed.
- *Set out the plenary process in the plenary thread.* This can be part of your welcoming message.
- *Ask the participants to review both content (their main focus) and the process.* Include setting up the group, the degree to which they found the task motivating, how they collaborated, their approach to feeding back as part of the learning points, so it becomes 'natural and normal' for them to reflect on not just their outputs but also on how they worked together.

Thanks to Naomi Lawless and David Shepherd for their input for this resource.

Resources for practitioners 18

Online participants: users with disabilities

In the spirit of wide diversity and empowerment, it is good that the disabilities of online users with special needs are not usually obvious online. It is normally impossible to tell from the messages in a conference that a participant or an e-moderator has restricted vision, hearing or mobility, unless that person wishes to write about it. People who have problems with their speech or hearing are not at a disadvantage in text-based messaging. Those who have problems with their vision or physical movement may well find that the keyboard and screen prevent them for doing as much as they would like. Dyslexics still have some difficulties online, even with electronic help available.

Blind and visually impaired users

Whereas many people with vision problems can learn to touch-type, they usually have problems in reading the screen. Windows software, for example, often requires precise placing of the mouse, even when keyboard commands are used wherever possible. An electronic screen-reader, that reads the text aloud at a steady pace and in a computer-generated voice, is valuable when long sections of text are onscreen, but useless when there is a diagram. The same is true of speech recognition software that enables users to speak the messages, for conversion into text by the computer. Taped instructions may help, but taped cassettes or material recorded on CD can prove difficult to manipulate.

Physically disabled users

Users who cannot freely move their hands and arms find that they cannot use the keyboard at a reasonable speed, even when the stiffness of the keys has been varied to suit. Speech recognition software may be better or semi-intelligent software that enables them to select whole words after the first few letters have been typed in. Exceptionally, users may need single-switch devices to control modified computers and their peripherals.

Dyslexic users

Spelling and grammar checkers can be very helpful to dyslexic users, particularly if their dyslexia is severe enough to put off non-dyslexic conference participants. The odd spelling or grammatical error worries nobody, but the condition may produce far worse effects.

Resources for practitioners 19

Online participants: induction

These suggestions may appear 'over the top'. However, from my experience, it is easy to make wrong assumptions about learners' previous computer literacy, levels of online competence and early behaviours and needs. The benefits of effective online induction and preparation are immense. When the course proper starts, the concentration of learners and teachers, participants and e-moderators can be on content, interaction and outcomes rather than passwords, software and lurking. Just as for a face-to-face group, making people comfortable and confident sets the tone for the course and leads to better learning.

Here are some suggestions for getting off to a good start:

1. Consider how much time you expect everyone will take to get up to speed – and double this.
2. Commence before the course proper starts (if you can, immediately you identify your participants).
3. Offer online induction for online learning.
4. Make it very clear to participants how the online induction and their use of online networking will lead to their increased success on the course. Some feedback suggests the need for serious 'luring' of online participants, eg shortcuts and ideas for time saving on the course, tips from course leaders about essential and 'nice to have' aspects of the course and the benefits of securing relevant wide-scale views and networking.
5. Get good helplines in place to solve technical and password problems.

6. Recognize that different people may need very different kinds of support at this stage (check this out – see Resources 2, 10, 20 and 21). Offer different streams and pathways for novices and the more experienced.
7. Ensure that each newcomer gets a friendly and individual greeting from an e-moderator (it's probably best to do this by e-mail to avoid clogging up the arrivals conferences).
8. Offer local support and motivation to get set up if you're dealing largely with remote users.
9. Offer the chance to conference in very small groups (up to 10) during the induction.
10. Remember that recent users of the induction programme (those who have progressed at least to stage 3, information exchange) make useful, patient and often enthusiastic supporters for newcomers. Perhaps set up an online mentoring system.
11. Keep navigation extremely simple and obvious, and provide direct pathways through the programme, stage by stage.
12. Keep the instructions very simple and as short as possible; use diagrams and illustrations that can easily be downloaded.
13. Focus induction activities on building confidence and socializing in the online environment.
14. Then focus on communicating and preparation for the course (not just the technology).
15. Ensure that there are worthwhile, authentic and relevant activities within the induction programme. Use inspiring questions to stimulate debate.
16. Don't assume that newcomers to the online system will find the answers they need to their queries in a mass of online instructions and FAQs – they need context-specific help (usually from a real person) in the early stages.
17. Ensure your e-moderators are friendly, supportive and that they visit their conferences often.
18. Ensure that each participant is pointed to permissible conduct, and codes of practice, and has a chance to discuss and explore their implications in the online environment.
19. Provide areas for 'junk' and practice messages.
20. Ensure that e-moderators and others with control of the look of the conferences leave them in an easy state for newcomers to navigate.
21. Track participation and follow up browsers and drop-outs by telephone or post.

Online participants: supporting and developing online novices

Many participants are novices at communicating, teaching or learning online, even if they are familiar with computing. In the early days, they need special attention. Based on my research, e-moderators can expect three types of response. I call these swimming, waving and drowning online.

The swimmers:

- dive in early;
- have conference-relevant experience, eg chat rooms on the Internet;
- are usually willing to help others;
- may become disruptive if they think the conferencing activities are not demanding enough;
- are likely to claim they know of better systems than the one you've chosen to use.

The wavers:

- need considerable help and encouragement to get started;
- depend on a telephone helpline or individual help even to appear online;
- arrive after the main group and need help in sifting through masses of messages;
- feel there is too little time to do everything;
- do very well and become enthusiasts once they've got logged on and are given support.

The drowners:

- find it very difficult indeed to log on and/or are reluctant to ask for or accept help;
- have little motivation to succeed;
- promise to log on but do not;
- complain at every opportunity that online work is irrelevant or too time-consuming;
- find the relationship building and socializing online difficult, especially if they are used to taking a leading role in face-to-face groups;
- do better if a supportive *swimmer* is allocated to them as a mentor.

To convert wavers and drowners to swimmers:

- build 'scaffolding' – steps towards success and confidence – into your induction programme;
- provide social and test areas within the online environment where they can experiment and continue to build up their confidence;
- build onscreen displays that be navigated fairly intuitively, without constantly reading instructions;
- address student expectations when providing online resources and activities;
- offer parallel ways of working (ie via print or telephone as well as online) where access is an issue, but only for the shortest possible time because you need to build up a critical mass online quickly;
- provide a telephone helpline for resolving access and password problems;
- prepare step-by-step instructions on how to use the software and ask a naïve user to try them out before you put them on screen (have paper copies for those who want them);

- provide an individual e-mail welcome to each participant in response to his/her first message and support each one in the early stages of learning conferencing;
- provide online help, instructions and an individual response from the course 'lifeguard' (possibly a postgraduate research student), backed up by support from recent novices, who can often help the new intake;
- engage as helpers individuals who have recently completed the e-moderator training or student induction (their help is highly valued in OUBS);
- provide students with full encouragement to learn by doing, by experimenting and by making mistakes in a supportive environment;
- emphasize the purposeful and relevant nature of conferencing for future learning on the course;
- e-moderate conferences often, with archiving of messages so that newcomers have only a few to read.

Resources for practitioners 21

Online participants: understanding lurkers

First, identify the types of lurkers you have and appropriate responses. There are three main kinds:

1. Those still trying to find out how to use the system, who lack access, skills or confidence to participate (ie those operating at levels one and two in the five-stage model). Check whether they need help to log on, or simply greater motivation or encouragement through one-to-one contact with you, by e-mail or telephone, or perhaps some written instructions.
2. The sponge – people who are needing a bit of time to come to terms with the environment, norms and ways of communicating online – ie those at levels two and three in the model. Give them time and support and they should start to take part.
3. The silent thief/freeloader – people happy to use other people's contributions rather than feeling the need to contribute. These people need a reason – even a requirement – to take part.

Here are some strategies:

1. Check that all participants know how to post and 'reply' to messages.
2. Provide a test area and an arrivals area.
3. Check that you have a free-flowing or social conferencing area.
4. Give participants plenty of time to become used to the online environment before insisting that they post their responses.

5.   Check across all your conferences – your lurkers may be participating (and using their time and energy) in a different conference from where you were expecting them to be.

6.   Reduce the number of messages in each conference – there'll be less to read so they'll be more likely to reply.

7.   Check you have a critical mass for the purpose of a conference (less than 6 participants or more than 15 active participants is likely not to work well, depending on the online activity).

8.   Try some humour rather than anger (eg don't be a lurker – be a worker).

9.   Check whether one or two individuals are dominating the conference – and deal tactfully with them to create a more open and equal environment.

10. Provide a structured evaluation questionnaire or an area for reflections and/or comments (some lurkers prefer safety in structure).

11. Explain to active participants what you are trying to do.

12. Allocate active participants to lurkers as mentors.

13. Rename 'lurkers' as 'browsers' and worry less about them.

14. Design for simple structured interaction where every participant plays a part (Salmon, 2002a).

15. Summarize, plenarize and re-present often.

Resources for practitioners 22

Online participants: valuing online diversity

The skills of relating successfully to the many different kinds of people we encounter through online conferencing are not those any of you reading this book were born with or acquired in childhood. They are, however, those that we need to achieve quite quickly. Those who find this difficult deserve support.

Our message about the value of diversity to trainee e-moderators in the OUBS's online training is reproduced below. Perhaps you can use it as a discussion document with your e-moderators to raise awareness and develop your own protocol?

One of the great strengths of the Open University is the diversity of its students and staff. On management courses in particular, this is a huge educational asset and assists with constructivist approaches. It means we have a uniquely rich variety of backgrounds, perspectives and experience to share and consider. But realizing this potential requires an environment in which people feel able to express what they really think – and, beyond that, to challenge each other and be challenged. This needs to happen in a context of mutual respect, enjoyment and support – a setting where differences as well as similarities are appreciated, and where disagreements are seen as an opportunity to learn, to understand other viewpoints better and to discover the limits of our own beliefs. This can be fun – but it involves risks and can be difficult.

So how do we propose to engineer this learning environment? Alas, there is no way we can ensure it happens – though happily it seems that, in varying degrees, the University does often approximate it. The equal opportunity policy, (which is stated in the student handbook and referred to in the Student Charter), expresses and underpins some of these aspirations. Nevertheless, it would be silly to suggest that we can, somehow, just make happen an honest, challenging and accepting environment.

We suspect that, in the end, the main thing we, as staff, can do is to set the best example we can – and this we will try to. In truth, your own contributions will be of far greater importance. We hope, therefore, that you will join us in trying to establish and maintain a climate in which everyone feels at home, and feels that their contributions are appreciated, even when (indeed, especially when) deep-seated differences are exposed.

Gilly Salmon and Roger Dence

The challenge to all participants: typing the talk

1. Each conference will develop its own 'cultural' norms. You can set the tone for this by making expectations abundantly clear from the beginning. E-moderators should clarify the conference's purpose and expectations, from the start, and if necessary remind participants from time to time during the conference.
2. When sitting at your keyboard, you may experience the illusion of isolation and safety, similar to that you may feel when driving your car. An e-mail message can then seem like an intrusion. If you are in a conference with others who are expressing views with which you cannot agree, that can be difficult too, but the conference is a more public forum, like being in a train or a plane where you and the other travellers recognize some basic behavioural rules.
3. Views expressed in text messages lack the non-verbal clues, such as facial expression, that add to our face-to-face conversations. This sometimes results in meanings being misinterpreted. Take care therefore with using irony and humour in case they are taken literally. Take account of this when reading the messages of others.
4. If someone accuses others of some incompetence or misdemeanour, there is a strong temptation to play the game of 'Yes! Me too!', 'Ain't it awful!' and 'What's more. . . !' without considering the impact of accumulative

accusations. This can create electronic bandwagons. Avoid doing this yourself, and take action against it very fast if you are the e-moderator.

5.   Use a short period of 'reflection' before responding immediately to a message that disturbs or upsets you, or even those with which you agree particularly strongly.

6.   It's great to pursue minority interests, complaints or opportunities with others online, and if appropriate to enable data collection and take action. However, avoid doing this in the middle of wide interest social or learning conferences. It's best to set up a conference for the purpose to which participants can migrate it they wish.

7.   It's rarely necessary to deprive someone of access to the conference because of inappropriate behaviour. However, this can happen if it's clearly in the interests of the majority.

Exploring online: a virtual learning environment parable

Would you like to explore multiple perspectives in the introduction of virtual learning environments (VLEs) through this little parable? I'll also put it on the book's Web site so you can use it as a discussion 'spark' if you wish.

I was walking over the bridge by the river on the campus, one fine spring day. I heard what I thought was a faint cry from a clump of daffodils near the path. On going to investigate, to my amazement, I found a tiny baby VLE, wrapped up in a carry basket. I took a cautious look, of course, and found that the foundling had a note. It read, 'My Name is BlaCT. Please look after my password. My licence expires in 28 days.' It was a rather odd sort of baby and seemed starved of proper feeding and attention.

I thought I really ought to try to find its real parents. Maybe its ancestors were from computer-based training, and more closely I thought I could discern the powerful Northern American instructivist nose. I carried it to the IT Centre, not far away, and asked the staff if they knew anything about it. They said, 'Oh no, it doesn't seem to belong to our family and we can't touch anything that's off the pathway . . . but it looks quite cool so you can leave it with us to play with for a while if you like.' However, they soon got tired of it, as it was demanding of attention. They said, 'We're really worried about its interoperability when it grows up. We need the academics to take responsibility for it, they said they wanted it.' I couldn't see any academics around at that time. Well, it was only 10.30 am.

So I wandered back towards my office and passed by the library. The information officers always seem such helpful friendly people; perhaps they would know what to do with BlaCT. They said they had to operate 24 by 7 so couldn't really help me, but could loan me some clothes and toys for it. They also agreed to start a search for its origins as soon as I returned some books.

I took it along to the administrators in my school. They were quite sweet with it really. They gave it a security badge clearly marked 'Visitor'. They said they'd seen all this kind of thing before and knew what to do about it. They said there were various forms I had to fill in about VLE foundlings, and then they would put my request it to the committee for funding, and if successful for adoption. They told me that its only hope was if it proved to be cheap to keep and was prepared to be centralized. However, they did warn me it would be number 36 on the agenda, and there were a number of other candidates.

By this time, I was getting quite fond of BlaCT and had a sudden thought. What about the university's development fund? After all doesn't that offer us a wonderful opportunity for piloting and creativity? I put the foundling on my desk while I downloaded the development fund papers. The baby shuffled around a bit and had a good chew on my FirstClass CD-ROM and a major sniff at my Blackboard user's manual.

A couple of postgrad students passed by and were absolutely delighted with it, saying, 'It's a real any time any place kind of babe, better than lectures any day. YES WICKED!!'

The development fund objectives looked pretty hopeless. It was clear that they thought VLEs too good to leave in the tender care of academics. For example they wanted to know if it had a daddy to provide matched external funding.

By then my academic colleagues in my centre had arrived to take a look, and were saying, 'Well, we could . . .' or 'Why don't you . . .' or 'Hey, my students would love that. Can I take a closer look and evaluate it? I've got an idea, let's check out its communication tools before we feed it. Wow, it has a slight Socratean look about it.' One gave it a search for a fast forward to promotion button, but no luck! I said, 'Who will help me with parenting this child?' They all said, We'd love to, Gilly, but you know we've no time at all this semester.'

I thought I'd try taking it to the Senior Executive Committee. They said I should define my terms against the university's global mission and explain why I had brought this unplanned resource to them. They asked in what way adopting foundling VLEs would help create better access to more students at lower costs and/or ensure greater competitiveness. I suggested that with nurturing it might grow up to take over Microsoft, but they said that do-gooders like me should be most careful, since the child might suffer from rampant featurism in the future, for which there is no cure. They told me that there were a number of more serious siblings who were likely to be supported, and they had to make their mistakes before any new approach could considered. I persisted but they said they said they were sorry. If they let me keep the foundling other teachers might want them too, and there was no proof it was cost-effective or even, horrors, scalable.

Finally I realized I needed to rely on my own resources, and that if I wanted this baby VLE to thrive, or even survive, I would need to be its champion. Perhaps I should build a shrine called Foundlingblog and become its missionary? Maybe not. What would you do?

Resources for practitioners 24

Exploring online: myth busters

I hope you can use this list as a discussion tool in online workshops for new e-moderators. It may save a lot of 'reinventing the wheel'.

- The technology we have available offers pedagogical tools (false). E-moderators add the pedagogy (true).
- E-moderators prefer to use simple rather than sophisticated technology (true). Avoid complicating well-rehearsed and successful online moderating approaches by complicated and maybe unstable sophisticated technologies. The value they add is minimal.
- E-moderators need lots of different kinds of training, time released to prepare and work online, technical support and good technology, and Web access (all true).
- Young instructors are easier to train and comprise the main group teaching online. (Not true, it has little to do with demographics or disciplines, much more to do with support and training.)
- E-moderators are willing to share their experiences and expertise with other teachers and similarly benefit professionally and personally (true).
- Online learning is here to stay, with up to one half of teaching taking place online over the next decade (prediction).
- Online education does not have to be either an online or offline mode of learning. Blending approaches works well if you wish. There are some claims that blended learning is the most effective. Of course, instructors still need to learn the skills of working online to be successful even with blending (all true).

- Successful e-moderators like working in a portfolio way (true of Curt's survey of US instructors and confirmed by others).
- There is considerable confusion still about who owns online courses (true). Copyright from online messages, however, remain with the author of them (true).
- The most successful e-moderators are flexible, foster participant interaction and engagement, and act as peers and co-learners (true). Less successful approaches include a lack of guidelines for students working online, didactical approaches to teaching, and discouragement of student knowledge sharing (all true).
- E-moderators need recognition for their success (true but not happening yet).

This resource was developed with Curt Bonk's collaboration and permission. It derives from his report on a survey of 222 US college instructors (Bonk, 2001).

Exploring online: a future scenario

How can we prepare people to work as e-moderators in the future? What kind of additional skills will they need? Try putting up this scenario for online discussion by e-moderators, e-mentors and e-trainers. In it, a manager working in the fashion industry, 5 years from now, recalls his day.

London, 12 June

I logged on first thing to get a weather forecast for our area of North London and found that a fine warm day was ahead of us. As always on Fridays, I stayed at Freya's nursery school for the first hour of the morning. I helped Freya and the other 3-year-olds with their keyboard skills and onscreen word recognition. I discussed with Mrs Barnes, the play leader, whether Freya should now move onto a full-size keyboard and whether her vocabulary and clarity of speech were sufficiently developed to start to use voice recognition software.

I decided to sit in the park on the way home and work. The first 250 e-mails took me 55 minutes to deal with. My new colour coding prioritizing software is successful though it had failed to convert some of the German titles properly into English again. I guess it's up to me to learn to programme it a bit better! I was pleased to see that this month's terrestrial meeting in Paris has been transferred to online again – I prefer to avoid the Eurotunnel when I can, although I'm still a little curious to see what my new director looks like. I e-mailed her and asked for a video profile. I ordered a pizza delivery, too. I enjoyed a few minutes laughing at the Pizza Zoo's new Web site "My Personal Pizza". It tried to persuade me I could smell the pizza as I saw it cooking but of course I couldn't! It arrived at the door just as I got home.

While eating, I logged into the global customer focus group who are test-wearing the current collection. It's my turn this month to e-moderate this conference. Their main suggestion is for small Velcro pockets in the lightweight Northern Hemisphere trousers to accommodate safely any form of multi-function electronic communicator. I summarized the discussion and e-mailed it to our designers. I downloaded a multi-media 'Happy Birthday' card from my granny: she's never got used to not allowing time for the post (my birthday is tomorrow). I enjoyed the e-collage she had created of my last 10 birthday parties. It's a good thing she wasn't present at one or two I've had! I quickly ordered the weekend shopping at the e-supermarket.

The CrossPond synchronous video meeting with our US partners started at 14.00 GMT. Steve, Jasmine and Andrew were looking very relaxed at breakfast by the ocean in San Diego, despite their early start! The agenda was somewhat dominated by the extent to which the new Internet domain names would be sufficient protection when launching our August interactive leisurewear catalogue. I felt annoyed with Andrew who always aggressively insists that using flowered printed fabric is not a unisex approach. I quickly e-mailed my mentor out of range of the video screen to get ideas on how to avoid conflict with Andrew in future. However, the collection looks great and will appeal to our customers throughout the Western world. Some additional red and yellow colour ranges are being added on the advice of our Beijing partners.

I am using the development of the promotional campaign for the August collection as a case study for my marketing assignment on my MBA. My collaborative learning group is very interested and supportive. The group's comparison with their experiences of promoting products such as books in Africa, medical services in the United States and railway travel in Australia is very instructive and useful. We still have so much to learn about global marketing. I wish that we had useful research and conceptual models to guide us. Our joint assignment on managing people transport networks is coming along well. Fortunately we're a well-balanced group in terms of collaborative and development skills. There're marks for group processes as well as content in the final satellite link presentation.

At 17.30 there was time for my exercise and fitness programme before leaving to collect Freya. The digital TV carefully tracks my small progress towards greater physical and mental fitness along with a 'Just in Time and Just Enough' aerobics and mind-games video. I'm feeling more alert and energetic! I downloaded a preview of tonight's movies at the same time and printed out the family's weekend diary. Call me old-fashioned, but I like all the appointments stuck up on the fridge!

Resources for practitioners 26

What will we call ourselves?

Many educators now talk about the 'Guide on the Side' rather than the 'Sage on the Stage' to indicate more facilitative approaches to teaching. We need to update this image for e-moderators to reflect the need for electronic conferencing experience.

I suggest you use this list for workshops and online discussion with e-moderators to explore the role in your context.

1. **E-moderator:** I've chosen this term to refer to online teaching and facilitation roles. The term moderator has grown up with computer mediated conferencing and has been used from the earliest days for online conference facilitators. Moderating used to mean to preside over a meeting or discussion. I have added the 'e' short for electronic to the front of it, borrowed from e-commerce and e-mail, to indicate the wider and special responsibilities that the online context adds to the role. Zane Berge in North America and myself in Europe appear to have started using the term e-moderator at much the same time, as the millennium turned. Zane Berge and Mauri Collins maintain a useful and popular e-moderators page that can be found at:
   http://www.emoderators.com/moderators.shtml
2. **Online negotiator:** where knowledge construction online is desired, the key role for the e-moderator is one of negotiating the meaning of activities and information through online discussion and construction.
3. **Online host:** since the social role of online working is important, you may want to have a social host (or hostess) as well as e-moderators for the

teaching and learning conferences. They do not need to run social events online as such (though they may) but ensure everyone is greeted and introduced to others with like-minded interests.

4. **Personal learning trainer:** this is a suggestion from Robin Mason. Learners may need a personal trainer to lead them through materials and networks, identify relevant materials and advisors and ways forward (Mason, 1998).

5. **Convenor** is a term that we've adopted in the OUBS and have used especially for online conferences and courses where there is a fairly wide audience. We also use e-convenor to mean a trainer of the trainers, e-moderator of the e-moderator in our online training courses.

6. **Online conductor:** this suggests the pulling together of a variety of resources as people (as in conducting an orchestra to produce a beautiful integrated sound) or perhaps electrical current conductors – if your conferences are effective and flow along, there will be energy, excitement and power!

7. **Online concierge:** to provide support and information on request (perhaps a map of the area. . .).

8. **Online manager:** much of e-moderating is also 'managing', especially in its up-to-date definition of coaching, supporting and leading. Managerial roles in conferencing include developing objectives, agendas, timetables, rules and group norms. Managing the interactions and capacity of a group is a key success factor in e-moderating, as in management.

9. **E-Police:** I hope you will not call yourself this, nor find the need to make laws and enforce them. You will of course need a Code of Practice and protocols for e-moderators.

10. **Online chair:** an E-chair would be useful if a structured meeting with clear action outcomes is needed. The skills of chairing online are similar to those of chairing a face-to-face meeting, with the added complexity and asynchronicity, that should result in more democratic decision-taking and hence more time than usual.

11. **Online leader:** this is a term I've not seen used. I expect this is because CMC tends to be a highly democratic medium and leadership may not be seen as quite appropriate. However, e-moderators are truly leaders – they need to set objectives and processes and provide and maintain optimum conditions online for the realization of these.

12. **E-teacher:** the terms 'teacher', 'trainer' and 'tutor' are generic and have the advantage of being in common use. Therefore adding 'e-' in front of them to indicate the electronic element probably makes them acceptable in most online courses and processes. I think the term then suggests a more facilitative and developmental role than traditional teaching.

13. **E-master:** The term master has come into use in recent years in terms of 'Web-Master' – someone who takes a particular responsibility for the technical, design and perhaps the editorial content of a Web site. The notion of CMC 'Master' could be introduced meaning the sporting term of 'master', ie someone who has previously won a number of games.

14. **Faceless facilitator:** this is a suggestion from Tan Lay In of Ngee Ann Polytechnic, Singapore. She reminds us that considerable skill change is needed in instructors experienced in face-to-face facilitation in order to promote online collaboration. (Tan, 1999).

15. **Tele-coach or tele-tutor:** from Germany comes a reminder that learning free of space and time needs a tele-coach (as opposed to a 'presence' coach) able to support learners into the new paradigms in the way coaches used to by being physically beside trainees (Mundemann, 1999).

16. **Online gardener:** this is an idea from the corporate training sector. E-moderators not only need to 'cultivate the garden' (by helping learners acquire knowledge) but also make the garden grow (by increasing the store of knowledge available) (Benque, 1999).

17. Try these metaphors out in discussion in your e-moderator training: E-ringmaster, Online priest, Agent provocateur, Devil's advocate.

Exploring online: conference text examples

If you have never taken part in a computer conference, the following three examples should give you something of the 'look' and 'feel' of being in one. They are extracts from conferences associated with the Open University MBA course, B820 *Strategy*. They have had to be harshly pruned to reduce the amount of space they take up in the book. A live conference may be a little more messy and variable than these.

You may find helpful my nine categories for analyzing such conferences, because they make it easier to see what's happening in the debate. Look for the code numbers [in square brackets] as you read the exchanges. You could use these categories yourself in conferences that you e-moderate.

Conference analysis

Individual thinking
1   Offering up ideas or resources and inviting a critique of them
2   Asking challenging questions
3   Articulating, explaining and supporting positions on issues
4   Exploring and supporting issues by adding explanations and examples
5   Reflecting on and re-evaluating personal opinions
Interactive thinking
6   Offering a critique, challenging, discussing and expanding ideas of others
7   Negotiating interpretations, definitions and meanings

8   Summarizing and modelling previous contributions
9   Proposing actions based on ideas that have been developed

Example I

This extract derives from a sub-conference on strategy in the Voluntary Sector. Note particularly how each participant contributes his or her experience and views. These participants are effectively using the technique of quoting the question to which they are responding in their first line of their message. The e-moderator is active in proposing challenging questions and throwing out ideas to get the conference started, but one of the students (PD) also helps stimulate responses and discussion.

There were nine individuals in the conference and the e-moderator is HB. The heading for each message indicates the initials of the sender and the date of the message.

PD 31 May

Thank you Susan, Diane, Cara and Tom. At last I feel we might be getting somewhere.

Anthony how are you?

If I were a profit-making organization providing services to a voluntary organization I would regard myself as a supplier and expect to get paid (mutually beneficial exchange). Much as I might like to do voluntary work, I can't afford to. My continued co-operation is dependent on the voluntary organization's ability to pay. [1] If I were influenced and persuaded by the not-profit motives and values of the charity (identification with norms, values and beliefs), I would become a donor or supporter. Is there a distinction between these categories? Would I be right in saying a donor provides cash whereas a supporter gives time or effort free of charge? [2] Excuse my ignorance, but what are Trustees? Are these the people who own the assets of the organization? What happens to the assets if the organization was to collapse? [2] And who are the customers? If the primary objectives are aimed at social good, are the customers the ones in direct receipt of the benefits provided by the organization, even though they may not be required to pay for these benefits? Or is it the state as Diane says, or are the donors customers, giving money in return for what? [2]
    Regards, Paul

HB 31 May

PD writes:

> *Excuse my ignorance, but what are Trustees? Are these the people who own the assets of the organization? What happens to the assets if the organization was to collapse?* [1]

Trustees own the assets of the organization and act as Directors would in a Limited Company, ie they are the Senior Management – even though they will not necessarily be managers in the day-to-day sense of the word. [4]

> *And who are the customers? If the primary objectives are aimed at social good, are the customers the ones in direct receipt of the benefits provided by the organization, even though they may not be required to pay for these benefits? Or is it the state, as Diane says, or are the donors customers, giving money in return for what?* [1]

Good question Paul. I have seen it suggested that charities have bi-focal stakeholders, ie when looking at funding the donors are the customers and the receivers are internal stakeholders. – When providing a service the receivers are external stake-holders and the donors internal (what they want will affect what the organization does). This for me is part of the fascination of the sector. That unlike the For-Profit and Public Sectors the use of stakeholder analysis is far more complex. Maybe we might develop this issue further [4].

Cheers, Haydn

CL 1 June

Identifying the main stakeholders will surely be part of the 'marketing audit'. [6]

The ICT required by each of these groups will be different – would it be an idea to 'segment' the market according to stakeholder needs rather than on the functional basis I suggested earlier? [5]

Would it be a good idea to decide on a process of how we tackle and construct the work for this Tutor Marked Assignment? [7] In reality we would be setting up project teams if we were embarking on a major market development? [9] Maybe there are those of you who have had experience in setting up such project teams – could you suggest a way forward? [9] Can we divide the task up in some way?

Any thoughts or suggestions?? Cara

PD 1 June

HB writes:

> *I have seen it suggested that charities have bi-focal stakeholders, ie when looking at funding the donors are the customers and the receivers are internal stakeholders. – When providing a service the receivers are external stakeholders and the donors internal (what they want will affect what the organization does).* [4]

Can a stakeholder be regarded as a customer if they don't have to pay? [1]
How about the idea that the receivers are the product, ie what the organization does, and the donors are the customers, ie those who buy and pay for the product? [1]

HB 2 June

PD writes:

> *Can a stakeholder be regarded as a customer if they don't have to pay?*

Yes, if their attitudes and feelings affect how the organization makes decisions. [3]
How about the idea that the receivers are the product, ie what the organization does, and the donors are the customers ie those who buy and pay for the product? [7]
What the organization does and who it does it for are not necessarily the same: as you might seem to imply. So is the product what it does, or for whom it does it? [7]
    Cheers, Haydn

MK 2 June

PD writes:

> *Can a stakeholder be regarded as a customer if they don't have to pay?'*

Haydn says 'yes' and I have to agree and would cite the following examples. (*Message gives examples from experience*) [4] Hope this helps. Meredith

PD 2 June

HB writes:

What the organization does and who it does it for are not necessarily the same: as you might seem to imply. So is the product what it does, or for whom it does it? [6]

A customer is one who buys a product or service.
A donor is one who gives.
A receiver is one who accepts/receives. [6]
Is the customer concept relevant to the voluntary sector? Could this be a case of force fit by the application of marketing logic and the dominant business paradigm? [6]
I am of the opinion that we could drop 'customers' from the stakeholder framework and substitute 'donors' and 'receivers' in their place. This would make five forces analysis more relevant, swapping 'customer power' for 'donor power' and 'receiver power' (6 forces analysis?) [7]
   Regards Paul

HB 3 June

PD writes:

I am of the opinion that we could drop 'customers' from the stakeholder framework and substitute 'donors' and 'receivers' in their place. This would make five forces analysis more relevant, swapping 'customer power' for 'donor power' and 'receiver power' (6 forces analysis?)

I can see the roots of your approach Paul, but am not convinced. I think the Voluntary Sector does treat donors as customers and receivers as customers, but at different times and in different focuses. I suspect we might be seeing the difficulty with the sector as an analysis – ie that it has two sets of stakeholders depending if you are looking at sources of funds or object of funds. Again they have two markets – to be seen to do the right thing and to gain attention to what is done. They also have difficulty with management based on the finance driven fund-raising (my own area of experience) and the delivery arm, whose mission aims and objectives cannot often be reconciled. Internal stakeholders are therefore also more fragmented than in other organizations. [7]
Who else would like to reflect on this dichotomy and its impact on the analysis of the sector? [2]
   Cheers, Haydn

(There were around 20 responses to this question.)

PD 4 June

There were some interesting comments on staff remuneration in the early chatter topics. [8]

- Unremunerated non-executive directors or management committee members. . . often bring their own personal agendas. DB
- Voluntary sector employees. . . offer them better salaries and conditions because we are not creaming a profit off before salaries.
- Their remuneration reflects the fact that they have some additional, say ideological, stakeholder interest in the company – they aren't paid the going rate because they care.

Do voluntary sector employees/managers have to take vows of poverty and commit to the ideology of the organization? [2]
Could we explore this further? There may be implications for the balance of stakeholder power and the effectiveness of strategies – question (b). [7]
Regards Paul

SD 5 June

Paul asks – Do voluntary sector employees / managers have to take vows of poverty and commit to the ideology of the organization?

Could we explore this further? There may be implications for the balance of stakeholder power and the effectiveness of strategies – question (b).

I don't take vows of poverty – I see myself as an earning employee, but I work for a large org which is well off – some employees of small and struggling organizations I know do work above and beyond the call of duty. . . voluntary organizations tend not to be unionized, but why would probably be a complex question. [3]
However, although I see myself as someone doing a fair day's work etc, I do sign up to the mission and values of the organization and indeed the organization expects congruence between my personal and professional values and theirs – there is a kind of symbolic signing up to these when appointed. . . This certainly seems different to the organizational 'values' thinking in our course which expected organizations would sustain considerable differences between personal/organizational values, though would expect loyalty when on the job to organizational expectations. . . [3]
I'm not sure how that relates to power of stakeholders, but employees are a considerably important lot. . . Perhaps more so than Trustees in some voluntary organizations. . . Though this gets complicated because in some voluntary organizations Trustees are also users of services (eg self-help networks like MIND) [4]
I think? I Susan

SD 5 June

> Re donors and customers. . .
>
> I think of resource providers (donors, individual and corporate and grant makers) (and purchasers of services)
> And Service Users (receivers of services who may or may not make a contribution towards cost but usually do not) [3]
> Donors are also customers of our objectives, donating fulfils their giving intentions, and they can shop around to find the organization that meets this best . . .
> Purchasers of services are also customers – mostly public bodies who buy our service provision to help them fulfil their duties. . .
> Then again some public bodies also grant aid the Voluntary Organization's – especially small ones – with no expectation other then the Voluntary Organization will carry on. . . [7]. . . Susan

PD 8 June

> Thanks to all who have so far responded to my plea for ideas on stakeholders. Please keep your thoughts coming!
> How significant are 'lenders' to the voluntary sector? Do voluntary organizations take out loans like private companies, and end up having to raise funds to pay bank interest?
> And who is the competition? Is there direct head on competition like Pepsi and Coke? Or is it more sideways competition, competing for lottery money or for the pound in my pocket against other things I might spend it on? [2]
> Regards Paul

CL 7 June

> Paul asks 'who is the competition?'
> I think competition in the VOLUNTARY SECTOR comes in several forms: Rival fund-raising activities, rival bids for contracts, rival bids for grants eg the national lottery, other service providers, selling its products merchandise (charity shops), education. I'm sure there's more!! Does that help? [4]
> Cara

PD 8 June

> Paul asks for scoring of stakeholders on the power matrix. [1]

At this point the conference continued with each participant contributing his or her views on a structured audit based on a simple model from the course material. Another 35 messages were posted. The conference ran for around a week, culminating in the entire group submitting individual assignments.

Example 2

This is a second example of knowledge construction through CMC, this time from the conference on the Brewing Sector. There were 10 participants. The e-moderator was AK. The sequence begins with AM's message on 30th May entitled 'Innovation'. The participants actively comment and build on each other's contributions while giving their own views and sources of information.

AM 30 May

> Hi, does anyone else out there see the changes in the UK Pub & Brewery business as an example of innovation (see book 6)? [2]
> This I would suggest strategies change in two ways.
>
> 1.   The arrival and rapid growth of the new Pub retailers.
> 2.   The growing importance of Brands and concepts to fill the gap of the businesses which had to be disposed of. [3]
>
> I believe that the second point is worth further debate as I think it is the key issue which will split the market in the next 10 years, with the big players at one end and the smaller regional brewer at the other. [6]
> Regards Arnold's suggestion: Meredith & Ben how about a meet in one of our great pubs shortly? [1] Anthony

MW 31 May

> Arnold, I believe the line you are proposing about the wider moves and consequent strategic ramifications are the best use of this conference. [6]

While I admire the effort of those who are digging out statistics and interviewing micro brewers I cannot help but think that is all far too detailed... the one thing this course has brought home to me is the idea of looking from above (yes the helicopter again!!!) thus preventing getting bogged down in the detail that the above kind of research will perhaps throw up. [6]

The analysis of the industry that I put up as a starter (see my strategic positioning table in my message of 20th May) I think combines well with Arnold's comments... Ie the industry participants are moving out of the middle of the table into one extreme or another and are specializing with brands and concepts etc... [7]

Maybe some comments on my table, coupled with Arnold's observations, will get some momentum??? [6]

Surely if we can agree that the table provides the scope of what we are looking at then we can really move forward apace??? [7]

   Meredith

IU 1 June

Meredith I think you are correct in that we need to take a helicopter view. [7]

But I have very little understanding of the industry and so I need a little statistical info to help me consider the total market. [3] Is it growing, shrinking, etc? [2] I live in a rural part of Scotland and so the nearest library that will have a copy of Keynote or Mintel will be over 200 miles away. I can find very little statistical info on the Web. [3] I am happy to discuss the wider issues with you too. [1]

Should we start here, maybe others will agree or disagree with our thoughts? [7]

As a starter I think the UK market has three/four brewers who control 90%. In the past they have controlled a high percentage of outlets whether by ownership of pubs, managed houses, tenancies and loans. Hence the Beer Order to break up this dominance. [4]

In recent years consumption in pubs etc, the Trade has been in decline, due to drink driving, health issue, change in social habits. In Germany 151 litres per head of population were consumed in 1976 down to 132 in 1996. [4] What are the figures for UK I wonder. [2] With a greater swing to beer purchases from Supermarkets brewers have moved position to being more in the leisure industry, satisfying the total leisure needs of consumers. Restaurants, hotels, holiday camps have all been good sources of profit and cushioned big players from decline in profits from beer. [4]

Maybe they saw that consumption would decline and there would be over-capacity and it would take some time for total production to balance with consumption. [5] I wonder if it will in the next 10 years, as over-capacity exists in European countries due to decline in consumption, see figures on Germany above. [5]

Yours and anyone else's comments would be appreciated. [1]

   Ivan

MW 1 June

Ivan

Re 'Is this why companies appear in certain spaces on your table?' [1]
I think you are exactly right. [7] because the industry is becoming fragmented and big
players specialising, the smaller players have to take a more focused position. [8]
(Enforced strategy??)... [6]
IMHO the answer to the TUTOR MARKED ASSIGNMENT questions could be hung
on a discussion such as yours as to why players are moving in the directions on the
table that they are... and what this means for strategies to the players in the various
segments... [8] Any comments anyone?? [1] Meredith

MH 1 June

Ivan and Meredith

To quote Grant pp 89–91, in the course book, Industry is an artificial construct;
therefore it is necessary to define what is meant by the Brewing and pubs as an
industry before taking a helicopter view. [6]
Meredith's 3X3 grid was a great help to me but the surrounding environment needs
looking at I believe. [7]
Nobody has considered the amount of beer that enters the market through supermarkets and the like, as home drinking must be a (poor) substitute for the pub. [6]
Also cider and spirits are substitutes for beer both in the pub and at home. [6]
Matt

AK 1 June

Re: supermarkets.

This is an interesting area... [6] Maybe it would help you to ask what do substitutes
do... [7]
They create a new industry at the expense of an old industry... as well as supermarkets there is the need to think about the effect of cross channel 'smuggling'... are
these substitutes? [7]
What do you think?
Regards, Andreas [6]

Nearly all the participants responded to the e-moderator's suggestion in this message. They then spent around another 10 days (and 50 messages) relating the sharing of their knowledge to concepts and theories in the course material. All successfully completed and submitted their assignments.

Example 3

Finally, have a look at this example of knowledge construction through interactive CMC in the Information Technology Sector of the same course. There were 11 participants in this conference. The e-moderator was BS, but he didn't intervene during these exchanges. AT (a student) recognizes the need to build a virtual team from the beginning and proposes a group 'mission statement' to get them started. The sequence ended with thanks and an apology from a 'browser'.

AT 19 April

If we rush into industry analysis too quickly we risk lack of focus. I think we still have work to do in defining the scope. [6]

'Mobile communications' could be further divided into the system providers (Orange, Mercury, Vodaphone, Cellnet etc) and customer equipment providers (Nokia, Ericsson, Motorola etc) plus the one stop shop businesses offering equipment and connection services. [7]

Should we address all of these sub-sectors or just one of them? [6]

My inclination is to address only the customer equipment provision sector. [5]

To give us a point of reference for the rest of the conference and the assignment, I think we need a mission statement. Here's my proposal: [7]

'The aim of this ITEC2 CMC conference is to analyze and research the attractiveness of the mobile communications customer equipment sector within Europe, evaluate potential strategies to compete within it and assess the sustainability of any strategic advantage. The Objective is to reach a reasoned consensus, within 9 weeks, that will form the basis of a report to the board of an international company entering the sector without infringing the TUTOR MARKED ASSIGNMENT submission rules, with regard to individual work.' [7]

Please feel free to amend, add, and delete etc. so we all know where the goalposts are. I suggest this statement be FROZEN ON 27th APRIL. [7]

Andrew.

JS 20 April

I agree with Andrew that we don't want to get into the analysis before we have agreed a scope. I also agree that we should freeze the objective by 27th April. [6]

However, I would like to add my view to the definition of scope. [6]

There is a further breakdown into Service providers eg Talkland who resell access to Vodaphone, Cellnet, etc. [7]

This may be a more interesting avenue of approach than equipment supply as they have the first line contact with the customers. They have to deal with the issues of churn and customer retention segmentation etc. [6]

Is there anyone else out there who might be interested in this area? [6]

Given that there are 81 people online interested in mobile telecommunications can we cover the three segments and give us all more of a chance to learn about different areas? [6]

Will be away until next week but will be interested in reading your comments when I return. [3]

    Jamie

Considerable discussion ensued about the focus on their analysis. At this point, AT attempted a summary:

AT 24 April

Three interest groups seem to be emerging: [7]

Mobile Comms (data and voice)

Internet Services

Communications service provision

Revised Mission statement: [8]

'The aim of this IT CMC conference is to analyze and research the attractiveness of the mobile multimedia service provision sector within Europe. This includes access to and delivery of voice, data, Internet and future multimedia services by a variety of mobile communications technologies. The conference will evaluate potential strategies to compete within this sector and assess the sustainability of any strategic advantage. The Objective is to reach a reasoned consensus, within 9 weeks, that will form the basis of a report to the board of an international company entering the sector without infringing the Tutor Marked Assignment submission rules, with regard to individual work.' [7]

Comments, counter-proposals, hate-mail? [6]

    Andrew

By the agreed date, they had achieved a joint mission. One of the participants thanked AT for his input:

JS 27 April

Andrew, I would like to echo thanks regarding your input to the Mission Statement. [6] Afraid I am only just managing to get the time to get into the Conference but what I have seen regarding the Mission Statement seems fine by me. [3] Like some others I do not have a technology background nor do I have any telecomms knowledge so I will have to rely heavily on those with the appropriate technical expertise for guidance and help. [3] I now look forward to making regular visits and input to the Conference. [4] Judith

References

Ahlberg, M, Kaasinen, A *et al* (2001) Collaborative knowledge building to promote in-service teacher training in environmental education, *Journal of Information Technology for Teacher Education*, **10** (3), pp 227–39

Ash, C and Bacsich, P (2002). The costs of networked learning, in *Networked learning: perspectives and issues*, ed C Steeples and C Jones, Springer-Verlag, London

Axelsson, L E, Bodin, K *et al* (2001) *Folkbildningnet: an anthology about folkbildning and flexible learning*, Swedish National Council of Adult Education, Stockholm

Azevedo, R (2002) Beyond intelligent tutoring systems: using computers as METAcognitive tools to enhance learning? *Instructional Science*, **30**, pp 41–45

Bakia, M (2000) Costs of ICT use in higher education: what little we know, *TechKnowLogia*, **2** (1) [Online] http://www.techknowlogia.org

Baptista Nunes, J M and McPherson, M A (2002) Pedagogical and implementation models for e-learning continuing professional distance education (CPDE) emerging from action research, *International Journal of Management Education*, Vol 2, No 3, Summer 2002, pp 16–27

Barker, P (2002) On being an online tutor, *Innovations in Education and Teaching International*, **39** (1), pp 3–13

Becher, T and Trowler, P R (2001) *Academic Tribes and Territories*, Open University Press, Buckingham

Ben-Jacob, M G, Levin, D S *et al* (2002) The learning environment of the 21st century, *IJET*, **6** (3)

Benjamin, A (1994) Affordable, restructured education: a solution through information technology, *RSA Journal* (May), pp 45–49

Bennett, S and Marsh, S (2002) Are we expecting online tutors to run before they can walk? *Innovations in Education and Teaching International*, **39** (1), pp 14–20

Benque, N (1999) *Online Training for Tutors*, Proceedings of Online Educa, Berlin

Biggs, J (1995) The role of metalearning in study processes, *British Journal of Educational Psychology*, **55**, pp 185–212

Biggs, J (1999) *Teaching for Quality Learning at University*, Society for Research into Higher Education (SRHE) and Open University Press, Buckingham

Billett, S (1996) Towards a model of workplace learning: the learning curriculum, *Studies in Continuing Education*, **15** (1) pp 43–57

Blumer, H (1969) *Symbolic Interaction*, Prentice-Hall, Englewood Cliffs, NJ

Bonk, C J (2001) Online teaching in an online world, CourseShare.com [Online] http://PublicationShare.com

Broadbent, B (2002) *ABCs of e-Learning*, Jossey–Bass Pfeiffer, San Francisco

Brown, S (1998) Reinventing the university, *Association for Learning Technology Journal*, **6** (3), pp 30–37

Brown, S, Bull, J and Race, P (1999) *Computer Assisted Assessment in Higher Education*, Kogan Page, London

Bruner, J (1986) The language of education, in *Actual Minds, Possible Worlds*, ed J Bruner, Harvard University Press, Cambridge, MA

Buckingham Shum, S (2000) *Lyceum: Internet Voice Groupware for Distance Learning*, internal document, KMI, Open University, Milton Keynes. A report on Lyceum and the Knowledge Management course is available online, *Lyceum: Internet voice groupware for distance learning*, http://kmi.open.ac.uk/publications/papers/kmi-tr-100pdf

Burn, J M and Loch, K D (2001) The societal impact of the World Wide Web: key challenges for the 21st century, *Information Resources Management Journal*, Oct–Dec, pp 4–14

Bygholm, A (2002) Understanding communication in text-based systems, in *Learning in Virtual Environments,* ed L Dirckinck-Holmfeld and B Fibiger, Samsfundslitteratur, Frederiksberg

Cann, A J and Pawley, E L (1999) Automated online tutorials: new formats for assessment on the WWW, in *Computer-Assisted Assessment in Higher Education*, ed S Brown, J Bull and P Race, Kogan Page, London

Castelfranchi, C (2002) The social nature of information and the role of trust, *International Journal of Cooperative Information Systems*, **11** (3 & 4), pp 381–403

Chenault, B G (1998) Developing personal and emotional relationships via computer-mediated communication, *CMC Magazine*, **5** (5) [Online] http://www.december.com/cmc/mag/1998/may/toc.html

Chisholm, I M, Carey, J et al (2002) Information technology skills for a pluralist society: is the playing field level? *Journal of Research on Technology in Education*, **35** (1 Fall), pp 58–79

Clarke, A (2002) E-learning 'close to being a core skill in the 21st century', *Adults Learning*, September, pp 12–13

Cloke, C and Sharif, S (2001) Why use information and communications technology? Some theoretical and practical issues, *Journal of Information Technology for Teacher Education*, **10** (1 & 2), pp 7–17

Coldeway, D O (2002) The success of advanced learning technologies for instruction: research and evaluation of human factors issues, *Industry and Higher Education*, Aug, pp 235–38

Collis, B and Moonen, J (2001) *Flexible Learning in a Digital World*, Kogan Page, London

Crystal, D (2001) *Language and the Internet*, Cambridge University Press, Cambridge

Csikzentmihalyi, M (2003) *Good Business: Leadership, flow and making of meaning*, Hodder and Stoughton, Chatham

Cuban, L (2001) *Oversold and Underused: Computers in the classroom*, Harvard University Press, Cambridge, MA, and London

Cuevas, H M, Fiore, S M *et al* (2002) Scaffolding cognitive and metacognitive processes in low verbal ability learners: use of diagrams in computer-based training environments, *Instructional Science*, **30**, pp 433–64

Cummings, J A and Bonk, C J (2002) Facilitating interactions among students and faculty via Web-based conferencing systems, *Journal of Technology in Human Services*, **20** (3/4), pp 245–65

Debenham, M D, Whitelock, M, Fung, P and Emms, J M (1999) Online educational counselling for students with special needs: building rapport, *Association for Learning Technology Journal*, **7** (1), pp 19–25

Dence, R D (1996) *Reviewing Conference Discussions on Participation and Contribution: Lurking or differently active?*, report for Institute of Educational Technology, Open University, Milton Keynes, January

Dibbell, J (1995) Viruses are good for you, *Wired*, **3** (2 Feb), p 15

DiPaolo, A (1999) *Online Education: Myth or Reality? The Stanford online experience*, Proceedings of Online Educa, Berlin

Dirckinck-Holmfeld, L (2002) Designing virtual learning environments based on problem orientated project pedagogy, in *Learning in Virtual Environments*, ed L Dirckinck-Holmfeld and B Fibiger, Samsfundslitteratur, Frederiksberg

Duchastel, P (1997) A Web-based model for university instruction, *Journal of Educational Technology Systems*, **25** (3), pp 221–28

Dulewicz, V and Higgs, M (2002) Emotional intelligence and the development of managers and leaders, in *Individual Differences and Development in Organizations*, ed M Pearn, Wiley, Chichester

Eden, C, Ackermann, F and Cropper, S (1992) The analysis of cause maps, *Journal of Management Studies*, **3** (29), pp 309–24

Edwards, R, Ranson, S *et al* (2002) Reflexivity: towards a theory of lifelong learning, *International Journal of Lifelong Education*, **21** (6), pp 525–36

Eisenstadt, M (2003) Marc's crusade could triple our output at keyboard, *Open House* (Milton Keynes) 387, Mar–Apr

Feenberg, A (1989) The written word, in *Mindweave: Communication, computers and distance education*, ed R D Mason and A R Kaye, Pergamon, Oxford

Fibiger, B (2002) Didactic design of virtual learning environments, in *Learning in Virtual Environments*, ed L Dirckinck-Holmfeld and B Fibiger, Samfundslitteratur, Frederiksberg

Friedman, A, Watts, D *et al* (2002) Evaluating online CPD using educational criteria derived from the experiential learning cycle, *British Journal of Educational Technology*, **33** (4), pp 367–78

Gold, J (1998) Disability and CMC, *Computer Mediated Communications Magazine*, **5** (1), p 1 [Online] http://www.december.com/cmc/mag/1998/jan/toc.html

Goodfellow, P, Lea, M *et al* (2001) Opportunity and e-quality: intercultural and linguistic issues in global online learning, *Distance Education*, **22** (5), pp 65–84

Goodyear, P, Salmon, G *et al* (2001) Competencies for online teaching, *Education Training and Development*, **49** (1), pp 65–72

Gray, C and Salmon, G (1999) Academic integrity in electronic universities of the new millennium: a practitioner's perspective, *Higher Education in Europe,* **24** (2), pp 259–64

Green, C A (2002) Reflecting on reflection: students' evaluation of their moving and handling education, *Nurse Education in Practice*, **2**, pp 4–12

Halliday, M A K and Hasan, R (1989) *Language, Context and Text: Aspects of language in a social-semiotic perspective*, Oxford University Press, Oxford

Haraway, D (1991) Cyborg manifesto: science, technology and socialist-feminism in the late 20th century, in *Simians, Cyborgs and Women: The reinvention of nature*, ed D Haraway, Routledge, New York

Harris, R A and Higgison, C A (2003) Reuse of resources within communities of practice, in *Reusing Online Resources*, ed A Littlejohn, Kogan Page, London

Harvey, F (2001). Knowing our precise place in the world, *Financial Times*, 13 Feb, p 12

Harvey, L and Knight, P (1996) *Transforming Higher Education*, SRHE and Open University Press, Buckingham

Hawkridge, D (1998) Cost-effective support for university students learning via the Web?, *Association for Learning Technology Journal*, **6** (3), pp 25–29

Hawkridge, D (2003) The human in the machine: reflections on mentoring in the British Open University, *Mentoring and Tutoring*, **11** (1), pp 15–24

Hawkridge, D, Morgan, A and Jelfs, A (1997) *H801 Students' and Tutors' Use of the Electronic Workbook and Electronic Mail 1997*, OU Report to the Electronic Tutoring Group, Milton Keynes, December

Hendry, G (1996) Constructivism and educational practice, *Australian Journal of Education*, **40** (1), pp 19–45

Henri, F (1992) Computer conferencing and content analysis, in *Collaborative Learning Through Computer Conferencing: The Najaden papers*, ed A Kaye, Springer-Verlag, Heidelberg

Hill, H (2003) Finding the Right Support, *E-learning Age* [Online] http://www.e-coaches.co.uk/mbtisurvey.asp

Holsti, O R (1968) Content analysis, in *The Handbook of Social Psychology: Research methods*, ed G Lindzey and E Aronson, Addison-Wesley, Reading, MA

Honey, P and Mumford, A (1986) *Using Your Learning Styles*, Honey, Maidenhead

Hopson, M H, Simms, R L *et al* (2001–2) Using a technology-enriched environment to improve higher-order thinking skills, *Journal of Research on Technology in Education*, **34** (2), pp 109–19

Hunt, C (2001) Shifting shadows: metaphors and maps for facilitating reflective practice, *Reflective Practice*, **2** (3), pp 275–87

Jackson, G B (2000) A new model for tertiary education in developing countries?, *Tech KnowLogia*, **2** (1) [Online] http://www.techknowlogia.org

Jewett, F I (1999) *BRIDGE: A Simulation Model for Comparing the Costs of Expanding a Campus Using Distributed Instruction Versus Classroom Instruction*, Proceedings of Online Educa, Berlin

Jonassen, D, Davidson, M, Collins, M, Campbell, C and Haag, B B (1995) Constructivism and computer-mediated communication in distance education, *American Journal of Distance Education*, **9** (2), pp 7–25

Kaye, R and Hawkridge, D (2003) *Learning and Teaching for Business*, Kogan Page, London

Kelly, G A (1955) *The Psychology of Personal Constructs*, Norton, New York

Kleinman, S S (2002) Methodological and ethical challenges of researching a computer-mediated group, *Journal of Technology in Human Services*, **19** (2/3), pp 49–63

Knight, P T (2002) *Being a Teacher in Higher Education*, SRHE and Open University Press, Buckingham

Lapham, C (1998) A mindset for the new millennium, *CMC Magazine*, **5** (10) [Online] http://www.december.com/cmc/mag/1998/oct/lapnp.html

Leach, J and Moon, B (1999) Recreating pedagogy, in *Learners and Pedagogy*, ed J Leach and B Moon, Paul Chapman, London

Leask, M and Younie, S (2001) Communal constructivist theory: information and communications technology pedagogy and internationalisation of the curriculum, *Journal of Information Technology for Teacher Education*, **10** (1 & 2), pp 117–33

Leino, A (1999) *Virtual United: Online course to 22 countries by an international team*, Proceedings of Online Educa, Berlin

Leonard, J and Guba, S (2001) Education at the crossroads: perspectives on distance learning, *Journal of Research on Technology in Education*, **34** (Fall 1), pp 51–57

Leung, W C (2002) The use of the Internet and information technology to facilitate teaching evidence based practice – a case study, *Nurse Education in Practice*, **2**, pp 181–89

Lippincott, K, Eco, U *et al* (2000) *The Story of Time*, Merrell Holberton, London

Little, S, Fowle, W and Quintas, P (2003) Building and maintaining distributed communities of practice: Knowledge management in the OUBS MBA in Kaye and Hawkridge (eds) *Learning and Teaching for Business*, Kogan Page, London

Macdonald, J (2003) Assessing online collaborative learning: process and product, *Computers and Education*, **40** (4), pp 377–91

Macdonald, J and Twining, P (2002) Assessing activity based learning for networked course, *British Journal of Educational Technology*, **33** (5), pp 605–20

Macdonald, J, Weller, M *et al* (2002) Meeting the assessment demands of networked courses, *International Journal on E-learning*, Jan–Mar, pp 9–18

Mann, S J (2001) Alternative perspectives on the student experience: alienation and engagement, *Society for Research into Higher Education*, **26** (1), pp 7–19

Margolis, J (2003) *The Implications of Virtual Teamwork Research for Virtual Learning: A case study*, Open University Business School Research Report, OU, Milton Keynes

Martell, C (2000) The age of information, the age of foolishness, *College and Research Libraries* (Jan), pp 10–27

Mason, R (1993) Written interactions, in *Computer Conferencing: The last word*, ed R Mason, pp 3–19, Beach Holme, Victoria, British Colombia

Mason, R (1998) *Globalising Education: Trends and applications*, Routledge, London

Masterton, S (1998) The virtual participant: a tutor's assistant for electronic conferencing, in *Knowledge Web*, ed M Eisenstadt and T Vincent, Kogan Page, London

Mathiasen, H and Rattleff, P (2002) The conditions of communication in computer-mediated, net-disseminated educational settings, in *Learning in Virtual Environments*, ed L Dirckinck-Holmfeld and B Fibiger, Samsfundslitteratur, Frederiksberg

McNaught, C (2003) Identifying the complexity of factors in the sharing and reuse of resources, in *Reusing Online Resources*, ed A Littlejohn, Kogan Page, London

Montieth, M and Smith, J (2001) Learning in a virtual campus: the pedagogical implications of students' experience, *Innovations in Education and Teaching International*, **38** (2), pp 119–31

Moon, S and Hawkridge, D (2003) Assessing student performance, in Kaye and Hawkridge (eds) *Learning and Teaching for Business*, Kogan Page, London

Morgan, D L (1988) *Focus Croups as Qualitative Research*, Sage, Beverley Hills, CA

Mundemann, F (1999) *Certified Training for Tele-coaches*, Proceedings of Online Educa, Berlin

Murphy, D (1999) *Still 'Getting the Mixture Right': Increasing interaction on the Internet*, Proceedings of 8th Conference on Open and Distance Learning, 'Learning and Teaching with New Technologies', Cambridge, UK, 28 Sept–1 Oct

Newell, A (1999) Enabling technologies, *Times Higher Educational Supplement*, p 13, 16 April

Norman, D (1999) *The Invisible Computer*, MIT Press, Cambridge, MA

O'Reilly, M and Morgan, C (1999) *Assessing Open and Distance Learners*, Kogan Page, London

Pidd, M (2003) *Tools for Thinking*, Second Edition, Wiley, Chichester

Potter, J and Wetherell, M (1989) *Discourse and Social Psychology*, Sage, London

Preece, J (1999) Empathic communities: balancing emotional and factual communication, *Interacting With Computers*, **12**, pp 63–77

Preece, J (2000) *Online Communities: Supporting sociability and designing usability*, John Wiley, Chichester

Pullen, J M (1998) ClassWise: synchronous Internet desktop education, *IEEE Transitions in Education* [Online] http://bacon.gmu.edu/pubs/ClassWse/tr98-06.html

Putman, R W (1991) Recipes and reflective learning: 'What would prevent you from saying it that way?', in *The Reflective Turn: Case studies in and on educational practice*, ed D Schön, Teachers College Press, London and New York

Remenyi, D (2002) As the first 50 years of computing draw to an end . . . What kind of society do we want? *Journal of Information Technology*, **17**, pp 3–7

Rheingold, H (1995) *The Virtual Community*, Minerva, London

Rheingold, H (2002) *Smart Mobs*, Minerva, London

Richards, C (2002) Distance education, on–campus learning, and e-learning convergences: an Australian exploration, *International Journal on E-learning*, Jul–Sep, pp 30–40

Roblyer, M D and Edwards, J (2000) *Integrating Educational Technology into Teaching*, Merrill, Upper Saddle River, NJ

Rodine, C R, Kotter, M and Shield, L (1999) *Voice Conferencing on the Internet: Creating richer on-line communities for distance learning*, Proceedings of EdMedia

Rogers, A (1993) Adult learning maps and the teaching process, *Studies in the Education of Adults*, **25** (2), pp 203–6

Rossman, M H (1999) Successful online teaching using asynchronous learning discussion forum, *Asynchronous Learning Networks*, **3** (2) [Online] http://www.aln.org/alnweb/journal/jaln-vol3issue2.htm

Rowntree, D (1995) Teaching and learning online: a correspondence education for the 21st century?, *British Journal of Educational Technology*, **26** (3), pp 205–15

Rumble, G (1997) *The Costs and Economics of Open and Distance Education*, Kogan Page, London

Rumble, G (1999) *The Costs of Networked Learning: What have we learnt?* Proceedings of Flexible Learning on the Information Superhighway (FLISH), Sheffield [Online] http://www.shu.ac.uk/flish/choice.htm

Rumble, G (2001) The costs and costing of networked learning, *Journal of Asynchronous Learning Networks*, **5** (2), pp 75–96

Salmon, G (1998) Developing learning though effective online moderation, *Active Learning*, **9** (December), pp 3–8

Salmon, G (1999a) Computer mediated conferencing in large scale management education, *Open Learning*, (June), pp 45–54

Salmon, G (2000) Computer mediated conferencing for management learning at the Open University, *Management Learning*, **31**(4), pp 491–502

Salmon, G (2002a) *E-tivities: The key to active online learning*, Kogan Page, London

Salmon, G (2002b) Approaches to researching teaching and learning online, in *Networked Learning: Perspectives and issues*, ed C Steeples and C Jones, Springer-Verlag, London

Salmon, G (2002c) Mirror, mirror, on my screen: exploring online reflections, *British Journal of Educational Technology*, **33** (4), pp 383–96

Salmon, G (2002d) Online networking and individual development, in *Individual Differences and Development in Organizations, Wiley Handbooks in the Psychology of Management in Organizations*, ed M Pearn, Wiley, Chichester

Salmon, G (2002e) Hearts, minds and screens: taming the future, *United States Distance Learning Association Journal*, **16** (5) (May) [Online] http://www.usdla.org/html/journal/MAY02_Issue/

Salmon, G (2003) Far from remote, *The Management Specialist*, **4** (9), pp 2–14

Santoro, G P (1995) What is computer-mediated communication?, in *Computer-Mediated Communication and the Online Classroom*, ed Z L Berge and M P Collins, pp 11–27, Hampton Press, NJ

Schön, D (1983) *The Reflective Practitioner: How professionals think in action*, Basic Books, London

Schreiber, D A and Berge, Z L (eds) (1998) *Distance Training: How innovative organizations are using technology to maximize learning and meet business objectives*, Jossey-Bass, California

Schwan, S, Straub, D *et al* (2002) Information management and learning in computer conferences: coping with irrelevant and unconnected messages, *Instructional Science*, **30**, pp 269–89

Scott, P and Eisenstadt, M (1998) Exploring telepresence on the Internet: the KMI Stadium Webcast experience, in *The Knowledge Web*, ed M Eisenstadt and T Vincent, Kogan Page, London

Seel, N M (2001) Epistemology, situated cognition, and mental models: 'Like a bridge over troubled water', *Instructional Science,* **29** (29), pp 403–27

Selinger, M and Pearson, J (eds) (1999) *Telematics in Education: Trends and issues*, Elsevier, Oxford

Selwyn, N, Williams, S *et al* (2001) E-stablishing a learning society: the use of the Internet to attract adults to lifelong learning in Wales, *Innovations in Education and Teaching International*, **38** (3), pp 205–18

Semaan, S (2000) Speech recognition: when people talk, computers listen, *TechKnowLogia*, **2** (1) [Online] http://www.techknowlogia.org

Sharples, M (2000) The design of personal mobile technologies for lifelong learning, *Computers and Education*, **34**, pp 177–93

Silverstone, R and Haddon, L (1996) Design and the implementation of information and communication technologies: technical change and everyday life, in *Communication by Design: The politics of information and communication technologies*, ed R Mansell and R Silverstone, Oxford University Press, Oxford

Simons, G F (2002) *Eurodiversity*, Butterworth-Heinemann, Elsevier Science, Woborn, MA

Slevin, J (2003) *The Internet Society*, Polity Press, Oxford

Somekh, B (2001) Methodological issues in identifying and describing the way knowledge is constructed with and without information and communications technology, *Information Technology for Teacher Education*, **10** (1 & 2), pp 157–78

Sorensen, E K (2002) Distributed CSCL: a situated, collaborative tapestry, in *Learning in Virtual Environments*, (eds) L Dirckinck-Holmfeld and B Fibiger, Samfundslitteratur, Frederiksberg

Spender, D (1995) *Nattering on the Net*, Spinifex Press, North Melbourne

Steeples, C, Vincent, P and Chapman, G (1997) *The Internet as a Collaborative Learning Resource*, CSALT, Teaching Developments Database, Lancaster

Stenhouse, L (1975) *Introduction to Curriculum Research and Development*, Heinemann, London

Tan, L (1999) *The 'Faceless Facilitator': An impossible learning approach?*, Proceedings of Online Educa, Berlin

Taylor, E W (2001) Transformative learning theory: a neurobiological perspective of the role of emotions and unconscious ways of knowing, *International Journal of Lifelong Education*, **20** (3 May/June), pp 218–36

Thorpe, M, Kubiak, C *et al* (2003) Designing for reuse and versioning, in *Reusing Online Resources*, ed A Littlejohn, Kogan Page, London

Tiffin, J and Rajasingham, L (1997) *In Search of the Virtual Class: Education in an information society*, Routledge, London

Tolsby, H (2002) Digital portfolios, in *Learning in Virtual Environments*, (eds) L Dirckinck-Holmfeld and B Fibiger, Samsfundslitteratur, Frederiksberg

Tsui, A B M and Ki, W W (2002) Teacher participation in computer conferencing: socio-psychological dimensions, *Journal of Information Technology for Teacher Education*, **11** (1), pp 23–44

Tsui, L (2002) Fostering critical thinking through effective pedagogy, *Journal of Higher Education*, **73** (6 Nov/Dec), pp 740–63

van der Heijden, K (1996) *Scenarios: The art of strategic conversation*, John Wiley, Chichester

Van Grundy, A B (1988) *Techniques of Structured Problem Solving*, Van Nostrand Reinhold, New York

Viera, F (2002) Pedagogical quality at university: what teachers and students think, *Quality in Higher Education*, **8** (3), pp 256–71

Waeytens, K, Lens, W *et al* (2002) Learning to learn: teachers' conceptions of their supporting role, *Learning and Instructions*, **12**, pp 305–22

Weller, M (2002a) *Delivering Learning on the Net: The why, what and how of online education*, Kogan Page, London

Weller, M J (2002b) Assessment issues on a Web-based course, *Assessment and Evaluation in Higher Education*, **27** (2), pp 109–16

Weller, M and Robinson, L (2001) Scaling up an Online Course to deal with 12,000 students, *Education, Communication and Information*, **1** (3), pp 307–22

Wenger, E R and McDermott *et al* (2002) *Cultivating Communities of Practice*, Harvard Business School Press, Boston MA

Index